GUNNA DAN

an angel for everyone

Patrick Moloney

WestBow
PRESS

A DIVISION OF THOMAS NELSON

WestBow Press books may be ordered through booksellers or by contacting:

WestBow Press
A Division of Thomas Nelson
1663 Liberty Drive
Bloomington, IN 47403
www.westbowpress.com
1-(866) 928-1240

Because of the dynamic nature of the Internet, any Web addresses or links contained in this book may have changed since publication and may no longer be valid. The views expressed in this work are solely those of the author and do not necessarily reflect the views of the publisher, and the publisher hereby disclaims any responsibility for them.

Any people depicted in stock imagery provided by Thinkstock are models, and such images are being used for illustrative purposes only.

Certain stock imagery © Thinkstock.

ISBN: 978-1-4497-0741-5 (sc)
ISBN: 978-1-4497-0744-6 (hc)
ISBN: 978-1-4497-0740-8 (e)

Library of Congress Control Number: 2010939753

Printed in the United States of America

WestBow Press rev. date: 11/12/2010

Contents

Chapter 1   Journeying into Mindfulness 1
Chapter 2   From the High Lands on High. 6
Chapter 3   From Where We Were to Where We Are 13
Chapter 4   Journeying into Knowingness. 21
Chapter 5   Reality All about Us 32
Chapter 6   Reality All within Us 44
Chapter 7   The Existence of Perfection. 54
Chapter 8   The Devastating Power of Destructiveness 64
Chapter 9   Who Is Who in This World of Ours? 74
Chapter 10   The Life of the Mind 88
Chapter 11   The Gift of Wisdom. 100
Chapter 12   Kindness in Our Lives and in Our Times 116
Chapter 13   Considerations on Oneself. 124
Chapter 14   Counteracting the Dark Side of Life. 134
Chapter 15   Hallowed Grounds, Holy Places. 142
Chapter 16   Towards a Global Ethic 152
Chapter 17   Ascending the Heights 162
Chapter 18   Listening and Learning. 171
Chapter 19   The Totality of It All. 179
Chapter 20   To the High Lands on High. 186

Index 193

Chapter 1

Journeying into Mindfulness

A man is always thoughtful when he goes into a pub. He grows more silent. He becomes more introspective. For a brief period in time, he is absorbed, even if the only thing on his mind is where to sit.

I was much more thoughtful than normal when I went into the Temple Gate Hotel pub in the town of Ennis, County Clare, Ireland. It was late afternoon in the first week of June, and I sat down at an unoccupied table away from everybody else. The waitress came quickly, and I ordered a West Clare bruschetta and a latte. I wanted to relax, but I was finding it difficult to do so. At sixty-four years of age, I'd just retired from a fulfilling and rewarding career in teaching. I was facing a new life and, to be frank, the prospect was more than a little upsetting. In fact, I felt a bit desperate.

With more time than ever to reflect and think, I came up against a problem: I didn't know my own thinking. I lacked both clarity and understanding, and that fact both saddened and surprised me. What saddened me as well was the realisation that we only know our own thinking from time to time. Each one of us has a mind for thinking – but, I wondered, for thinking *what*, exactly? As I sat, waiting to be served, I reminded myself of what I believed about the mind – the beliefs that had formed the foundation of my entire career. While our sense organs are clear about their business (other people generally hear the same things we hear, see what we see, etc.), our minds have no such limitations. Others cannot know what we are thinking unless we choose to reveal it. What's more, the very mind that works perfectly in its relationship with one's body – mastering, controlling and conducting all the activities of physical life – can also be rebellious and pugnacious. The mind can refuse to follow its owner's directions and instead choose to create mayhem with wild, freaky and fierce thoughts. Humans spend a great deal of time controlling the battles going on within their minds, and on that sunny morning in Ennis, I was surprised to realise I was engaged in just such a battle.

Throughout my teaching career in Dublin, my teaching strategies and tactics invariably revolved around a single theme, that of *importance*. The first aspect of any subject I taught was its importance. The second aspect was the importance of each individual student. I wanted every learner to embrace what I saw as meaningful self-importance. To that end, I praised and encouraged, coaxed and cajoled. My approach could be summed up in the old Gaelic proverb *Mol an óige agus tiochfaidh sí*, or, 'Praise the youth and they will grow.' My goal was for everyone to respond well and happily to the magic and mystery of life.

The whole idea of anchoring one's thinking on importance became more significant for me as I got older. I grew to realise that self-esteem and self-confidence can only happen when we think well of ourselves. Thinking well of ourselves is a powerful weapon against negativity. It helps us cope with depression. It gives us solace in times of anguish. More than those, it helps us adjust more knowingly, ably and calmly to the realities of life and living.

That's what I needed to do with this concept of retirement. I needed to reduce it to a state of mind and apply the very same principles I'd based my career on in order to manage it – sooner rather than later. I reminded myself that my self-esteem, self-awareness and self-confidence were more valuable to my thinking than anything else in my life. After all, my status had changed. I was no longer the professional at large. The erstwhile burdens of obligations and commitments had vanished, but that didn't have to be a negative thing, did it? I could cultivate a freshness of spirit and openness of mind. And wasn't that exactly what I'd done when I ordered bruschetta? After all, I'd never eaten bruschetta, but here as I sat at the table I was being adventurous.

I was delighted with myself. *Bruschetta and … a new house. A* new house in the lovely little village of Inagh, just east of Ennis. It was the perfect place to relax and *get away from it all*. Why was I so worried? I was beginning to make things happen. I was going to be fine.

Resting easily in the armchair, I opened the *Irish Times* and spread it before me on the table. Instead of reading the news first, I turned to the second last page and tackled the crossword. I particularly like the calming and restful effect crosswords have on my mind. From time to time I get a delightful burst of insight and inspiration from them.

As I waited for my bruschetta, I set to solving my puzzle. I happily wrote in the answers as they came, but when I met the tiny little clue, *pto (3,6)*, it stumped me. The answer consisted of two words, the first one having three letters and the second, six. I tossed the letters over and over in my mind. How could they be interrelated? *P-t-o ... please turn over?* Please turn over ... what? A page? Previously, I would have given up, but retirement meant my time was my own. The table next to me was served a pot of tea. And it suddenly struck me. *Pot ... pot pourri!* I completed the crossword with a flourish and settled back to await my bruschetta and latte. All the time, however, that splendid burst of inspiration thrilled me. My carefree mind danced happily with notions, words and phrases. *Carefree.* What a wonderful concept – possibly because of another word: *retired.*

I was still savouring my crossword success when I saw him. At first, I pretended not to see him. The empty coffee glass and the bare plate on his table indicated that he had finished his meal. He was reading a newspaper, the *Irish Times*, in fact. At least, this is what I thought he was doing. Then I couldn't help but notice that he was not reading it at all. Instead he was, like me, solving the Crosaire crossword. Down on the floor by his table he had Tesco bags full of shopping, just as I did. Very suddenly, our glances met. We smiled at each other in acknowledgment and politely immersed ourselves in our own private thoughts.

That was when I began to wonder. An uneasy feeling came over me. I had seen that gentleman somewhere before. *Seeing people and meeting people are everyday events*, I reminded myself. *Why should I become concerned at this time?* But, I was concerned. I realised that I had actually felt his presence even before I saw him. This unnerved me a little bit and made me recap the day's events. Earlier, I had gone to the beach in Lahinch. It had been a lovely, warm day. It had been over twenty years since I had gone into the Atlantic waters off the west coast of Ireland for a swim. The water had always been too cold for me. The sand had been too gritty.

Now, in my new-found freedom, I wanted to take on new adventures and be more daring. The liveliness of the Atlantic waters was so inviting. Because of the fine weather's continuous and lasting spell, the coldness was gone from the water. With the delight of a child, I went into the ocean. I thoroughly enjoyed that swim. The energising waters lifted me and vigorously massaged me. I ducked under the smaller waves, and I backed into the bigger ones. I ignored the jellyfish. I ignored them until I walked back onto the beach and then noticed that the inside of my right knee was bright red and a little swollen. Then the pain started, so I tried to soothe it with the salty water. A gentleman passed by.

'Jellyfish,' he ventured to say.

'Yes,' I replied, 'and the sting is quite painful.'

'Only one thing for it,' he said. 'A brisk walk eases the pain quickly. The fresh air will evaporate the poison and the serum. A good walk and you will be right in no time. And look! My blister – here on the inside of the right knee – is nearly better.'

His blister was very similar to mine. It was in the same place, inside the right knee, it was the same size and it was very red. I did as he suggested, and off I went walking. I must say that his advice was good, and in next to no time, the stinging pain began to abate. One thing I must admit about myself is this: I would make for a useless witness at any scene of activity. My powers of observation are not good. Maybe this is not quite correct. Maybe it is that I do not use them. One thing I can say is that if I were asked to describe that man on the beach, I wouldn't be able. Certainly I could talk about his blister, its size, its colour and its location. He was wearing blue swimming trunks. He was about my height, probably about my age, as well. He was a little grey-haired and slightly balding. And he was friendly and courteous. I liked that about him. But after that, my recollection is poor and my memory is genuinely vague. Of course, I had no earthly reason for remembering him. I more or less had forgotten about him by the time I finished my walk. I didn't delay, because I wanted to get to Ennis for light fittings, and the blister had surprisingly disappeared. It was in the Tesco supermarket that I got the newspaper. The queue was long at the checkout, and while I was waiting for my turn, I read the lead article about the arrival of immigrants into Ireland. It outlined the revised plans and processes to be implemented for the speedier handling of applications.

The correspondent listed the immigrants' countries of origin, and the list was long. *From wherever will they come next,* I thought to myself.

When I stretched out my legs, I inadvertently kicked the plastic shopping bags and upended some of the items onto the floor. I got up from the chair, collected the items and bags and put them into a neat pile away from my legs. It was then that our eyes met, this time directly. His were the kindest eyes I ever saw and the almond colour of the irises was deep and strong.

'A beautiful day,' he said.

'Most enjoyable,' I replied.

I tried my best to be as nonchalant as I could. It was he, the man I met on the beach.

The waitress came with the food and coffee, and she placed them quickly on my table. She immediately went over to the gentleman and gave him his bill. 'West Clare bruschetta and a latte! That will be seven euro fifty please.'

Occasionally I have had the experience of thinking, *Cripes, let me out of here.* This was certainly one. I was beginning to come to conclusions about the day's events. *Coincidences are coincidences,* I thought to myself, *but this is too much.* I will readily admit that life is strange. But, for a man like myself who is very comfortable with the mundane, the banal and the ordinary, this was far too strange.

The gentleman got up and left. We wished each other well. But, I was not relieved. I can tell you I was much more thoughtful leaving the pub than when I had entered it. Somehow or other, I knew that we would meet again.

Chapter 2

From the High Lands on High

The next day, I went out to Cloonmacken Lake in the evening to sit for a while at one of the two picnic tables. The lake is home to a great variety of birds and fish, and I love to sit at a table there and spend time looking around me. The odd time, I might feed the ducks. The ducks at Cloonmacken Lake expect to be fed every time a human appears, but this time I ignored them. I had no particular purpose in mind other than to sit and relax. Down through the years, whenever I left Dublin for a break in the country, I always enjoyed the spaciousness of the countryside all around me. I so looked forward to it. *A holiday for my eyesight*, I always reminded myself. Now, here in Cloonmacken Lake, I was taking it all in. The yellow of the evening light was soothing and restful. In the distance, I could hear the rhythmic sound of the engine of a tractor.

Then I saw him coming – the same man. He was wearing a loose-fitting lemon-coloured linen suit. The looseness of the fit and the creasing of the fabric gave him a casual yet elegant appearance. The white shirt and shiny brown shoes presented him as a classy type. I assumed that he had to be a vacationing visitor to the area. He walked quite leisurely from the roadway towards me. I gave him a welcome, and he sat down at the table with me.

He told me his name was Gunna Dan. His voice was clipped and clear. I looked at him closely. He was not unlike me in age or shape or size. Indeed, there are a huge number of men in Ireland who are like me – in their sixties, about five feet nine inches tall, grey-haired, big-eared and in various stages of baldness. He seemed to me to be at ease with himself, and, to be very honest, I was pleased to see him. We began slowly, talking about the weather and the lake. And, as is usual with me, I said one of my inane remarks about life being good. I often think about life, and, deep down, I know that life has been good to me. Somehow or other, though, my gratefulness seems inadequate to me, and I am not happy about this. Gunna Dan surprised me in his reply.

'Yes,' he said, 'life is good. Oh! It is so good.' He kept repeating himself, as if the repetition would give him an easier fluency in what I immediately knew to be, for him, a new language. He then went on to enthuse about the abundance of life on and in the lake. He admired the trees. He commented freely on the profusion of the peripheral leaves on each and every one of them. Even as I was looking at him, he was watching the insects flitting above the surface of the lake and noting the birds flying overhead. All the time while he was talking to me, I thought *now here is a man who has sensibility*. It also seemed to me that while he was possessed of a serious inward disposition, he was fully in tune with the fullness of the natural world. He commented on the greenness of the grass in the fields. He saw loveliness in the shapes and sizes of the trees, the bushes and the hedges. He was wide-eyed as he took it all in. I felt sure that he must have come from some barren land. It was clear to me that he was not used to this landscape at all. Then, after a period of quietness, we both agreed that Cloonmacken Lake was a heavenly spot.

I took to him immediately at that first lakeside encounter. Somehow there seemed to be an inner harmony and serene depth to him. I delighted in his company. The world of work and the busyness of life had always prevented me from taking time out to just stay still. I had heard a lot about quiet and stillness, to be sure. I had even read a lot about it. I would readily admit to anyone who would care to listen that stillness within oneself is the source of great peace and harmony. My lifestyle while working prevented this from happening to some degree. I was always frenetic. I got up early every morning, and, until I went to bed later at night, I was always rushing. I had so much to do. I had so many agendas. Now I was finally beginning the process of slowing down, and beginning to like it. I was settling into my new-found slowness here at the lakeside with my new-found friend, a friend whom I discovered, without fully understanding it, to be strangely affirmative and supportive.

On our next visit to the lake, we jocosely yet meaningfully greeted each other with 'How's life?' At this second visit, I found myself telling Gunna Dan about my life and times, a conversation I hadn't expected to have. I told him I recently retired from a career in teaching, a career that spanned all of thirty-seven years. I, as is often usual for me, said another one of my apologetic remarks – 'and now I am counting my blessings.' He surprised me with the ease with which he tuned into my sentiment. He invited me to share my story with him, but first he made an admission. He told me he was from abroad, from a place called Onavistan, a district northeast of the Himalayan mountain range. The name, he explained, literally means 'the high lands on high', so called because the whole region is an elevated plateau. He also told me that even though there are many languages spoken in the area, chiefly Pandi and Folbo, everybody learns English, and nearly everybody can speak it to some degree. This, he explained, is in response to the ever-growing influences of American and British politics on the area.

He then told me that he had suffered mental and personal upheavals, but he did not want to go into any details about them. He mentioned to me that the ineffectiveness of previous efforts to discuss these upheavals had saddened him. This sadness became apparent when he commented rather wistfully and vaguely on 'the uselessness of it all'. As I looked at him, I kept quiet. I did not want to upset him. He told me that the power unleashed by negative thinking is very strong and damaging. He even seemed afraid of it. He explained that he so wanted to elevate his own thinking. Including me, if not everybody, in his next statement, he again repeatedly commented, while tapping the middle of his high forehead with the index finger, 'we must raise our thoughts, and we must raise our thinking in a much more resolute and steadfast way.' His firmness and sureness surprised me.

He must have noticed my hushed demeanour. He turned towards me and reassuringly began emphasising to me that he was so thankful to be in Ireland, even though he found it a strange country. The more I listened to him, the more I realised that he was not in the least bit sorry for himself. Rather, he was pleased and grateful to be among us and especially pleased that his application to stay in the country was processed quickly and successfully.

He was, however, puzzled by our mannerisms, our speech, our language and even our place names. He knew that he was among people who did not understand him, but he was anxious to learn our ways. His move to Ireland was a great opportunity for him to make a clean start. He assured me that he was so happy to have landed not only in Ireland, but especially in the county of Clare. The people he had already met were so kind to him.

In a moment of great seriousness, he then told me that he wanted to know more about life and reality in the here and now. Getting fixed up with social welfare was all good and fine. Having food, shelter and other life necessities were important. However, he wanted to understand his life and the purpose of his life in a much more meaningful way. He told me that he had a lot of doubts about nearly everything and that he spent a lot of time wrestling with them. I noticed that he became a little sad, and there was a touch of lonesomeness about him. Then he told me that he often feels he's not really present here at all, even though he knows full well that he is physically present. He said that he knew a lot about the planets, the stars and the galaxies, but very little about the details of life all around him. I knew that some people could maintain great long-term memories as they aged, while their short-term recall might become faulty. Gunna Dan's better memories seemed to relate to far off space and time. I felt sorry for him, and I internally acknowledged that he was honouring me by confiding in me. I empathised with him greatly.

Then he told me that his people were directly descended from a wise people of ancient times who gave the symbol zero (0), that strange and acceptable face of nothingness, to the world of mathematics. He explained to me that the sages among them had given a lot of thought and importance to the concept of nothingness, to the understanding of nothingness and to its place in man's thinking. These ancient people meditated on nothingness religiously, but at no time in Gunna Dan's life was it ever seriously discussed. I was able to tell him that I knew that the introduction of the symbol zero into the decimal number system revolutionised the study of mathematics in Europe when it first appeared in the twelfth century AD. It also transformed the world of business, trade and commerce. He was amused when I told him that Europeans, at first, greatly resisted the introduction of this Indian symbol, as well as the other so-called Arab mathematical digits, into the Western

World. These decimal digits, invented by the Hindus,[1] were condemned as 'infidel symbols' by the European establishment of the time[2] because of Europe's religious and cultural climate. Another important cause for the condemnation of these symbols was Europe's attachment to the ancient Roman number system. A symbol for zero, I told him, was badly wanted. Without it, the Roman number system was disadvantaged. Multiplication and division were well-nigh impossible. How could you multiply II (two) by V (five) and come up with X (ten)? Gunna Dan found this amusing. For a man who seemed to have suffered much, lightness and laughter welled up in him easily. This pleased me greatly, and I was delighted to be there with him, a man I now detected, because of his perceptive and supportive comments, to be wise and knowledgeable in a special way. He continued talking to me for some more time about his upbringing. He was proud of his people, and it was obvious to me that he admired their resourcefulness, as they eked out an existence in what I gathered to be the hostile and arid plains of their countryside. Eventually, he told me that he was anxious to hear about me and who I was.

I had no trouble telling him briefly about my early childhood in the village of Shanagolden in County Limerick. He couldn't believe it when I told him that in the 1940s and 1950s, life in many parts of Ireland was harsh. Conditions were tough, and people in their thousands left the country seeking a better life for themselves and their children. I told him about my early education in the village national school and later, from the age of twelve onwards, my experience attending boarding schools in Mallow in County Cork, Castletown in County Laois and Faithlegg House in County Waterford. Throughout my explanation of these years, Gunna Dan enquired and probed, but he seemed to be much more interested in people rather than events, in their personalities rather than in their activities. This became very apparent when I told him that I had great admiration for the De La Salle Brothers, the teaching order of many schools in Ireland and of the boarding schools I attended. I told him that, except for the occasional human weakness, they were exceptionally honourable men totally dedicated to the work of the Christian mission.

---

1   Eugene P. Northrop, *Riddles in Mathematics* (London: Pelican, 1975), 41.
2   See Peter L. Bernstein, *Against the Gods: The Remarkable Story of Risk* (Hoboken, New Jersey: Wiley, 1998), XXXV. The city of Florence, Italy passed an edict in 1229 that forbade bankers from using 'infidel symbols'.

Our education, I told him, was all embracing, extensive and varied. The vast vista of learning, of knowledge and especially of holiness was opened up before us. The men who looked after us led the way freely and without self-consciousness. They were very open and transparent about their vocational aims, their work and their lives. As a child, I loved all of it. What I particularly loved was how adventurous they were in introducing to us a host of sports, particularly hurling, football, handball and, when the weather permitted, rounders, volleyball, lawn tennis and even swimming. And when the weather did not permit sports, we engaged in indoor games of ludo, snakes and ladders, chess, draughts, darts, rings, table tennis and even blow football.

I even told my friend that when I was in school with the De La Salle Brothers, it was my wish to grow into a man like them. I told him that from a young age, I was convinced that any cohort of men or women who would go down on their knees each day to pray for the salvation and ultimate happiness of all of humankind was deserving of the highest respect and greatest honour.

Gunna Dan then begged me to let him know what vision and foresight is possible in the minds and lives of human beings and what it is that gives them purpose and meaning. 'One of the things that puzzles me,' he confided, ' is that I do not know what people think, what people feel or what it is that is important to them.' There and then at the lakeside, he entreated me: 'Please explore with me, please find out with me the significance and importance of human life and human living. Please let me know. I know you have insights. I know from what you have said that you have benefitted from inspirational teaching and guidance, and I know that you have spent a life in the world of teaching and of knowledge, of reading and of study.'

This entreaty silenced me and seriously upset me. One thing he had said stung me: the assumption that teachers more or less know everything. Even from the beginning of my teaching career, I had been well aware of my own limitations and, as I got to know other teachers, I began to see theirs. I began to see that the expertise we had was terribly segmented and compartmentalised. It was with no little disappointment that I realised that teachers – and this would probably apply equally to the other professions – reflect society and in the process reflect both the good and ill in society. All of this internal rambling was going on in my mind, and I realised that out of courtesy to Gunna Dan, I could not remain silent anymore.

So I told him that I would give serious consideration to his plea. I told him that it was too important to ignore and that sooner rather than later I would refer back to it. Somehow or other, though, I was discomfited by the challenge of the task.

We got up from the table and walked towards the water's edge, scattering a few ducks on the way. Gunna Dan looked closely at me and his gentle smiling face disarmed me totally. I quickly eased up in mind and spirit, surprisingly so, and then I could see that Gunna Dan was happier. Not long afterwards the two of us began looking for flat stones, and we engaged ourselves in trying to throw them as far as we could across the surface of the water. I could not but notice that Gunna Dan was very skilful, even stylish, as he spun his well-chosen stones across the water. On one particular occasion, we both whooped with great shouts of glee when a stone he threw danced and hopped seven times before it sank into the waters of the lake. We grew very fond of the activity, and the boyishness of it all gave us great delight. There was nobody around but us, and we laughed and joked and teased with carefree happiness.

When we were leaving Cloonmacken Lake, Gunna Dan turned to me and said that he was coming down to the lake again on the following afternoon and that if he found himself all alone, he would spend the time reading one of his books. I detected the implicit invitation and told him immediately that I would come as well.

Chapter 3

From Where We Were
to Where We Are

The following day was lovely and sunny. When we arrived at the lake, mothers, children and dogs were there aplenty, and children were feeding the ducks. In the company of all of this, we remained silent. Gunna Dan walked away a little bit and contemplatively looked into the water. It was only when most of the people had left that Gunna Dan told me that he wondered a lot about my later education, and he was curious to know how I got into teaching. We both sat down at the lower table, and I told him. When I graduated from University College Dublin with a science degree and later with a higher diploma in education I was appointed a teacher on the staff of Pearse School, later Pearse College of Further Education, in Crumlin, Dublin. There I taught chemistry, physics and biology, and in later years, a variety of courses in computer studies.

For many years, I explained to him, I presented and chaired courses in the appreciation and understanding of philosophy, particularly for the older students who enrolled in the school's cultural studies programme. Gunna Dan was as keen as could be to find out about the adult education programmes we had at the college, and I had to spend some time responding to his many excited queries. He was agog when I told him that I had incorporated the principles of philosophic thought into an environmental science course that I delivered for over twelve years. In fact, I told him that for practically all of the thirty-seven years that I had spent teaching and lecturing, I always gave importance to reflective issues, knowing that they would evoke thoughtfulness in my students.

Gunna Dan asked me if I was proud to be part of Ireland's great scholarly tradition. I started explaining about how I belonged to the vocational education system in Dublin and how my colleagues and I explicitly acknowledged that our students were of central importance. As members of the City of Dublin Vocational Education Committee (CDVEC) system, we had many opportunities to respond to the changing needs of the time. I had a great time telling Gunna Dan about how I was involved in the introduction of computer technology into the college; about my part in the development of further education courses; about how I, along with others, ensured the timely delivery of a wide range of work-related training programmes; and about the wonderful colleagues with whom I worked. I regaled him with stories of our achievements and successes. As I was saying all of this to Gunna Dan, I became aware that I was bragging somewhat and I quickly stopped.

Gunna Dan ignored the sudden silence. He began asking me about the meaning and the rationale of education in the western world. It had to be something more than just coping with the practicalities of life, he argued, and as he discussed the topic with me he revealed himself to be a man of discernment and purpose. I told him that I particularly admire the primary school teachers in Ireland because, for the most part, they are very effective in delivering their education programmes in a holistic, learner-centred manner. But the second level system, I voiced, leaves a lot to be desired.

'I'll put it to you this way,' I said. 'A teacher of French or Irish or Spanish is very happy, and considers it to be a great success, if students learn the irregular verbs of the language. A mathematics teacher is delighted when the complexities of quadratic equations are understood, and the geography teacher is very satisfied when the Aztec names and pronunciations of Mexican mountains are correctly absorbed.'

I explained to him that in my view, the education system – certainly at second and third levels – has turned out to be pragmatic and utilitarian. It is pragmatic, I said to him, in that the teachers have a programme to deliver within a certain length of time. It is utilitarian in that the benefits are mostly measured according to their usefulness to society, specifically to the economic good of the country and to how well foreign investment can be attracted into the country. Employers and managers have a vested interest in this kind of education system. Owners and managers of industry need highly trained and competent recruits for the workplace, and so much the better if their recruits' required training is given in the country's schools and colleges at the taxpayers' expense.

Gunna Dan was astounded to be told that here in Ireland no courses of study exist on how to live life and on how to live it well. Without prompting, he exclaimed, 'What are they taught after learning the facts?' Then he revealed to me his great desire. 'I have so many questions. I am a mature, grown-up person. I know so little, not only about life, but also so little about myself. I do not know where I came from. I do not know where I am going. And it upsets me not to know where I belong. I am so ignorant of the important things in life.'

There, sitting at the table beside Cloonmacken Lake, he renewed his previous afternoon's plea, which was more of a prayer. He wished me to discuss with him the issues of life and truth and reality. I kept quiet in the face of his seriousness and his earnestness. To be honest, I could not reply there and then, because his challenge numbed me. My numbness meant that anything I would say would be trite and silly, if not stupid. However, I had always accepted that the experience of true knowledge is innate knowledge, and that this knowledge consists of the emergent eternal truths that can enter our minds. I had always assumed that understanding and clarity could only come once we had engaged in our own internal questionings and conversations. And, in order to achieve any kind of success in this area, I had always accepted that resolute and steadfast thinking was essential. Therein was my problem. I was reluctant to admit it, but my own serious thinking was only a part-time activity. I wanted better. Our great journey from the state of grand ignorance into the realm of true knowingness starts and continues only within us. It is through our own internal engagement that we can, like the philosophers of old, connect with the eternal and with the principles of truth[3]. Gunna Dan knew that in spite of my silence, I would answer his plea, and when I looked into his kindly eyes, I knew I could not refuse.

Later that night, I reflected on the day's events. I began to seriously wonder what I was engaging in. I was newly retired, and more than

---

3   See Socrates (470–399 BC), for example.

anything else, I needed time and space to settle and to adjust to my new life. Since I had come to Inagh – and I confess it freely – I was spending a lot of time, more time than I would have liked, recalling my past, including my childhood, my schooling and my years as a teacher. I knew I was journeying retrospectively, and yet I also gave a lot of time and consideration to my continuing journey in life, a journey now in need of much ease, refreshment and enlightenment.

There was one thing about which I wasn't at all calm. A lot of my thoughts and notions could, at times, be turbulent and furious. I could dwell on them passionately, and I often found myself in fierce internal arguments. I would try to justify myself against all my perceived wrongs. Of course, my battling self would repeatedly be victorious in my mental wiles. My false victories sustained the spurious arguments, and somehow or other I found myself fighting the same ones over and over again. Where had the gift for clear logical thinking gone to? However, I had tactics to help me manage, as it were, the wild circling thoughts and all the misplaced activities going on in my head, activities that always hijacked my energy and tired me out. One tactic in particular I liked involved my going on long walks, moseying along the country roads. In the beginning, I would be absorbed in my own thoughts and feelings, thoughts and feelings completely unconnected with the surrounding independent landscape. However, I would quickly ease into the real and silent countryside. I would soon feel quietness within myself. I would become thankful, even thankful to the countryside for allowing me in.

Quickly I would find that I felt free. I was released into a world of calm and serenity, of solace and soothing. Then, more than anything else, I would begin to see and feel the expansive spaciousness of the outdoors, and I would drink it in. I would indulge. I never argued with myself when I was on long walks. I saw no wit whatsoever in walking the roads while cultivating an agitated mind. My mind would open, and everything would become agreeable. Combative and antagonistic thoughts would be dispelled. I could see greatness and grandeur all around me. When I returned home from such walks, I would be refreshed, soothed and happy.[4]

---

4   See William Hazlitt's (1778–1830) essay, 'On Going a Journey,' which I studied (and loved) as a student at boarding school. Periodically, staff and students would go on long walks in the countryside.

Another thing that I got to appreciate in my life, which also served as a tactic for quieting an agitated mind, was the comfort to be had in the routine of daily life and in the mundane. I have found rest and solace in the ordinary tasks of life. Therein I could do all I wanted to do – read books, visit places, dine out, go on holidays, and yes, visit the churches and say my prayers. Nothing spectacular. Nothing exceptional. All these thoughts and notions were flooding into my head as I thought about Gunna Dan. Strangely enough, all my reservations about being able to help him soon faded. I liked the man. I trusted him. I felt safe with him. And I surprised myself at how easily I decided there and then than I would discuss the importance of life and its implications with my new-found friend. I decided that I would go on this journey with him with hope and expectation. I told myself that it was essential that I declare from the very beginning that our pursuit would have to be that of truth and openness with ourselves and with each other. And another thing I planned to tell him and to tell him earnestly was this: that the important issues of life, truth and reality are the very same issues, in my view, that are sadly, ignored and neglected.

The next time we met was in a pub in Inagh. Well, correctly speaking, it wasn't in a pub; it was in the Biddy Early Brewery. It was mid-afternoon, and we were the only patrons in the place. We ordered two coffees and two small ones (the standard serving of Irish whiskey). We settled down, and when I looked at Gunna Dan, I immediately knew that he was pleased to see me. 'I feel as if I'm about to go on a journey,' he said, eerily echoing my own thoughts from the night before. He seemed very confident in me, which made me somewhat nervous.

I could see immediately that Gunna Dan was forthright about his ambitions and his intentions. I felt that it was necessary for me to tell him my perception of reality in Ireland at this time. So, I gave him fair warning that the time had come for straight talk between him and me, and mostly on my part. Since he came into my life, I told him, he had actually upset me to a great extent. He had unwittingly made me confront my own thoughts and opinions; my own views and ideas. He had, to some extent, forced me to think more deeply about my life and its purpose. Now he wanted me to reveal and discuss with him all I that I knew. This made me uncomfortable. Gunna Dan quickly reassured me, however, and told me he wanted me to realise as fully as possible how important I was to him. He told me that he knew very few people, and the officials at the welfare offices were the only people he knew well. I was, he plaintively confessed, the only conversational companion he had. He needed me. He needed me badly because he found the simplest of things in Ireland to be complex. Everything we did and said perplexed him and disturbed him. There and then, I felt pity for him. I knew that he was as old as I, if not a little older. Despite his age and the difficulties associated with ageing in a new and strange country, I had the certain knowledge that he was anxious and eager to start out on a pilgrim journey and he wanted me to be on the road with him.

My first response to his plea was to address our language, our place names and our speech, all of which he found astoundingly bizarre. He had questioned me several times about the meanings of our place names, in particular, and wondered why they were so difficult to pronounce. When I told him that Cloonmacken[5] literally meant 'the place, or field, for parsnips' and that Inagh means 'an ivy covered place', he was astounded. He was more surprised when I explained that we were living in a country where almost all the place names were in a different language to the language spoken by the people. The language of our place names is that of the ancient Gaels, called Gaeilge or Gaelic. Anyone would come across numerous examples of this language in place names all over the island of Ireland – from Shankill in Belfast to Glounthaune in Cork; or from Terenure in Dublin to Oranmore in Galway. Even the name of our capital city, Dublin, as I explained to my friend, means a 'black pool'. I assured him that most Irish people, because of our schooling and education, would be aware of the Gaelic influences in our place names, and would have some insights and understandings for our historical and linguistic past.

I did not want to exclude the importance of the Latin language in the lives of the people who lived in Ireland long ago. Because of this, I began telling him that I was reading, or, rather, re-reading a book, *Life of St. Columba* by Adomnán of Iona.[6] This book, presented in modern

5   James Frost, 'The History and Topography of the County of Clare: Appendix VII – County of Clare: Irish local Names Explained,' *Clare County Library: http://www. clarelibrary.ie/eolas/coclare/history/frost/appendix7_c.htm*.

6   Adomnán of Iona, *Life Of St. Columba*, trans. Richard Sharpe (London: Penguin Classics, 1995).

English, is a translation of the original manuscript written over thirteen hundred years ago in Latin. The original is now housed, after many years of wanderings, adventures and escapes, in the Stadtbibliothek in Schaffhausen, Switzerland. The manuscript, which dates from before 713 AD, is written on goatskin vellum and comprises sixty-nine folios. I showed Gunna Dan my translated copy of the book, and we both had a good look at the lengthy introduction and the copious notes with great interest. I told my friend that the book gives a great description of Saint Columba's self-imposed exile in the year 563 from Ireland to the island of Iona, which is located off the mid-west coast of Scotland. The book gives a sincere, and yes, a pious account of the saint's impact on the lives of the people of that time, not only in Iona but also in mainland Scotland, Ireland and the north of England.

I also told my friend that the book describes Saint Columba's efforts to resolve the dissension between the Celtic church and the church in Rome over the dating of Easter. The Council of Nicaea had, in 325 AD, ruled that Easter Sunday be the first Sunday after the first full moon after the twenty-first of March, but in Ireland, the Irish maintained firm allegiance to the older methods and had a certain aversion to mandates coming in from abroad. Throughout my explanation, Gunna Dan was in thrall to the realisation that we in Ireland have such an ancient cultural and literary inheritance. In his own excited way, he exclaimed, 'you have … you have … you have … first-hand information, and … and … first-hand sources on the lives and times of people who lived so very long ago.'

His great interest in the spiritual and cultural riches of our past encouraged me and I couldn't help but tell him that I was also reading about *An Cathach*,[7] considered to be the oldest extant book written in the Gaelic language. It was produced about fourteen hundred years ago, and it is acknowledged to be the world's second most ancient copy of the Psalms. At Gunna Dan's encouragement, I explained my views on the ancient history of Ireland, especially the history of the church from the time of Saint Patrick onwards. I then told him that just the previous week, I had spent some time on the Internet in the public library in the near-by town of Ennistymon, gathering some information on the life of Saint Patrick, one of the three patron saints of Ireland[8]. I told him all I knew about the 'Confessio', a document that Saint Patrick composed in

7   Michael Slavin, *The Ancient Books of Ireland* (Dublin: Wolfhound, 2005), 104.
8   The other two patron saints are Saint Bridget of Kildare and Saint Colmcille of Iona.

Latin over fifteen hundred years ago and how it was transcribed some four hundred years later into *The Book of Armagh*. As I recounted my tale, I conveyed to Gunna Dan my own impressions of this great apostolic man, explaining that Saint Patrick was possessed of a remarkable Christ-centred spirituality. He was especially determined to impart to the people of his time in Ireland the knowledge of God's glorious gift of his divine Son, Jesus, for the redemption and salvation of humankind. His purpose was again evident in the way he used the three leaves of the shamrock plant to explain the mystery of the Holy Trinity. All told, Saint Patrick was a man of writing and letters, a poet and a visionary, ever-steadfast and resolute, a true revolutionary who dramatically changed the social and spiritual orders of Ireland in that ancient time.

I was delighted with how Gunna Dan kept commenting on what I was saying, and I knew instinctively that he was very willing and anxious to listen and learn. His demeanour was reverent and respectful, and this surprised me because in one way, I was still being the teacher. But this did not bother him in the slightest. He was always responsive to me, and he was especially so when I argued that it was Saint Patrick who gave rise to the birth of Ireland's literary and scholarly accomplishments. Saint Patrick did this chiefly through his introduction of the Roman script and alphabet to the country, but also through his spiritual and poetic writings – all of which, and much more, we have so fortunately inherited.[9]

---

9   See Magnus Maclean, "The Literature of the Celts," *St. Patrick, The Pioneer of Celtic Writers*, (London: Senate, 1998).

Chapter 4

Journeying into Knowingness

We left the Biddy Early Brewery and crossed the road. Because it was now a bright, sunny evening, we decided to go for a walk along the back road towards Kilnamona. The white woollen clouds were high in the sky. The blue overhead was full and pure. We noted the meaning of the name *Cill na Móna* (as spelled in Gaelic) – the 'church of the bog land' and pondered the people of ages past who had trod on the same road we now were on. Gunna Dan was delighted when I told him that Cormac McCarthy, who was king of Munster from 1118 to 1127, had a shrine made to preserve the arm of Saint Lachtain. The shrine was kept in Kilnamona's church until 1640, when it was moved to Lislachtain Abbey in Kerry. A holy well dedicated to Saint Lachtain is situated south of the burial ground in Kilnamona, and his feast day is celebrated on 19 March, the same day that his festival used to be celebrated in Freshford, County Kilkenny. Gunna Dan was amazed to learn from me that the shrine built to house the relic of Saint Lachtain almost nine hundred years ago was at present in the museum of the Royal Irish Academy in Dublin.[10]

We walked leisurely along the road looking at the fields, the hedges and the hills. We were aware of Slievecallan Mountain behind us as we walked up the sloping road. We casually commented on all we saw, and I couldn't help but tell Gunna Dan that our walk along this country road reminded me so much of my home village of Shanagolden. In my childhood, my grandmother, Bridget Mullins, lived on a farm on the

---

10   See 'Churches of County Clare,' *Clare County Library*: www.clarelibrary.ie.

Old Abbey Road. Many times I walked, trotted or ran the one-mile distance to that farmhouse. Every time, I did so happily, delightfully, and it was only in later years that I recognised why. My grandmother was the kindest person any child could meet and know. My whole spirit would dance the very minute I left the village to go to her house. Gunna Dan noted with surprise that the road's name, the Old Abbey Road, was as English as you could get. But, what I told him next astounded him. Just beyond my grandmother's farm, up at the crossroads, were the ruins of a monastery that used to be called Manisternagalliaghduff Abbey or, as it was more commonly known, Mainister na gCailleach Duff, which means the 'monastery of the black-veiled nuns'. Extensive ruins of the monastery, which was reputedly founded in the first half of the thirteenth century, still remain. Pope Martin V ordered its suppression in 1432 when he got reports that the nuns were leading 'loose and dissolute lives'.[11] However, the monastery continued to function until the middle of the sixteenth century, when it finally closed, a victim to the legislation enacted by King Henry VIII of England to suppress all monasteries and nunneries.[12]

Talking about the variant names for the monastery led us eventually to discuss the language that is spoken by the people in Ireland today. I told him that the English language is one of hundreds in the world. It was imposed on us from a neighbouring island, an imposition that was colonial in the extreme. English was then a relatively new language on planet Earth. It still is. When it was imposed on Ireland, English replaced the ancient Gaelic of our forefathers, and a great treasure of Gaelic literature was lost. The remnants we have tell us that our ancient ancestors had great oral traditions, complete with their epics and stories. They had their societies, their laws, their systems of rule and their methods of governance. The various clan members were of royal lineage. In their assemblies, the clan leaders addressed their people regally with 'A Dhaoine Uaisle' meaning 'O Noble People'. The phrase, 'A Dhaoine Uaisle', is still used nowadays particularly when leaders of society stand up to address their audiences. Unfortunately, as I explained, the ancient Gaelic order was cruelly destroyed. Gunna Dan was pained to hear of man's brutality to man. He found it hard, first, to understand how human beings of the world use hundreds of languages, second, how one society would force another society to adopt its ways even to the point of slaughter, and third, how a

---

11   See 'Shanagolden-Robertstown-Foynes Parish,' *Heritage Project: Diocese of Limerick:* www.limerickdioceseheritage.org

12   The suppression of monasteries in England, Wales and Ireland began in 1536.

new, untried and untested language like English could replace an ancient tongue and all its wisdom. I had earlier told my friend about the great English writer William Shakespeare. I told him that Shakespeare wrote many sonnets and plays about four hundred and twenty years ago, and how in doing so, he felt obliged to bring over two thousand new, and now current words, into the language[13]. I also told him that in Shakespeare's time, the Bodleian Library in Oxford, England, had almost six thousand books. All of them, however, were written in Latin except for thirty-six[14].

Gunna Dan understood that our formulation and expression of ideas depends on the language we use. He spoke authoritatively to me on this, and I knew that, because of his own multi-lingual background, he was speaking from experience and knowledge. It is not easy to express one's ideas purely, cleanly and accurately, he acknowledged. He explained it this way: verbal expressions of anything are at best literal translations, so any nuances of feeling, knowledge, wisdom and insight can be lost. I agreed with him and told him that in the *Concise Oxford Dictionary*, I had counted nine different definitions of the noun *love*, four different definitions of the verb and a large number of entries for the derived words.[15] He then explained to me that when he was first learning English, he could not get the hang of 'It is raining'. He would have preferred the phrase 'Drops of water are falling from the sky', a phrase much closer to the structure and meaning of his native Pandi language. Then, in jest, we vied with each other to produce more examples. We had great fun with 'It is raining cats and dogs', 'The kettle boiled', 'The train stopped', 'the train fare' and 'I'm after my dinner'. Indeed, we merrily dissected each of the phrases for far longer than we realised. This game kept us occupied all the way back on our return journey to Inagh crossroads. Howsoever, we both accepted that we would be using the English language to express our ideas and notions in the search for truth. We even went so far as to recognise that every language is limited in the way it can reflect reality and some more so than others. We promised each other nonetheless that any difficulty at this level would not stop us in our explorations.

And, as if I didn't know, he told me there and then that he was having difficulties with the English language. He wondered why there was so much

---

13   See Bill Bryson, *Shakespeare, The World as a Stage* (New York: Eminent Lives, 2007) 112.
14   Ibid., 114.
15   *Concise Oxford Dictionary*, 9th ed., (New York: Oxford, 1995).

liberty and looseness when we were speaking among ourselves. He found that a lot of the time people were illogical, irrational and emotive, while at other times they were very reasonable. In his travels, he experienced wide variations in accents and inflexions, and he told me that what he heard puzzled him greatly. He could never understand the energetic repetition of sharp monosyllabic words that constantly streamed from the younger people in particular. He could only conclude that these were violent and vulgar expressions. On too many occasions he felt confronted with contrariness and contradictions. His expectation of polite conversation and clear thinking was constantly thwarted.

And there on the road as we walked back to the village of Inagh – it was now late evening – he pondered all of this aloud. He particularly queried me as to how man's thinking can be so full of errors, seemingly involuntary and yet, he felt, wilful. I, for my part, was silenced by my friend's emerging sadness. I tried to affirm the uniqueness of man's power for thinking and how all of us can imagine ourselves doing glorious things in any place at any time. But I couldn't. I so wanted to argue out that the basis of true living can only be found in the mind and that there is a necessity now more than ever for clear, purposeful thinking, which would enable us to see more and know more, to see better and know better. But again, I couldn't, and strangely, I felt impelled to remain silent and keep my thoughts to myself.

We met a few days later in Ennistymon. We both liked coming to this bustling town, and we loved looking at the quaint and varied shop fronts stretching along the length of the main street. We decided that we would walk up to the graveyard and the church ruins situated on top of the appropriately named Church Hill. Right from the start of our visit, we noted and respected the graves of the dead. Gunna Dan couldn't start walking anywhere until he first prayed for the departed, and then we walked slowly beyond the old ruined church and around to the far side of the hill. From our vantage point, we could see like birds. Down below us was the Inagh Road. Looking all around us, we could admire the fields, the houses, the shrubs and the trees stretching way out into the distance. Oh! The spaciousness of it all!

When I turned around, I could see the cars carefully negotiating the old narrow bridge and successfully avoiding the architecturally interesting but abandoned houses situated uncomfortably close to the roadway. A wedding party was boisterously filling the entrance to the Fall's Hotel. Down in the distance, I could see and hear the cascading Inagh River. Yonder, behind the hotel, the river, now coming to the end of its journey, meandered much more evenly, serenely and calmly towards the sea. The Atlantic Ocean, in its glorious vastness, was not too far away, and I could easily see the headland of Liscannor in the further distance. The views all around were impressive. We viewed the surroundings in wonder and stared for a long time at the many features we found appealing. After our little adventure, we decided to go back down into the town and go into a café, An Teach Bia, for a coffee. We decided to order some apple pie and ice cream as well. Once we were served, I wasted no time in giving vent to views that were, I must now admit, robust and animated.

My earlier intention to keep my private thoughts private went out the window, but Gunna Dan was tolerant and relaxed. 'We humans on planet Earth,' I boldly asserted, 'are shockingly deficient in knowledge and knowingness. We actually know nothing. We are born naked and ignorant. For many years, we stay ignorant. Our society, considered civilised and enlightened by most people, appreciates that our children should attend school until they are at least sixteen years old – preferably eighteen – and that's just to learn the very basics; the rudiments of reading, writing and arithmetic. In our age, the art of reading for learning is greatly ignored. The development of self-confidence and sound judgment is purely by chance. The importance of self-esteem and inner sanctity remains ignored. The accumulated knowledge, wisdom and skills of the people who were here before us are not passed on to the hearts and minds of newer generations. In truth, future generations in Ireland will be born into a country that has lost the practices and values that were revered for centuries, if not millennia.'

I paused to have a sip of coffee and without ado, I continued. 'I am ashamed to admit it, but we humans can be extremely limited. We know so little about ourselves. We do know, of course, that we were given life. And we know that after a short life span our earthly life will end. Then, should we live this short life span in darkness, should we fail to benefit from the wisdom of our ancestors, and should we remain indifferent and neglectful of the gift of revelation given to us over the ages we will end up knowing very little about our true selves and the purpose of our lives, about truth and about reality.'

At this point, my friend winced just a little, yet he encouraged me to continue. One thing I had grown to recognise and like was that Gunna Dan never argued with my assertions. I knew that while he was keeping silent, he was, all the time, absorbing what I was saying. I also knew that he was enjoying the apple pie, the ice cream and the coffee.

'Gunna Dan, you have challenged me to tell you about Ireland and its people. The great reality for most people in Ireland today is the material world. Possession of the material things of life, the goods of this world, is alas, what seems to count the most. All of us, all over the country, have a great appetite for property, houses, land, cars and appliances of all kinds. Everybody wants comfortable jobs and big pay. Even the children are taught to want possessions of all kinds. They must have the latest Nintendo Wii, up-to-date Apple iPods and the most elaborate of mobile phones.

And yet, for a people immersed in materialism, the essential dynamic going on in the material world is not understood. Indeed, the essential reality of the material world is ignored.'

I paused to nibble at the pie. I sipped the coffee. Then I continued with my spiel. 'Let me explain it this way. Living on this island are cattle of all kinds, including cows, bulls, heifers, bullocks, steers and calves, numbering approximately seven million animals in any one year. There are also roughly as many sheep. Pigs account for well over a million and a half. The total number of poultry is in excess of twelve million, almost thirteen. Then there are thousands of horses, ponies, donkeys, mules and jennets.[16] And we cannot omit the animals of the wild, including otters, stoats, badgers, red and fallow deer, pine martens, red and grey squirrels, hares, rabbits and foxes. This list, of course, does not include goats, cats (of which there are well over a million in Dublin alone[17]), dogs and the birds of the air. And, of course, there are the almost six million people living out their lives in Ireland. Let us face it. Every day of the year, each and every one of these animals, along with us ourselves, offload thousands of tonnes of crap and millions of litres of wee onto the land and into the waterways of this lovely green country of ours. And this has been happening for thousands

---

16 *Statistical Yearbook of Ireland 2005* (Central Statistics Office, An Príomh-Oifig Staidrimh), 219.

17 Jimmy Cahill, General Manager of Dublin Society for the Prevention of Cruelty to Animals, 'Programme to neuter feral cats and stop spread of disease urged.' Published 02 February 2008, *Irish Times:* www.irishtimes.com.

of years, and it continues to this very day. It goes on day after day and year after year. In fact, the whole world is saturated with the stuff.'

Gunna Dan's eyes were popping, but I kept going. 'And every year, thousands of tonnes of potatoes, oats, wheat, barley, fodder and root crops of many species, green crops of great varieties and fruits aplenty – apples, pears, blackcurrants, raspberries and strawberries – are extracted from this same saturated land. By far Ireland's greatest plant products, which you admired for their verdant emerald colour, are the grasses and clovers that cover our fertile isle. All this is cultivated, managed and farmed with this principal fact in mind that the more crap and the more wee that is dumped on the land, the more and the better is the food that comes from it. All of us, including the animals of the land, then eat this food. We devour it in huge quantities. If no refined chemicals are used in the cultivation, we say that the food is organic. In fact, the more crap and the more wee that we spread on the land, the more organic is the food.'

I let that bit sink in, but I noted with amusement that what I was saying didn't in the slightest deter either of us from enjoying the apple pie, the ice cream and the coffee.

I felt encouraged to continue, and with a flourish I asked, 'And, here in Ireland, what happens to the animals themselves?' I paused dramatically, but quickly continued. 'The animals themselves, a year or two after they are born, are slaughtered in the slaughterhouses. Butchers cut up their carcases with hatchets and knives. Every day, hundreds of thousands of chickens are decapitated, de-feathered, gutted, washed and packaged. Every day, hundreds of thousands of pigs are electrocuted. A similar number of sheep and lambs are killed, and every day thousands of cattle are knifed and hacked. Then meat in the form of lamb chops, beef off the round (sliced from the bums of cattle), steaks, rib beef, shin beef and what have you is offered for sale in the shops and supermarkets for our consumption. This is our material life on planet Earth. This is truth. This is reality. This is certainty.'

I hesitated a little. I looked at my friend. He was open-mouthed. And then, I couldn't help it. I decided to layer it on. I told him that the worldwide number of animals killed for food in the year 2000 was forty-five billion (45,000,000,000), according to the Food and Agriculture Organization of the United Nations. This included 306 million cattle, buffalo and calves; 1.2 billion pigs; 795 million sheep and goats, and 42.7 billion chickens, ducks, turkeys and geese. And then I continued by telling him that these numbers do not include the fish or any of the other animals from the sea, simply because they are too numerous – in fact, incalculable.[18]

'This is unbelievable,' said Gunna Dan. 'Forty-five billion animals!'

Except for a satisfying smile, I did not react much to his amazement. I did not want to discuss or explore the implications of this information while we were eating at the table. I lifted my mug to my mouth and discovered that without realising it, I had already emptied it. Gunna Dan, the gentleman he was, got up with alacrity. As he was standing, he gasped, 'I wasn't expecting this at all!' He made his way to the counter, leaned over it and directed a loud 'hello' towards the kitchen. He politely asked the startled waitress for two more mugs of coffee and soon resumed his seat.

'I have to take this approach,' I blurted. I did not want to be apologetic, but it came across as if I were trying to be that way. 'You see,' I said to my friend, 'we need to have an understanding of the natural world we live in, first and foremost. We cannot give allegiance to anything unless we understand it and know it. All of us belong to the world in some fashion or other and to give it allegiance, if not fidelity, without knowing anything about it is, to say the least, foolhardy if not truly dangerous.'

'The truth that I want to get across is this: throughout the world, a great cycling and recycling of biological materials takes place, particularly of crap and wee. Because of this, all material life is connected. Earth is a more or less closed system. The natural world, except for the input of energy from the sun, is a closed system. The law of conservation of mass-matter tells us that the amount of matter in this closed system remains constant. No new matter is ever created. The world is no heavier today than it was in ancient times. All that happens is that the same materials are recycled over and over again. The constituent parts can only be rearranged, built up, broken down and built up again. We are all made of this same material, which is how plants and animals are closely related even though we live in a world where all matter is constantly changing and nothing ever remains the same.'

Every now and then Gunna Dan would stop me in my tracks and question me intently. At this point he begged me to be more specific. After a moment's thought I continued.

---

18 'Animals Killed for Food in the United States in 2000 (millions),' *United Poultry Concerns, Inc.: www.upc-online.org/slaughter/2000slaughter_stats.html.*

'All the materials that a head of cabbage needs for its growth and development are the same substances required by our bodies. So, we eat cabbages. A whole host of proteins, fats, salts and nutrients that are in abundance in the bodies of animals are the same materials that we need for our own growth and development, so we also eat animals. We never eat sand. The materials now making up the nucleotides in the cells of my body were probably active in the liver of some other animal in the green fields of Ireland a few months back. The nitrogen now in my muscles could, last year, have been stored in a plastic bag at the back of some creamery somewhere in County Clare prior to having been scattered onto the grasslands. It could also have come from a much less salubrious source!'

Gunna Dan was agog. He listened intently to everything I was saying. Every now and then, he would make a comment or repeat a phrase I had just uttered. This comforted me a lot because I knew that he was with me all the way. At times our comments to each other could be very speculative. Nonetheless we accepted that all of us are obliged to recognise the intelligence at work in the world of nature. We need to stop short in our tracks at moments in time and answer for ourselves what it is that enables us to be beneficiaries of a great universal provision. Gunna Dan pondered a lot on this. Then he told me that throughout his life he saw differences everywhere and had always assumed that everything in life was haphazardly different. Now he was pleased to learn that all life is one. He pleaded with me to explore and expand on, what was for him, an astounding issue. After a mouthful of coffee, I continued.

'The internal processes going on in plants, animals and humans are the same. There is only one chapter on aerobic respiration in biology textbooks because for all oxygen-breathing organisms, the process is the same, the enzymatic reactions are the same, the end products are the same and the trapping of released energy from the food is the same. The constant chemical respiratory activity that goes on in every living cell of a mouse or a rat or an elephant is the exact same process that goes on in every living cell in our bodies. All the domestic mammals that we breed and rear and kill and eat are very similar to us in design, even though you may not think it just by looking. The pig has seven bones in its neck. A mouse has seven bones in its neck. A rat has seven bones in its neck. A horse has seven bones in its neck. Seven cervical bones are also found in the necks of a cow, a whale and a giraffe, and we humans also have seven bones in our necks. We are only distinguished from each other by slight variations in the basic mammalian design plan. Not only this, but at the molecular level, the differences are extremely slight. For years, pig insulin was used by diabetics simply because it worked as well as human insulin. A molecule of pig insulin, exactly like a molecule of human insulin, is constructed and arranged in two chains, one of twenty-one amino acids, the second of thirty. They differ from each other in only one amino acid.[19] The DNA structure, which is on a much bigger scale altogether than any protein and carries within itself a huge amount of information, is extremely intricate and complicated. Yet, this very complicated molecule is universally similar in the cells of all mammals.'

I was anxious to emphasise to Gunna Dan the enormity of the information that is stored in our DNA molecules. Because of this, I referred to the question that Eckhart Tolle asks in his book, *The Power of Now*. In his appreciation of the intelligence of life on Earth, he rhetorically asks, 'How can a single human cell, measuring one thousandth of an inch across, contain instructions within its DNA that would fill one thousand books of six hundred pages each?'[20] This enlightenment bowled Gunna Dan over completely. For some time, he was speechless at the implications of it all.

By this time, more people had come into An Teach Bia. Gunna Dan had so many questions for me, but the increasing noise level upset us. We left the café and went across the road. We decided that before we would part for the evening, we would walk along the right bank of the Inagh River on the grounds of the Fall's Hotel. Gunna Dan was particularly anxious for the walk. No sooner had we started than he blurted: 'I am astounded to realise that we are all born into a material world that is closed in on itself and where everything in the world of nature keeps going round and round. All the materials underpinning life on Earth are constantly breaking down so as to be built up and used again. And then, and then, all this activity goes on with perfect precision, perfect timing, and not unimportantly, with complete independence.' Then he was silent. He was silent as if he wanted to meditate on his thoughts. At times such as this I

---

19 DocCheck Medical Services GMBH, 'Insulin.' Last updated 2002. *DocCheck Flexikon: www.flexikon.com/insulin.*

20 Eckhart Tolle, *The Power of Now*. (London: Hodder & Stoughton, 2001), 20.

had begun to notice that he had a particular characteristic. He would join his hands in front of him and twirl his thumbs like mad. This is what he was now doing, with vigour and with anxiety.

After a deferential period of quiet I began. 'Look, Gunna Dan, the material world exists. It is. In fact, it is laughable to suggest otherwise. But then too, we have our minds. We have our minds for thinking. Our ability to think enables us to give meaning and importance to our place in this world of ours.'

'That's it', interjected Gunna Dan. 'That's what I need to explore. I need to explore the meaning and importance of this life. I need to experience truthful personal responses to the issues of life and of living.'

The sound of the cascading waters did not disturb him in the least so intent was he on what he was thinking and on what he was saying. In the silence that followed we continued walking. I felt that Gunna Dan needed the silence to reflect and to ponder. I too became reflective. I could not help admitting to myself that I loved the company of Gunna Dan, especially then, when we were ambling by the riverside. The silence between us was magical – to me, for certain, it was. I often wondered about the man and about what he was feeling and thinking. However, every time I was with him, I found that it was sufficient for us just to be together, and my curiosity about him was not greatly aroused. Strangely, I was always more curious about him afterwards. Eventually, we arrived back at the front of the hotel. We walked down the avenue and out onto the little road. We passed the vocational school on our right, and soon we were in the village square. As we parted, Gunna Dan assured me that he would be thinking quite a lot about what we had discussed and with a 'see you soon again', he was gone.

Chapter 5

Reality All about Us

A few days later, we met at the car park of the Rambler's Rest and decided that we would go for a walk along the Corrofin road out as far as the crossroads at Mauricesmills. Once we got away from the busy Inagh to Lahinch road, we were able to relax and enjoy the countryside. I like nothing better than to be able to look all around me. I am always in a state of expectation, wishing that something spectacular would happen in the midst of our isolation and aloneness. And more often than not, I am not disappointed. This time, however, I was amusing myself by observing the hedgerows and the fields. Gunna Dan agreed that the hedgerows were distinctly pleasing, and he found them to be in sharp contrast with the dry stone walls further up in the county. I couldn't help but tell him that in the olden times in Gaelic Ireland, hedgerows would have been maintained on top of banks or mounds, now called ditches, to mark out the boundaries of the townlands. Only remnants of such hedgerows remain now, because from the mid 1700s onwards, Ireland's forced colonisation and enclosure of land took place. New hedgerows were planted with the intention to delimit fields and to claim ownership of them. The fact that by 1870 nearly 10 percent of the country of Ireland was owned by just twenty people and that only 3 percent of all Irish householders owned any land tells us that the efforts of the colonisers were hugely successful. However, since the 1880s, a great land revolution has taken place in Ireland. Even by 1916, the year of the Easter Rising; the year that saw the opening act in the War of Independence, 63.9 percent of the land was back in the hands of the country's people.[21] This warring over land mystified my friend because, as he explained it to me, the land in his country was held in common for all people, and the idea of personal ownership of small units of mountainous land was meaningless.

Gunna Dan was especially bewildered with the way I could, as in this case, look at the hedgerows and the enclosed fields and then tell him with conviction that they were a very modern landscape feature. And then again, I could look at other features and say with assuredness that they were old. In fact, he said that he was very appreciative of my comments because I was enabling him more and more to realise that information, and the knowledge that comes from the processing of information, has great depth. Realising this gave him a sense of great profundity. He was surprised by how easily he was able to perceive that the obvious reality on the surface of things more often than not hid a deeper reality of greater significance. He added with just a slight hint of sadness that we humans can often experience knowledge at a very shallow level, and, because of this, we remain unaware of deeper realities and more extensive truth. This took me very much by surprise, and then Gunna Dan took over the talking.

'What puzzles me greatly is this,' he said. 'Why is it that the vast majority of us do not have much insight into the great universal reality of sameness and commonality that we were talking about the other day in Ennistymon? Why is it that we cannot see the material world for what it is? Why is it that we cannot give importance to a great issue? Are we not all members of one extremely close family? Are we not all brothers and sisters to each other? Should it not be a mark of civilised society that we are affectionate to and for each other? Tolerance here is not a virtue. It is simply obligatory. Can I not assume that at least the learned people know this? The writers and the poets, the scientists and the university dons, the leaders of society, the politicians, the doctors, the teachers and the clergy? In fact, anyone with a little wit and understanding; should not all people be aware of this? And yet ... and yet, this certain knowledge seems to be inert and ineffective. It seems that this profound knowledge only skims our minds.'

Gunna Dan was very serious in his manner and his speech. He maintained the same demeanour as he then continued. 'Furthermore, we

---

21 David Hickie, ed., *Irish hedgerows: Networks for Nature* (Networks for Nature, 2004), 14.

are not aware that everything is cyclical, circular and connected. We block our thinking and our feelings from realising that not only are we all alike and similar at the personal and microscopic levels, but we are also close to the same nature and share common origins. We are actually part of the earth and soil. Indeed, we are truly the earth and soil as one great family in one great nature-hood. This nature-hood is deserving of greater recognition and a greater respect. In truth, it is deserving of a holier celebration. Our wonderful planet is sustained and energised by the sun. Its energy is abundant and free. It is always there for us. It warms and uplifts us all the more after a period of darkness and cold. Its energy ensures that we are provided with food, oxygen and water, so that we can live life.'

Sometimes we would stop and look at the bushes, the hedges and the fields. We particularly liked observing the only species of whitethorn, also called hawthorn, native in Ireland and wondering whether we could we see the turn of the season in the developing haws (hawthorn berries) – fruit that would sustain birds and field mice in the winter to come. Sometimes we would be looking down at the ground while talking. This time, however, Gunna Dan kept looking skywards.

The loveliness of being out in the sun was not lost on Gunna Dan. He now asked me if I could tell him more about our nearest star. He was astounded when I told him that the sun, a relatively young star and one of the brightest in the galactic complex, makes up 98 percent of the mass of our particular solar system and that the remaining 2 percent consists of all the planets (of which Earth is one) and the lunar satellites. Every second, seven hundred million tonnes of hydrogen gas are converted into helium products. In the process, the equivalent of five million tonnes of pure energy is released.[22] This happens every second of every day. Furthermore, the sun has enough fuel to burn for another four and half billion years! What impressed Gunna Dan a lot was that no matter how great the quantities of gases and no matter how long the time, this whole event is a diminishing finite process. More than that, the unceasing burning process is an accelerating one. The consequence of this is that the sun continues to glow brighter at a rate of roughly ten percent every billion years or so. Gunna Dan had his own insights into this accelerating diminishment, and he surprised me when he deliberately and slowly accentuated to me that

---

22   Calvin J. Hamilton, 'Sun.' Last updated 2009. *Views of the Solar System: www.solarviews. com/eng/sun.htm.*

one can only wonder at the great intelligence that directs and maintains the whole solar system and the universe itself.

He then queried me on how exactly Earth's green plants capture the sun's energy to make food. Gunna Dan asked me this, as much mischievously as enquiringly, because on other occasions, I had held forth on the importance of the grasses growing in the fields. He did not know that all the hundreds of thousands of species of plants on Earth, with their millions of subspecies and families, could practically fit into one of only four groups: algae; mosses (and their allies); ferns (and their allies) and seed bearing plants. The one special family of plants among them all is the grass family, which provides the bulk of feedstock for the world's community of animals and humans: rice, corn, maize, wheat, barley, rye, oats, pearl millet, sugar cane, sorghum and the common grasses, of which there is a tremendous variety[23]. We continued talking about the issues for some time, and in our rambles we considered world hunger, famines, global warming and climate change. It was Gunna Dan who always wished to find out how things were meant to be, and so it was that we admired the natural fact that green plants manufacture huge quantities of high energy foods. We reflected on the fact that they provide copious quantities of oxygen into the atmosphere, much more than they require for their own needs. And in the process, we noted that these same plants absorb vast quantities of carbon dioxide gas from the atmosphere.

We had long reached the crossroads at Mauricesmills. The evening was clear and cloudless, and rather than turn back, we lingered there. We sat down on a low-lying, dry stone wall. We drank water from the plastic bottles we carried with us, and before long, we were chatting about the availability of fresh water on the planet. We noted that only 3 percent of the world's water is freshwater (most of it is saline), and only one third of this freshwater, just 1 percent, is available for human consumption.[24] Nobody should complain – we suggested to ourselves – if we were ever to get a prolonged wet summer! No wonder all the populous cities of the world must have water recycling and conservation systems in place.

Eventually we walked homewards. To emphasise my point about recycling and conservation, I told Gunna Dan that back in the late 1960s,

---

23 'Flowering Plant.' Last updated 28 May 2010. *Wikipedia: en.wikipedia.org/wiki/ Flowering_plant.*
24 'Freshwater Crisis.' Last updated 2010. *National Geographic: environment. nationalgeographic.com/environment/freshwater/freshwater-crisis*

while a student working in London, I was made aware of the conservation of substances when I was told, while drinking a glass of water in one of the city's pubs, that my kidneys would more than likely be the twelfth pair through which this same water would be passing, simply because of the intensity of the recycling processes going on in London. The hydrogen and oxygen atoms making up the water molecules would, of course, have been billions of years old. The water molecules themselves could probably have travelled hundreds of millions of times around the world. In fact, they could have travelled anywhere. They could have travelled everywhere. In its great process of purification, the heat of the sun constantly energises the molecules of water in a process called evaporation. The water molecules go high into the sky, leaving behind the debris and the dirt. Then, after the accumulation and aggregation of the clouds, the same water pours down on us, pure and clean. Gunna Dan was taking all of this in, and even though we were now reaching the car park in the village of Inagh and were about to part, he declared to me, all the time looking intently into my face, that the implications of what I was saying were enormous.

'Why is it that humankind has difficulty recognising the great intelligence behind the dynamic activities of the world? Did we not revere the sun, did we not treasure the land and the landscape and all its animals and all living things, and did we not worship the source of all this life and sustenance? Did we not realise that we are seriously part of the dynamic world through and through? Do we not know that when the birds sing and ducks quack that we, with them, are closely in touch with a single universal reality that sustains all of us? Does not everyone on Earth rejoice every morning when the sun rises because it rises to nurture us?'

I could not answer him. I did not want to answer him. In one way, I felt that he did not expect me to expand on his comments. Instead, I was preoccupied in my mind with the notion that I was seeing an emergent spirit that was full of concern. I was seeing a man who was thinking about things more and more. And as I looked at him, I knew he was fretful and concerned. He had become very reflective and, to be very honest about it, this was to my liking. We parted, and as we left, he surprisingly acknowledged that it was a most rewarding ramble up and down the road.

I spent a lot of time thinking to myself afterwards. I knew that I would soon be concentrating on other aspects of our lives when we met for these discussions. While we were at the crossroads, I was reluctant to keep the focus on the material side of life. I had started to explain to Gunna Dan that all the materials of the world that enter our bodies have only a very short stay. In the case of the air, it is only a few seconds, the case of water only a few hours. And we must eat every day because the food we eat only lasts a short time. I continued explaining that our white blood cells have only a life of two weeks or so; that all our red blood cells are spent and gone after three months; that our skin has a similar length of life, as the clearing of scars and scratches testifies; that our muscles, blood, bones, brains, heart and guts are different ages with different life spans. Even then, as I was talking, I knew that Gunna Dan was aware that what I was saying was not the whole picture. I knew that he was pondering on other realities besides the reality of the material world and the reality of our physical presence on Earth. I think I unsettled the poor man because I spoke so convincingly and rapidly. I became upset that night, not because my fond friend – I had grown more attached to him by now – was upset, but more because I knew that within a short time I would have to radically give greater importance to the scope of our discussions.

We met the next evening, a Saturday, in Inagh. I was going to the eight o'clock Mass in the local church. The sound of the church bell was pure and clear. I invited Gunna Dan to come with me. I found it easy to do so because I knew that by now he had a significant awareness of the historical event of Christianity itself. The lives of the saints especially that of Saint Patrick were a marvel and a delight to him. Then he told me that the ringing of the church bell reminded him of his homeland. His people, he emphasised, still have a great respect and reverence for the sonority of the bell. Bells ring from the tents when babies are born, and bells ring when anyone passes out of this world. There is a ready acceptance among his people that the sound of the bell harmonises with the still existent energies of primordial creation and, because of this belief, bells are tolled at the beginning of life and at the end of life. Bells, he told me, are the great message carriers of this world, communicating the realities of our lives with the realities of other worlds. Tolling bells call out to other worlds, telling them that we want their notice and approval, their help and protection. Gunna Dan was remarkably sure about this, and he went further. He explained to me that this was why his people always put bells and gongs around the necks of their animals, confident that the kindly spirits of the next world would hear the pure, clear, clean sounds ascending as prayers, beseeching these spirits to protect the animals and their people. I couldn't help but tell my friend that it was Saint Patrick himself who brought the first bell to Ireland, and that the iron bell of Saint Patrick (now in the National Museum, Dublin) is at once the most authentic and the oldest relic of Christian metal work. It has an unbroken history through fourteen hundred years.[25] The ringing of the church bell in Inagh, I explained, maintains an uninterrupted tradition and practise that links every one of us on the island of Ireland to the ancient past, and now in the present time, it brings us into contact with as yet unknown spiritual worlds, if not into contact with our future destinies.

By this time, we had drawn nearer to the church. I encouraged him to come in with me but there was no need. He was quite willing, and, he laughed when I told him that we would be out again in half an hour. There was a lovely smile on his face as he went in. What I admired about him was the fact that he was adventurous, open-minded and free-spirited. Afterwards, as we were walking away from the church, he thanked me profusely for asking him to come. He was very much pleased by the occasion, and he was not in the least bit overawed by the symbolism and mysteriousness of the service. He told me that he was impressed with the saintly aged priest who conducted the service of the Eucharist. And, in special way, he admired the holy women of the parish who prayed the rosary beforehand. Noteworthy for him was the recitation of the *aguisín*,[26] or supplement, at the end of each decade. 'It is so noble,' he said quietly to me, 'to pray that all souls will ultimately enjoy the happiness of heaven.' He was delighted when a similar sentiment of universality was stated more emphatically during the consecration of the Mass.

He then began recapping the ideas and statements that occupied our minds on the previous day. He now wished to know how attached any of us should ever be to the earth, since all matter, and in particular the matter of our physical bodies, is constantly changing. Further, he wanted to know if, as a society, we really accepted the implications of all of this. He

---

25 Richard Lovett, 'Ireland's Eye Continued: Shrine of St. Patrick's Bell,' *Irish Pictures Drawn with Pen and Pencil. Library Ireland: www.libraryireland.com/IrishPictures/I-9.php.*

26 *Auguisín* means addition or addendum in Gaeilge, according to the Irish-English dictionary (*An Roinn Oideachais*), *Gearrfhoclóir Gaeilge-Béarla*, (Dublin: Irish Department of Education, 1981).

wondered if the ephemeral nature of the world had any impact on man's thinking at all. I told him that the transience of the material world is very old knowledge given to us in the Bible. The first book, the book of Genesis, deals with primordial history, and there, in this very ancient document, we get the information bold and true. On Earth 'shall you eat your bread until you return to the soil as you were taken from it. For dust you are and to dust you shall return.'[27] During this time, Gunna Dan remained sombre. It didn't help when I added that this very truth was recalled every year on Ash Wednesday at the blessing of the ashes. I knew, however, just by looking at him that he had a lot of questions for me. I knew, too, that he had come to some conclusions of his own, but I wished him to wait. I continued my discourse, and I addressed Gunna Dan as follows:

'My dear friend, I trust that you will stick with me while I tell you what life and truth and reality are all about. It is not an easy task. Again, all of us here are born ignorant and helpless. Yes, we are undeniably a part of the earth and the soil. Even still, some wags will be heard to say that we are nothing but pieces of crap on a gigantic merry-go-flush-around of constant recycling and rearrangement; that we are here only to utter a wondrous "Aw!" when new variations pop up. One thing is sure,' I said as I looked straight at him, 'our personhoods are not made up of atoms of carbon, oxygen, nitrogen and phosphorus, nor of the molecules of proteins, carbohydrates, fats and salts. Neither are we just an accumulation of blood and guts and bone and muscle. All the chemicals, compounds, tissues and constituent substances that make up our bodies are there for only an infinitesimal amount of time, relatively speaking. The atomic constituents of these materials are billions of years old – indeed as old as the universe itself. They belong solely to the earthly world, and they will stay with the world and in the world as long as Earth itself persists. A material view of our make-up abandons our much longer lasting personhoods, our enduring personalities and our inner living entities.

'Yes, the material or the chemical make-up of our bodies is important, but it is so extremely peripheral. While we are on the topic of our material make-up, we cannot forget that Earth is now, for all practical purposes, a closed system. But billions of years ago, the planet that we now live on was formed from only a tiny part of the 2 percent of the solar nebula that was left over after the formation of the sun[28]. Gravitational forces

---

27 Genesis 3:19, JB
28 'Earth.' Last updated 29 May 2010. *Wikipedia: en.wikipedia.org/wiki/Earth.*

brought about the concentration and accumulation of galactic dust and gas, and from this material, our planet, along with all the other planets and associated moons, emerged.

Gunna Dan was so pleased to hear me talking about our wider global context, and he encouraged me to continue. He so wanted to explore wider vistas and grander aspects. It was easy for me to see that he loved the inclusion of the solar and galactic dimension in our discussions.

He interjected, 'Now, I understand from you that, even at the material level, we are as closely a part of the astral world as the stars themselves. The very dust and soil of the ground is of the stars. We are of the same astral matter. We come from the stars. We are of the same origin. Yes, we surely are of the same origin. From the cosmic perspective, we can be seen as discrete celestial entities.' Echoing my earlier comment, he joyfully continued: 'And the origin of our inner living entities is way beyond all of this.'

Immediately, I saw that Gunna Dan realised that our realities belong to a wide, magnificent spectrum that stretches from the very dirt in the fields way out to the furthermost stars and beyond. He began to realise that the true story of who we are can only be revealed when we travel from the microscopic to the cosmic, from the ordinary to the sublime. He then knew that no issue could be excluded and that all aspects had to be examined. He went home happy that night. He was chuffed that the cosmological dimension was opening up. He felt more at home in this realm. He was particularly happy when I agreed, at his insistent cajoling I may add, to meet him at the lakeside the following day. I was more apprehensive, however. The cosmological dimension of which I was thinking would be more adventurous and challenging.

Cloonmacken Lake was a beauty on the Sunday when we next met. The lake, settled in a broad basin some little distance from the slopes of Slievecallan Mountain, was incredibly quiet. The clouds overhead were reflected finely and distinctly on the mirror-like sheet of water. The beautiful vista accentuated the brightness and the lightness of the world around us. And when Gunna Dan smilingly joined me, he immediately expressed his delight at all he saw and felt.

We both agreed that it would be advantageous if it were possible to go for a long walk all along the lakeshore. Instead, we looked all around us in unison and admired the full flowering of the surrounding diverse species. The sunlight enhanced their colours. The nearby ducks watched us hungrily. We made an unusual pair, wearing sunglasses and sun hats. We could not sit down at the table. The seating itself and the table were too wet. Just before we arrived, we had one of those sunny summer showers one is often likely to experience during Ireland's summertime. The glistening wetness gave a heightened freshness to everything. In the distance, a rainbow threw its regular smooth arch of colours over the whole landscape, and we both commented on the strength of its hues. We both appreciated that the natural phenomenon we were looking at was a miracle of light. Gunna Dan was especially taken by the clarity of the violet light. I even thought he was excited about it. He surprised me when he explained that in Chinese culture, a culture that has a strong influence on his home country of Onavistan, violet light is considered to be a harmonising power in the universe because of the combination of red (yang) and blue (yin). Then he started to tell me that violet energy is the energy of healing and that its power extends throughout the whole planet, including the atmosphere, the seas, the lands, the rivers and the lakes. All plants, animals and humans absorb its power, and, verve and vigour are subtly heightened in everything. All the time while Gunna Dan was talking to me, I stood there actually astounded, and I knew, as if I hadn't already known, that I was in the company of an exceptional man. I even began to wonder if he was actually part of the light and the energies of the whole world. I began to wonder more when he casually commented that it is the solar energy from the red and blue ends of the spectrum of light that make the high-powered compounds of carbohydrate in the photosynthesising cells of plants. He then explained how the unabsorbed green light is reflected outwards, and so, he said as much jocosely as in earnest, 'This is why green plants, though not being green, appear green.'

In the distance, the yellow flowers of the gorse (called *furze* in some parts of the country and *whin* in others) beamed out a terrific golden colour. The reeds on the lake, for some odd reason, were sloping almost northwards. At the water's edge could be seen emerging irises, never called anything but *feileastrams*[29] by my father when I was growing up. Red and white flowering clovers were abundant in the grassy areas. I then brought Gunna Dan's attention to a small patch of yellow flowering shamrocks that I saw growing nearby. The plant we were looking at was *Trifolium dubium* (in Gaelic, *an seamair bhuí*), more often referred to as the lesser yellow trefoil. This led to the start of a pleasant interlude. I explained to my friend that while the shamrock (from *seamróg*, originally *seamair óg*, meaning 'little clover') is the national plant symbol for Ireland, nobody actually knows which plant is the real shamrock. In 1892, Nathaniel Colgan, the botanist and author of *The Flora of County Dublin* (1904), went about finding out the answer. He invited contributions of the true plant from all over the country. He received specimens from some twenty of the thirty-two counties of Ireland, and the numerous varieties sent in included white and red clovers, the lesser yellow trefoil that we were now admiring, some spotted medick and other similar plants[30]. Then I told him about another survey that was carried out by the botanist Charles Nelson at the National Botanic Gardens in Glasnevin, Dublin in 1988. Charles Nelson invited people to send in to him specimens that they thought were shamrock[31]. This time, 46 percent of the contributions were *Trifolium dubium* (the lesser yellow trefoil), but white clover came in second at a substantial 35 percent. Of course, as I explained to Gunna Dan, one could not be too surprised, because all the plants that were submitted have the trifoliate leaf, all were similar looking and each one of them could easily represent the plant that Saint Patrick used to give insight into the mystery of the Holy Trinity.

Then, all of a sudden, our composure was disturbed. Right besides us, a big, fat, hairy, bulbous bumblebee landed on the purple red flower of a clover plant. How the bee could fly to the flower was a wonder, but once it settled down, it began working feverishly. Gunna Dan was elated to see and meet with our little visitor. His delight showed all over his smiling face. Excitedly, he told me that whereas there is only one species

29 The term is also used in the *County Clare Biolological Records Centre*: *www.clarebiodiversity.ie*.

30 Anna Pavord, *The Naming of Names: The Search for Order in the World of Plants* (London: Bloomsbury, 2005), 396.

31 'The Truth Behind the Shamrock.' Last updated 17 March 2004, *BBC News: news.bbc.co.uk/2/hi/uk_news/3519116.stm*

of honeybee in Ireland, we are blessed with nineteen different species of bumblebee. I knew that Gunna Dan had been over to the Aran Islands off the Galway coast in late springtime. I knew he took part in an outdoor study programme on the flora and fauna of the island, and I knew, too, that he was always ready to share his new-found knowledge with me. Now, by the lake in Cloonmacken, he further surprised me when he told me that there is a bumblebee sub-species, *Bombus muscorum var. allenellus*, on the Aran Islands, which is the only location in the world where this black-haired specimen lives. I knew that the west of Ireland, particularly areas around the Burren, was rich in various bumblebee species.[32] I also knew that their long tongues could reach down inside the flowers of the red clover and, as a result, could easily effect pollination, a task that the shorter-tongued honeybees are unable to do.

Gunna Dan went leisurely over to the clover plant. He stooped down, ever so gently, to see the industrious bee. My friend then settled himself on the grounded gravel and stretched out his finger as if to touch and rub its hairy back. However, just at the point of contact, the bumblebee slowly rose, like a laden helicopter, took off into the air and flew away into the distance. Gunna Dan rose, and in his rising, I saw a man transformed and enraptured. He was euphoric in the true meaning of the word – full of goodness and happiness. I saw, too, as we turned and walked back towards the lake, that he was a man now more noble in stature. He was so cheerful, and his gaiety and high spirits were infectious. His posture and bearing revealed his constant engagement with an elevated state of rapture. I was so chuffed to be with him. I felt great. I wanted it to last. And to a greater extent, an extent that surprised me, I began to value my fellowship and friendship with Gunna Dan more, so much so that I promised myself that from now on I would be less hesitant, less self-protective and much more daring.

We walked briskly towards the lapping water's edge. The ducks didn't expect this, and they ran helter-skelter in all directions into the water. What surprised me was that feathers of all shapes and sizes flew in all directions, up and down and over and back. One feather in particular seemed to have ascended the highest; it was all on its own as it descended downwards from the sky above. Gunna Dan was pleasantly amused, and I, for my part, loved it.

---

32 'The Irish Fauna,' *Bees of Ireland*. Last updated 12 February 2010. *Trinity College Dublin: Zoology:* www.tcd.ie/Zoology/research/Bees/fauna.php

Chapter 6

Reality All within Us

I didn't meet Gunna Dan again until the following Wednesday. He was coming out of the Mace supermarket in Inagh just as I was going in. I was delighted to see him. Before I could say anything, he casually said to me, 'Look at what I got in the surf shop in Lahinch yesterday' – and from his inside coat pocket he pulled out a little blue book. It gave the dates and times for high and low tides for the whole year. 'This is a great little book,' he said. Tomorrow afternoon, at a quarter to three, is the low tide. Are you on for a walk on the beach?' I needed no prompting whatsoever. I spent the rest of the evening in great expectation, and when I went to bed that night, I began to realise that my friendship with Gunna Dan had become an important, if not an essential part of my life. I can assure you that as I went to sleep, I spent a lot of time counting my blessings and was so thankful.

Gunna Dan was already on the Lahinch beach when I arrived. Both of us blended in well with the holidaymakers. We looked splendid in our shorts, T-shirts, sunglasses and hats. I made no mention at all of the wonderful day at Cloonmacken Lake. Neither did my friend. For me, it was a precious occasion. By the lakeside I had felt, for the first time in a long while, the joy of elemental simplicity. I had enjoyed doing nothing other than looking at flowers and weeds and birds and insects. It had been soothing to my spirit to stop and look and stare. I had been easy and contented in myself. I instinctively knew that, for Gunna Dan, that sojourn was truly special. I knew, too, that when Gunna Dan had reached out to touch the bumblebee, he was reaching out from somewhere special within himself.

We soon began walking. The whole wide-ranging vista of the expansive beach extended before us. We became fascinated by the persistence of the surfers as they came inwards, trying to ride the crest of the waves, and we noted their continual trudges out to the sea in order to come back in again. Eventually, we arrived at the lower reaches of the beach. Fewer people were about and this seemed to trigger Gunna Dan to start discussing the issues on his mind.

'I've been thinking a lot about the constantly changing nature of the material matter of which we are all made. You amazed me when you told me that the elemental constituents of all of this matter are billions of years old. Essentially what you are telling me is that for billions of years, all that is happening is only a recycling of everything, and that this recycling keeps on a-going irrespectively and independently of how we live out our lives.'

He halted and composed himself. I thought that I even heard him gasp. He prepared to speak again, and what a preparation it was. He was breathing quickly, and then, at first stutteringly, he began, 'you see ... you see, the energy of the material world is precisely and narrowly focused. It is specifically closed in on itself. It is limited. It is limited because of the imposition of strict non-material external laws that limit all action to precise, predictable and restricted outcomes.'

Abruptly, he turned towards me. By now, I had become used to his mannerisms, but the feeling I had was more than just becoming used to him. I had grown to like the man a lot, and I just loved being there with him. This time, however, I detected seriousness in his looks, and this was confirmed for me when he, in a slow and deliberate manner, said straight to my face, 'Paddy, we need our thinking.' He only paused for a second. Then he continued. 'We need our thinking badly. We need our thinking to free us, and we need our thinking to keep us free. Without this freedom, we will never be able to see.' He paused again. 'The material world says nothing to anyone. It belongs to itself. It stays within itself. It only goes round and round in circles, and this is what it will do for billions of years to come. In fact, that is all it can do.'

He said this latter phrase with certain desperation, and actually, he emphasised his seriousness with a garnish of crossness. It encouraged me to present a considerate contribution. 'Yes, that's it. The laws of nature and science, working with starting materials, govern all the physical outcomes, whether they are products or residues. The material world is overt, so much so that it engrosses our thinking, our feelings, our wants and desires. This engrossment, particularly of our minds, can be so great that we cannot meet with other more constant realities in our lives. We cannot see them. They are blocked out. When this happens, other-worldly realities are blocked out, higher aspirations and goals are greatly reduced, and what we now want above all are the victorious possessions of the so-called good life: houses, cars, holidays, good jobs, plenty of money and admiring audiences.'

As we walked along the beach, we talked all about these issues, and Gunna Dan made a telling point. 'We ought to be living out our lives independently of the closed, transient material world. Our attitudes and our thinking should be elsewhere. It is our thinking, at whatever level it is, that gives meaning, direction and guidance to our lives. In fact, it is our thinking that makes us the people that we are. And, it is our thinking that makes the society we live in. Sadly, as I see it, today's society is strongly materialistic, which limits each and every one of us. It confines us. Dare I say it? It imprisons us. Truly, we are not free.'

We continued to speak about all of this for quite some time, and eventually we came to conclude that each individual person must develop an understanding of his purposeful place in the whole scheme of things. Rather, Gunna Dan urged me to go with him into this conclusion. He had often spoken about the impoverishment of his own inner self. Even though he admired every insight he attained with regard to the grandeur of this world, he knew and felt that this was not the only story, let alone the important story. He instinctively knew that there were other realities. He so wanted to connect with them. The uncommon experience we had by Cloonmacken Lake indicated to me that he had already begun the process.

'What I would love to explore,' he said to me, 'is the importance of the individual human being. I would love to understand more about the human condition.' Normally I would keep my views to myself, but because I knew he had, by now, a great regard for me, I felt encouraged to express and explain myself. It became easier when he said, 'Talk to me about it. I get comfort and gladness in your forthrightness.' In these circumstances, I felt free and carefree. Not only that, but I had the new-found confidence that as I expounded on issues and expressed my ideas,

I would get terrific insights from him. I soon found myself talking about the human condition.

'When we are born, we are born with needs. We need food, shelter, warmth, parental care, friends and love. We express our needs fully and forcefully. We cry loudly and with the totality of our being. Our comforts must be met. One pertinent fact that needs to be appreciated is this: our bodies possess tremendous knowledge. Our bodies, right from the very beginnings of life, know everything required for successful living. There is no learning needed. Babies instantly know how to suck, how to take air into their lungs. All of our bodies' systems typically work perfectly: the circulatory, digestive and nervous systems, to name just a few. Any system that is not active until later in life, especially the reproductive system, waits in abeyance. But the end issue is this: the body has all the knowledge it needs for a successful life within it. It regularly works perfectly. It knows everything. It does not need to learn anything.'

And then, to his great amusement, I told him that even the knowledge of our own baldness was safely stored away in the cells of our baby bodies for later implementation and expression.

At this point, Gunna Dan stopped me. 'Do you remember the time we were in An Teach Bia in Ennistymon? Did you not emphatically tell me then every human being is born ignorant and helpless? And yes, you also said that we have to spend years in school learning and studying in order to get out of this state of ignorance. This is a great difficulty for me. What I'm hearing is that at one and the same time humans are full of great ignorance and of great knowledge. This is really something.'

We stopped walking. I looked at him and told him that apparent contradictions will crop up all the time. I wanted to assure him that I would do my best to be factual and accurate, but that I needed his help. I needed to benefit from his insights. I wanted to benefit from his queries and questionings. I wanted his input into my talking. I told him all of this more to comfort myself than anything else. I was fully aware of the extent of man's ignorance, in general, and I was acutely aware of my own, in particular.

Strangely, the softness of the beach's sand comforted me. I noted that we were still some way off from the confluence of the Inagh, Cullenagh and Derry rivers, the point at which they enter the sea, and soon we began walking towards it.

As we walked, I started explaining to my friend that we are not our bodies. He readily accepted that we are multi-faceted, made up of minds with ideas and notions, of hearts with feelings and passion and of bodies with strength and power. It was difficult at first for him to come to terms with the notion that when we are born, our minds know nothing and our bodies know everything. 'How are you to know the meaning of life then?' he asked painfully. Then he laughed. He knew that this was the reason why we were walking along the beach and having these discussions. He also knew that as time passed, we would go over all the issues, indeed repeatedly, and tease out as many of their implications as we could. He urged me to continue.

'Right from the very first second of our birth, even though our minds are virtually empty, we have high standards. Independent of mind and independent of whatever little thinking we engage in, we want nothing but the best. As we grow and age, we demand the biggest, the nicest, the noisiest, and so on. It is in our natures, our feelings, our spirits and our minds to want the best. A major recognition is required here of you, Gunna Dan: there is far more to life than the material world. What I mean is, there are many other realities that are intangible and cannot be seen by our bodily senses. The desire to strive for what is best is innate in all of us. In all of us, there is a need and a wish for perfection. To attain full understanding of us as human beings, we must not only recognise, but also accept this principle. Time and time again, we see this principle at work in children. Children will be most unhappy if parents give them toys that are inferior to those of their bigger brother or sister. Children know the difference instinctively between the good, the better and the best. Disabled and disadvantaged children can be very expressive in this regard and their responses can be quite intense. All of us can become angry when restrictive circumstances confront us. All of us can be enraged when faced with obstructive intention. Exasperating and tear-inducing frustrations can reduce us all to helplessness. This happens because each of us, in truth, always wants what is best, and we are saddened if not maddened when denied it.'

Gunna Dan questioned me intently on this. He wanted to know more about the superlative hunger within all of us, within our minds, our spirits and our psyches. 'Am I to take it that excellence and seeking the best are innate forces within us? Am I to take it that these same innate forces are enduring, persistent and all embracing? Do these forces cause us to want to extend our human cognitive capacities way beyond ourselves? Do they compel us to go deep within ourselves and way out beyond? Am I to take it that truth and reality cannot be fully experienced unless we acknowledge the importance of excellence as a standard in our lives?' I was relieved when I realised that his questioning was rhetorical. It seemed that he just wanted to think aloud, all the better to dwell on his thoughts and confront them.

I also knew that he wanted to understand human behaviour more and more. He was eager to find out what motivates us, namely what impels us to do the things we do and to say the things we say. The thought that we are all disabled by frustrations of one kind or another puzzled him. The thought that we are always on some kind of emotional roller coaster saddened him. And, the thought we still have high standards despite these disabilities and rollercoaster rides baffled him. 'Is it not,' he asked very seriously, 'truly natural for every member of the human race to strive for the best? Is this not a mere mechanism for survival?'

I put it to him that the pursuit of excellence, of what is true and real is a pursuit far beyond mere survival. 'We must admit to the energy of our spirit. We must acknowledge that there is a constant urge in our spirits to see things perfectly and to want things to be perfect. But, I must do more than that. I need to concede that I can only be true to myself when, from within my mind and heart, I adopt and foster the concept of perfection.'

I paused and stopped walking. So did Gunna Dan. I deliberately stopped because I wanted to stress something that I wished him to consider and examine. Very seriously I declared to him that despite our human frailty, despite our human condition, despite our frustrations and weaknesses, we are in essence perfect beings. 'We are made that way,' I added.

Gunna Dan remained silent, looking way out into the distance. I went about repeating myself, but it came out differently. 'Because of our human condition, because of our limitations, something is always wanting in us. There is no completeness and there is no fullness, much as we would strive for it, much as we would love to have it.'

I was thinking on my feet as I walked along the beach. I was actually wishing that Gunna Dan would interrupt me, but he was pondering what I was saying. I argued that certainly it is natural for every one of us to want the best. 'What is certain is that in all our circumstances, we can know what is best. We can also know how to achieve the best even when resources are scarce and opportunities are few. Doing our best in trying circumstances does not diminish the excellence of our efforts. In no way is the essential nature of our inner beings compromised just because we face challenges.'

For some strange reason, Gunna Dan was very quiet. He was deep in thought, and yet I felt he was absorbing everything I was saying. I was overtly aware that he was in step with me in our strides. As I slowed, he slowed. As I veered to avoid pools and rivulets, so did he and I knew that as I spoke, he listened. By this time, I could see out beyond Lahinch golf club, out as far as the green fields and their hedges. Some inland trees were sheltering an unusual number of noisy crows, but the distraction only encouraged me to continue.

'I want you to look at those trees over there,' I said. 'The leaves that we see on them are wonderful examples of perfection in action. Their design and internal structure is fine and pure. In the light of the sun, they constantly absorb carbon dioxide, manufacture high-energy carbohydrate food and pump out oxygen into the air. All the chemical processes within the cells of the plants work perfectly all the time. The sequencing of these plants' bio-chemical activity is perfect. Starting materials, catalytic substances, substrates, products and bi-products all act and interact with true coherence and perfect orchestration. This perfect state is the natural state of vegetative life. It has to be. Any deviation or any imperfection in the process leads to disaster. The internal processes of green plants and vegetation on our planet sustain the world and all life in it. They do so abundantly, way beyond the requirements for their own needs. A huge quantity and variety of plant food is produced, so much so that billions of human beings and many more billions of animals are fed every day. Abundance flourishes naturally. Plants do not live just to survive. In fact, there is great majesty in their living.'

By this time, we had turned and started walking back to the promenade. Gunna Dan was stunned once he realised the significance of green vegetation on the planet and the tremendous work rate involved in the production of food. Before long, he wished me to talk more about the human condition. He encouraged me to continue because, as he said, it helped him to think more clearly. So, I continued.

'No adult will buy a new car with scratches on it, or worse, if it leaks oil, no matter how little. Each of us wants what's right, what is best, what is perfect. Every one of us will demand that the CD or suit of clothes or saucepan that we are buying is flawless. Manufacturers know this, of course. This is why so many companies nowadays boast in their mission statements that they provide products, services and/or solutions of the highest standard and of the best quality. No purveyor of goods will ever state that they are producing second-rate stuff. All manufacturers want it to be known that their products are of the highest standard. All will declare allegiance to excellence. In our personal lives, we demand excellence from doctors and surgeons and from pilots and bus drivers. We demand excellence from the mechanic who services the car.'

I paused. The two of us stood and looked all around. The beach had become a very lively place. The number of surfers had obviously increased. More families had colonised more areas of the beach and had put up tents, spread out their towels and organised a huge variety of colourful paraphernalia. Children and youths were running hither and thither. Some played hurling; others, football. Many ran into and out of the water. A diffident few stayed at the water's edge. We took our time. We walked more slowly, as if reluctant to join the throng, but in truth, we were more reluctant to finish our walk.

As I watched, I became more thoughtful. I surprised myself in the way I became so reflective, and because I wanted to get a reaction from my friend, I began talking to him again. 'It is true that all of us are much closer to the state of perfection than we realise. Perfection is found all around us in nature and even in our own human efforts – in the manufacture and piloting of aircraft; in the construction of roads and buildings; and in the production of all kinds of electrical appliances. Millions of people are engaged in the pursuit of excellence in their workplaces, and by and large, they are extremely successful at it.'

Gunna Dan turned towards me. His expression was serious, and his whole bearing was thoughtful. 'You are a constant challenge to me,' he said. 'Human beings can live their lives any and every way they like, but if they do so, they must somehow acknowledge to themselves that only the best is really good enough for them.' He said this with conviction. 'I'm sure that a lot of frustration follows when this does not happen in their lives.' He then turned to me and added, 'You've given me something here.'

We arrived at the promenade shortly afterwards and rested there. As we leaned on the wall, we watched the waves, the sea and the enthusiastic surfers. I scanned the horizon. I looked out into outer space. Then I expressed my need to visit the washrooms. We both went. On our way back, we could see an elderly man walking hurriedly towards us in what I guessed was actually his same walk towards the same washrooms. All of a sudden, he fell. He seemed to have kicked or hit an unevenly raised concrete tile on the pathway. His left hand and two knees took the full brunt of the fall. Gunna Dan raced to his help. It became clear that the man was more embarrassed than hurt. Gunna Dan checked him all over. He then raised him up to his feet and got him to walk slowly a little this way, and again, a little that way, all the time consoling and coaxing him. We accompanied the hapless man to the washrooms, and while we were waiting, Gunna Dan told me that he could feel the pain of the man's fall himself as it was happening.

When the man came out of the washrooms, it was clear to me that he was somewhat distressed. 'I have never fallen before,' he started. 'Why did this happen to me? Why wasn't I able to stop myself from falling? I should've been able to stay up on my feet.' I felt sorry for the poor fellow. The man had become aware of his own infirmity, as all of us will do at some time or other in our lives. His state of personal wellness, a state that he had probably taken for granted for so long, was rudely disturbed. His mental and emotional well-being was, for the moment, shattered. And there in front of us, despite the best efforts of his will, he sobbed. Gunna Dan, however, was great. He walked back with the man to the promenade, all the time comforting him and talking to him. As I walked behind the pair, I knew instinctively that Gunna Dan was actually healing and empowering him. I knew this when I noticed that their walking became a little livelier, more sure and more in tune with each other. When we left him back at his car, the recovered man was smiling and couldn't thank us enough.

It was great for me to be there with Gunna Dan. I can tell you this very sincerely. There, on the promenade of Lahinch beach, I saw a man fully alive and fully free in spirit. There was no limitation or restriction whatever in anything he did. He was strong and full of authority. Everything he did and everything he touched was wholesome and invigorating. I was captivated by the thoroughness of it all. I couldn't but wonder in amazement at my own realisation that the more he gave of his time and effort and energy, the livelier he became. I knew I was with a man with wonderful inner resolve and courage.

However, he quickly interrupted my private innermost thoughts and told me – taking me completely by surprise – 'I love being with you, Paddy. You are easy with me, and when I am with you, I can be truly myself in every way. Thanks for being with me when we helped that poor man.'

I was happy to be so honoured. Indeed, I was overjoyed. I felt that I was with a magnificent man, and I admitted to myself that it was not only the unfortunate fallen one that belonged within the ambit of his care and benevolent guardianship, but that everybody else did, as well.

Chapter 7

The Existence of Perfection

A feature that I liked about our meetings was that they were very matter-of-fact. Neither of us bothered with any complicated agendas. This is why I wasn't in any way surprised when my friend suddenly asked me, 'Could we meet again tomorrow evening sometime, say … after four o'clock? The tide will be out far enough to give us access to the wide-ranging expanse of the beach.' When I responded immediately and positively, he, with a slight wave of the hand, left me, and soon he was gone out of sight.

In fact, I was pleased with his decisiveness. I was also pleased because I knew I would be getting more exercise and taking in more seaside air. I was noticing already that the exercise I was getting was doing me good. I was more active. I was eating better. And, I was sleeping well.

We duly met on the promenade of Lahinch beach on the following evening. For the want of something to say, I began by telling Gunna Dan that I have always liked going to the seaside. Then I began telling him about my memory of the first time I ever went. He was as keen as could be to hear of it. I told him that the district nurse for the area of Shanagolden, Nurse Kitty Mulcahy, stayed in our house. She was an outgoing and lovable person, ever-generous in spirit and mind. Whenever she had time off in the summertime, she would pack a crowd of children into the back of her Morris Minor and take off for the seaside town of Ballybunnion in County Kerry, a distance about thirty miles away. Back then, in the early 1950s, that Morris Minor would have been about one of the three or four cars in the village. Even at that time, it was a lovable specimen of a car. The back seat was tremendously roomy and the flag-like traffic indicators always amused us when they were in operation. I told Gunna Dan that the very first time that I had seen the Atlantic Ocean I was enthralled. We had been almost a mile from town when the seascape first came into view, and as we drew nearer and nearer, I got more excited. The vastness of the seascape in the far distance made me wild-eyed. The grandeur, the wildness and immensity of the vista in front of me was lovable and attractive. And, while on the women's strand later that afternoon, (the second adjacent beach in Ballybunnion was called the men's strand) we spent time whooping and shouting, prancing and splashing. Even then, as a child, I knew that some outside force was energising and uplifting me. I felt the energy of the sea within my mind, body and spirit. I turned to Gunna Dan as I was saying this and added, 'I still feel that way to this very day.'

By this time, we had got down from the promenade onto the beach and had started walking in the direction of Liscannor Head. The evening sun was bright and gentle. Then, probably because I was still in a mood for reminiscence, I told Gunna Dan that, as I was growing up, I always felt very uncomfortable with the notion of perfection. Even as a child, I had reservations about those people I thought of as perfectionists and purists. One particular example stood out in my mind, and as I told it to Gunna Dan, he became fascinated. My childhood was a wonder to him. The story I told him was this: It had been common when I was growing up for my dad to help out on the farms of our uncles and aunts, his brothers and sisters, at hay making time. He would bring my brothers and me along with him. He was a great believer in the saying 'Many hands make light work.' Our job began when the haycocks of hay were made. We had to kneel down and pull out a small quantity of hay from all around the base of the haycock. This had to be done in a particular way and in a particular direction to achieve the right result.

On one occasion, we looked for a detailed explanation for this process and were told that it was necessary to have a gap all around the base of the haycock. Then when it rained, the rain fell onto the bare ground. I detested this pulling. More often than not, I would pull at a prickly thistle or, what was equally bad, a stinging nettle. After this explanation, I turned to my brother John. 'Come on,' I said. 'Let us turn the forks around, and instead of pulling out the hay, let's shove it in with the top of the handles.' Without a bother, we started. It was much more comfortable. The handles of the forks worked a dream. Standing apace, in ease and in comfort, we went around each haycock in no time. The end result was *perfect*. We were so happy.

Then our uncle saw what we were doing. We had to go back down on our bended knees, and he ordered us to undo all our work. With tears in our eyes, we were obliged with our bare hands to pull out the hay, the thistles and the nettles. While we were working, he constantly harangued us. The gist of it was, 'Do you not know that this is how I did it myself as a child? Do you not know that this way has been passed down from generation to generation? Do you not know that this is the right way to do it and that there is no other way?'

Gunna Dan laughed when I told him that for a long time after that, I disliked perfectionists intensely. I saw them as contrary people inflicting an inhuman and unnatural standard on innocent and harmless victims. Now, here on the beach in Lahinch, I was earnestly talking about perfection with admiration. 'Perfection has its own existence. It is as real as real can be. It expresses itself within and without. The existence and the expression of perfection is a natural guiding phenomenon in the universe,' I said. 'Perfection is everywhere. Its driving force is everywhere. All our dynamic systems, our bodily organs and tissues, work constantly with 100 percent perfection. Just consider the aged among us. Their livers, lungs, hearts and kidneys have been working perfectly for every second of every day of their lives. We know this because we are well aware of the effects of just one microscopic cell going awry. The presence of one rogue cell can and often does give rise to serious and terminal illness.'

Gunna Dan was in his usual thoughtful mood – serious and silent. I knew that the understanding of reality was a persistent engagement of his mind. Turning towards me he said, 'Perfection has its own existence.' He repeated ever so slowly the words I had said earlier. I knew he was examining the statement, pondering and wondering about it. 'I am admitting to myself that what you are saying is indeed true. You know, my earlier wish was that I would know reality, and your words about perfection give me fabulous insight. Now I see that truth and reality have many layers, visible layers that can be obvious and invisible layers that can be less obvious. What I wish for now more than anything else is to know truth in all its indications and in all its correspondences with reality. That is, I want to know it when it hits you straight in the face and also to know it in its silent manifestations.'

And, as if he were clarifying his thoughts for himself as much as for me, he added, 'Long have I thought about the pigs and mice and rats, the horses, cows, whales and giraffes you mentioned to me earlier, and how they all have got seven bones in their necks. Long, too, have I thought about the various bio-chemical and physiological processes that constantly work perfectly inside our bodies throughout our lives. Despite being full of doubts and uncertainties, I am coming to my own conclusions. Despite many contradictions in my life and in my mind, I am becoming more firm and steadfast about certain views and notions. I do admit to myself all the time that my own doubts and contradictions need quite a lot of unravelling, but having said that, I must also admit that truth comes to us with power and clarity. It comes into our minds pure and bright, and it remains there to be seen and known. More than that, it awaits our adoption.'

There on the beach, as we left our footprints behind us, Gunna Dan began expounding excitedly on the admission of truth into minds, and I must say that I was thrilled to be alongside him. What pleased me to no end was the fact that I was seeing that rare event: I was seeing a man thinking. He was struggling in his thinking and struggling in the admission of obligation into his thinking. I did not interrupt him. I couldn't. When he was silent, so was I, and when he resumed thinking aloud, I listened attentively.

'One reality that I have recognised is the sure and certain existence of the philosophical imperative. It is no use talking about issues unless we accept and respect whatever truth is revealed to us. We have spent time exploring and identifying the concept of perfection. We have spent some time talking about the human need, indeed drive, to seek what is best. The time has come for us to accept the truth of these issues and to acknowledge the implications that follow.' Then, firmly and seriously he declared, 'Truth imposes imperatives on us, and the first imperative is that we accept it.' Wishing to expand on the theme, he persisted. 'Truth allows for no variability. It is never arguable. It is immutable, objective and exclusive.'

Gunna Dan kept talking, but essentially he was repeating his thoughts, I surmised, to help him to become more cogent and decisive in his conclusions. Finally, and chiefly because of his endeavours, we both came to explicitly recognise that philosophical imperatives exist; that they cause human knowledge; that they are authoritative; that they order us;

and that they exhort us to accept them and all their implications. Gunna Dan then convincingly said to me, 'Philosophical imperatives are quite synergetic. They bring with them extra power and sway to enable us to willingly accept them and to even want them to direct our lives.' Gunna Dan was much more talkative as we strolled along the beach. He was more energetic and lively than I had ever seen before. My sense of time and space and place faded from me, and I was far more aware of my dancing spirit as it was lifted upwards.

With renewed vigour, Gunna Dan repeated, 'Philosophical imperatives are serious, truthful conclusions demanding acceptance. They emerge from continuous, serious reflection on the fundamental issues about human life on Earth. They emerge into our minds, and we can know them.

By this time, we had moved much further away from the crowded areas and were more or less alone. We stopped and, in silence, looked out at the sea. I must say that I, for my part, admired anew the vast spaciousness of so grand a seascape. The few white clouds in the sky were so high above us that its vastness was augmented. Then I took notice of my friend and instinctively knew that he was absorbed in his thoughts. I was struck by the clear impression I got of a man full of confidence. All of a sudden, he turned to me and earnestly said, 'Look, Paddy, there is no effective intelligence without light. There is no effective understanding without illumination. Every philosophical imperative has luminosity, and it is this luminosity that enlightens us. It is this luminosity that fills our minds with light. This is the luminosity that enables all of us to see and to know.'

I was taken aback. I had thought Gunna Dan had relaxed and that now he was pondering the reality of the sea and the land. I had thought that he had been preoccupied with plants, animals and people. Here on the beach, he was actually expounding on ethereal realities. More correctly, Gunna Dan took me into a new world of luminosity. I could not but notice that he felt so comfortable and happy. It was as if he had found a lost treasure, he was so unrestrained in his glee. It was great to be here with him. Then, he continued to astound me:

'Truth is revealed in the luminosity of imperatives,' he said. 'This enables us to see. Now I understand it. Human beings must experience the luminosity of philosophical imperatives in order to know truth completely. This is great. This is a new landscape for me. This is a landscape for everyone. Paddy, you have opened up the realm of perfection for me. I must tell you this as well. Ever since we started our discussions, I have thought often and long about many issues, and they are beginning to occupy my mind a lot – or, rather, I am dwelling with them in my mind more and more.'

Then he stopped. He looked at me intently. 'I want to say something that is full of meaning for me, and I hope you will see some sense in it yourself. I now realise that the frustration of perfection in this life is the sin of the world[33]. The whole world of humankind, and all human life within it, is frustrated. Because of our human frailty and our human condition, and because of our limitations, something is always lacking, something is always wanting. There is no completeness. There is no fullness. There is no wholesomeness. And when there is no patience, no tolerance and no understanding unknowing and unthinking reactionary responses spring up within our darkened minds and give rise to all the badness and wrongdoing going on in the world. Because of our darkness and unknowingness, we, all of us all over the world, continue to cause rumpuses, responding to our frustration and annoyances more often than not fiercely and intensely, extravagantly and wildly. One thing is sure; the wrongs of the world and the badness that is in it belong solely to us. They belong nowhere else.'

Gunna Dan looked at me intently. He even stared at me penetratingly. Then he continued. 'And yet and yet and yet, it is because of this frustration that the whole world and all human life within it, are, and always will be, struggling and aspiring towards excellence. And consequently – and let me emphasise that this is true as much for myself as for everybody else – the banal and the common, the mundane and the ordinary are much more frustrating, and always will be, than the spiritual and the supernatural, the mystical and the holy. Therein is to be found an understanding to our salvation. Therein is to be discovered the blueprint for our deliverance. And Paddy, let me emphasise especially that it is only by coping with the frustration of perfection that humankind can advance its own certain perfectibility.'

He was quite firm, calm and dispassionate. His impact stilled me. I was dumbfounded, yet I was delighted. I can tell you that there and then I again treasured knowing my friend and I felt honoured by him. Without fully understanding it, I knew too that my inner self was uplifted and strengthened by being with him.

---

33   See 'Glory to God in the Highest', a prayer from the Mass. See also John 1:30, JB

We walked along in silence for a little while. I watched him. Here was a man on a mission. He was possessed of a strong, quiet demeanour. He inspired confidence. He relished the contemplative experience. His earlier diffident assumptions were now firmer conclusions. I admired him all the more. Here was a man who realised that all of us are purposefully destined for better things. I could perceive that he wanted everybody to know this. How I wished and willed that I could grow into his stature.

By this time, we had started on the return journey to the promenade. We were surprised to notice that the younger people were still surfing. Many older people were out walking, enjoying the cool of the evening and the refreshing breeze. By the time we got back to the promenade, I noticed that he had become very quiet.

'Is something amiss?' I queried.

'Yes. When I think of all the people in the world, when I ponder on my everyday experiences, nothing but sadness, conflict, tragedy, illness, not to mention poverty and famine, stares me in the face. We get so little evidence of people striving for the truth and for what is best for themselves and everyone. Children get a raw deal. Personal conflicts between so-called educated people are often violent. Two people can be married for ten, fifteen or twenty years. Then in one moment of madness, everything can be shattered. All the painstaking good work of previous years is gone. What actually is happening?'

We continued walking towards the town. When we reached the Waves café, we decided to have a coffee. We sat down in a quiet corner and rested body, mind and limb. We both needed the rest. I waited for some time. I knew that in all fairness, I was obliged to address my friend's concerns. I did not, however, want to echo his sad tone or dwell on it too much. The coffee helped us to relax, and we settled down.

'Millions of parents and guardians are involved in the tremendously creative work of rearing and supporting children,' I said a bit lightly. 'Week in and week out, parents bring their children to music classes, games, sporting events and all types of creative activities. The adults also pursue all types of hobbies and activities. Evening courses are always popular. Self-improvement programmes and holistic health classes continue to be in demand. These kinds of long-term, persistent activities are essential for bringing the human spirit into touch with its true self, a self which came from, and which resides in, the world of divine silence. Shakespeare knew this state very well, as he started his thirtieth sonnet with the line, "When to the sessions of sweet silent thought".[34] As individuals and as members of societies, we need more and more to engage ourselves in purposeful creative pursuits. We need to saturate our minds, hearts and bodies in the fineness of spiritual silence. Gunna Dan, there are many realities that we still need to know.'

Gunna Dan took another sip from his coffee. He agreed with what I was saying. With certain sadness, he offered, 'A disappointing fact remains, however. The appreciation of and desire for perfection in our lives do not dominate our thoughts at all, and certainly not in places or in situations where perfection matters most. Relationships between people are often horrible and fraught. Fathers, mothers and children can all be caught up in acrimony. Newspapers, television and radio stations constantly report on atrocities, killings, shootings, robberies and drug addiction.' He then turned to me and plaintively said, 'You have read about it all yourself, Paddy. Many are the times that you have raised this issue with me. And many a time, too, we have spoken about it. You know only too well how it saddens me. I am very sad for all people who suffer and are suffering in so many ways. We have an apparent inability to travel on our personal journeys from the state of not knowing anything into the state of light and truth. This is our mission here in this life. This is what matters.'

He looked down at the table, took another sip of coffee and then sighed.

'Importantly, too, there is another aspect to my sadness. I know that each and every one of us has a great ability to be creative, good and true. It is not beyond our means as a human race and especially as individuals to be creative in all spheres of our lives. The human race has produced magnificent masterpieces, and the world is blessed with our many created wonders. So many inventions are taken for granted. In today's world, our comforts are protected by our reliance on electricity and technology and by our great ability to manufacture almost anything from raw materials. It must be acknowledged that humans can be very creative. Even thousands of years ago, humankind revealed brilliance and, time and time again, wonderful insights.'

I impulsively interrupted his train of thought. My own thoughts were bubbling in my head so fiercely that I was itching to let him know them.

---

34 William Shakespeare, *Sonnets*, ed. Levi Fox (Norwich, England: Jarrold, 1993).

Before he could continue, I had already started. 'In ancient times,' I quickly explained, 'the Babylonians worked out that our planet took 360 days to go around the sun in a circular orbit. Ever since, we have measured complete circles in degrees of three hundred and sixty. The people in Stonehenge in England reached similar conclusions three thousand years ago. Even much earlier than that, in 3200 BC, more than five thousand two hundred years ago, a megalithic passage tomb was built in Newgrange, County Meath, Ireland. Every year at the winter solstice sunrise, the interior chamber and passage light up. A shaft of sunlight shines through the roof box and illuminates the interior. The event lasts for approximately seventeen minutes. It is estimated that the passage tomb at Newgrange took a work force of three hundred people at least twenty years to construct[35]. People in those times had no paper, pens, notebooks, electricity, running water, central heating or supermarkets. There were no sophisticated tools or machinery, let alone calculators or any fine instrumentation. People then had to have brilliant minds to visualise, plan and make decisions. Their computational and communication skills must have been superb. Their mental capacities must have been considerable. Much later, in ancient Rome, eleven major aqueducts were built to supply copious quantities of water to over one million people then living in the city. The longest one of them, Anio Novus, was fifty-seven miles long[36]. Roman engineers used a mathematics system that had no zero, no multiplication and no division. Yet, they managed all the calculations involved in the planning and design of these massive constructs.'

Then I echoed Gunna Dan's earlier remarks and asserted that a knowing person is obliged to acknowledge and revere the brilliance of our forefathers on Earth. Despite all the hardships of the time, despite all the restrictions and privations in their lives and in their living, they still aspired to greatness. And they were great.

Gunna Dan listened to me the whole time with great interest and curiosity. He took me up on my positive concluding remarks. He remarked quite firmly that problems are never the issue. The issue is how we relate and react to them. And it is in reacting to them that all of us can first relate to our inner greatness. Everybody has inner greatness, he said convincingly.

---

35   'Newgrange Megalithic Passage Tomb,' *Knowth.com: www.knowth.com/newgrange.htm.*
36   E.J. Dembskey, The aqueducts of Ancient Rome (master thesis, 2009), Aqua Anio Novus: http://www.romanaqueducts.info/aquasite/romanovus/index.html: July 2010

Gunna Dan always took the opportunity to emphasise the inherent grandeur and potential excellence of the human condition to me. On many occasions, he briefly mentioned to me that love for ourselves and for our fellow humans is an important and essential virtue, and without it, we would never know truth. He would love nothing better than to see mothers, fathers and children allowing for more love and tolerance in their lives. Goodness requires it, he often said.

We had finished our coffee and left the Waves café. I decided that I would visit some friends out at Moy, but before I parted from Gunna Dan, I got him to promise me that we would explore the difficulties and negativities that can make our lives so troublesome and painful. I wanted his help in facing down the wrongs of life. I also wanted to discover ways and means to enhance my own knowledge and understanding. There was one thing that bothered me, and I told Gunna Dan of it before we parted. My friend had triggered it when he said that humankind could be quite creative. What bothered me was that we could be very destructive, as well.

Chapter 8

The Devastating Power
of Destructiveness

The following Thursday, we met outside the Rambler's Rest at the crossroads at Inagh. It was early afternoon. We both wished, once more, to go for a ramble along the back road to Kilnamona, partly because we liked the quiet byways, but especially because no one would disturb us and we could chat away in a carefree manner. This time, I found the initial rising slope more of a challenge, caused, no doubt, by the fact that I had woken up late. Then, I had eaten breakfast rather too quickly. What helped me to cope, oddly enough, was walking backwards up the slope, all the time admiring the view that stretched westwards and south-westwards before me. Soon, Gunna Dan was likewise shuffling backwards up the hill. The Milltown-Malbay road seemed very far away in the distance as we continued backwards. The vista Slievecallan presented was remarkable. The mountain seemed broad, strong and wide. Its width was impressive, neutralising somewhat the impact of its height of 1,283 feet above sea level. We also noted the new houses in Annagh Dún, the still newer crèche, the sturdily built church, the supermarket and, further away from these but nearer to us, the pubs at the crossroads. We stopped and spent a little time looking all around us, and from our vantage point, we were able to admire and appreciate the wonders of Inagh.

We turned around. We could see that beyond us, the road was narrower. The green grass that was growing in the middle of it told us that we were going into even less travelled terrain. This appealed to us to a great extent.

It certainly helped me start talking about an issue that was on my mind. I reminded my friend of the confidence we had spoken about of the human spirit to be creative. I didn't hesitate to tell him that I have always admired creative people myself, whether they are composers, musicians, artists, poets, playwrights or performers. I told him that I had a particularly high regard for singers and musicians even though as a child at school I was considered to be tone deaf. Even to this day I still wonder how musical people can be totally au fait with the individuality of the notes of the octave and how, on hearing them, can recognise them immediately irrespective of the source of the sound.

It had become a pattern in our walks that when one or the other of us wanted to say something that was considered important and serious, we would stop and visually engage each other. The higher hedging on both sides of the road accentuated our isolation and our intimacy. I stopped and faced Gunna Dan. 'There is an issue that I want to get off my mind. I want to face it because it disturbs me greatly, and it has always disturbed me. I know you have declared that the frustration of perfection in this life is the sin of the world. I have pondered an awful lot on this. And I will tell you this: our power to be destructive is one mighty frustration indeed.'

The kind man just smiled. One thing I liked about him was that he always made it easy for me to let rip. What I mean is, he was very tolerant of any high-octane rant that would come from me, and he had been helpful to me in similar situations before. Because of my confidence in him, I felt free. And I must admit it; I did not spare him in my harangue.

'We can destroy anything and everything – be it animal, vegetable or mineral; or be it person, place or thing. Worst of all, we are quite capable of destroying ourselves. Being positively creative is, oh so difficult, laborious, painful and time-consuming. Writers, poets, dramatists, composers, architects and builders spend years and years in the creation of their masterpieces. The splendid cathedrals of Europe's continent were designed by architects who had been long dead by the time the foundations were complete. Those who laid the same foundations were long dead by the time the roofs were started, and when the first religious services were performed, the priests were presumably praying for the souls of the long departed creators and installers of the stained glass windows. Then, during wartime, the bombs from aerial onslaughts destroyed these same buildings in seconds. With rapidity, whole cities were destroyed, and hundreds of thousands of people were killed. Destructive power is overwhelming, brutal and sudden. For some strange reason, we have a sneaking admiration for destructiveness. We go in droves to the cinema and complain loudly when the pyrotechnics and the destructive effects are not more shockingly dramatic. Television programmes reveal constant abrasiveness and hostility in the lives of the characters meant to depict our daily lives. Rarely is a kind action highlighted, and one will almost never hear a prayer or a blessing. But, Gunna Dan, let us remind ourselves that other realities exist and that each of us can be positively creative. Our positive creative forces are gentle, kind and quiet. They are never hurtful. Our ability to achieve greatness can be limitless when we are tolerant and open, aware and insightful.'

There, in the quietness of the isolated country road, I held forth. To be honest, I wanted to do it. I wanted to emphasise to myself as much as to Gunna Dan that creativity and destructiveness are not *equal* opposite forces. Life, I know only too well, is full of opposites – of good and bad, of right and wrong, of praise and blame. The list is endless. But what always disappoints me terribly is that negative forces are very strong and powerful, way out of proportion to everything else in life. And worse, these dreadful forces are embedded in all of us. All of us carry within us obscure and abstract violence. The energy of violence is a ruthless force of extreme power. When unleashed, it has fierce and brutal vigour. Violence creates an irresistible urge to destroy and to continue destroying until destruction is complete.

I so wanted to talk about this. I so wanted Gunna Dan to hear me out, and without the slightest hesitation, I continued. 'Look, Gunna Dan, there are influential people among us who are unaware of the great disproportion in the two contrasting realities of creativity and destructiveness. Radio and television managers, newspaper editors, film and video producers all claim to virtuously maintain a balance in the presentation of arguments and debates. They do no such thing. Every creative proposal and project intended for good (whether it be material, political, religious, cultural or even personal) ought to be allocated hours of supportive time and energy. Its contrary destructive position should not be treated with equal respect. Consider again the hundreds of years required to build a cathedral and the single second it takes to bomb it into total destruction. There's balance for you! This imbalance is especially highlighted when a national referendum is taking place. We often experience the government being unable to freely explain why a certain course of action should take place. Legislation now prevents government parties from spending taxpayers' money to promote their well thought out proposals in support of good governance. The leader of our society, An Taoiseach, can only speak on television to the nation when the opposition have the right to reply and counteract.

And why is such the case? It is simply because the gainsayers have argued that allowing the government to freely communicate with the citizens discriminates against them. They make the claim that their oppositional views are not heard. But the system is worse than that. The opposition in any democratic system can only gain power by destroying those who are currently in power. Unbelievably, the system supports them. Opposition parties in democratic countries all over the world now claim the right to have equal time, equal resources and parity to counteract and disparage, to denigrate and contradict. Many argue that this oppositional system is mature, modern, intelligent, wise and civilised. It is no such thing.'

I paused for breath. By this time, Gunna Dan had picked up a thorny stick that had been lying on the roadside. He began waving it gently over and back in front of him in deep silence and in a constant rhythm. I got the impression that he was using it like someone who uses worry beads or a stress bag to relieve tension. But, I remained unrestrained.

'It is fashionable for us in the Western world to sing the praises of our governing methods. Our leaders venerate the concept of democracy so highly that they are prepared to equip teenage boys and girls to travel thousands of miles laden with guns, bullets and firepower to kill men, women and children all around them, so as to impose a democratic system of government, a system that is considered advanced, modern and enlightened. Successful feudal systems of government from the past and the present are considered to be de facto abhorrent and must be destroyed. The truth is otherwise. The democratic parliamentary system is based on winners and losers; it is based on those who govern and those who oppose; it separates out those who do from those who don't. To put it briefly, the whole system is based on the nefarious foundation of destructive opposites. Essentially, our democratic process engages dangerously with destructive and damaging forces. Opposition politicians are paid by taxpayers who devise damaging tactics with one aim in mind – to derail if not prevent constructive action from taking place. The good name and reputation of another is fair game. The good work that thousands of dedicated people have put forth in schools, hospitals, churches and sporting arenas is blithely rubbished. Those institutions that hold out the highest ideals for us are belittled. In short, we are a self-destructive people. Thus, the prospects of improving, achieving and creating are formally circumscribed by destructive and opposing forces.'

I paused. By now I was sure that Gunna Dan would be irritated by my tirade. I had certainly held forth, because I had felt I had to – more so for myself than anything else. I quietly continued thinking about it, as I could not stop. *Nobody gets to the later stages of life without witnessing, if not experiencing, life's raw, dark, harsh and painful side. You would have to be a fool not to realise that we live in a violent, vicious world. And I know this much: there are very many people out there who would be far more authoritative than myself in any discussion associated with destructiveness and violence, and especially so when it comes to matters of personal and family relationships.* Gunna Dan soon interrupted my thinking.

'It is necessary to say and admit these things,' he said very quietly. 'Not only is it necessary, but also it is good. It is all very fine to keep telling ourselves that we should think positively and ignore the negative around us. But it is vital to understand the energy involved. All the destructive energy within us comes from our frustrations – frustrations that arise when situations and things and people are not better and not to our liking, when they are not perfect and harmonious to our minds. And the more we dislike them, the more frustrated and the more nasty we become. It makes little difference whether significant issues cause our frustrations or whether they are simply 'storms in a teacup'. No matter what, we can expend a huge amount of angry energy. The uncontrolled intermingling of wild thoughts, emotions and actions impels us to do crazy things. Because of our mental upset and our emotional upheaval, we can become very dangerous people. In truth, we need to be able to see ourselves while we are thinking and feeling and doing, so that we can dissipate our angry energy. We can only see ourselves, however, when we are enlightened.'

Gunna Dan paused for a short moment and then, looking directly at me, he continued. 'And a strange thing is this: when all our energy is expended on our frustrations, very little is left for badness, or for goodness, either, for that matter. In general, people are not evil, but our goodness is baulked. Our frustrations dampen and darken our creative spirits. They dull our creative spirits, and worse, they vitiate them. Our frustrations suck in and retain our energies. The pure, clear energy that is required to enable us to be creative and good disappear. We need to know this. We need to understand it.'

I can tell you that I was relieved and comforted as I listened to him. I was relieved because there was no hint of discouragement in his response to me. I was comforted because it dawned on me that Gunna Dan had a tremendous empathy for the human condition. By now, we had come to a gate that led into a field. We rested our arms on it and took in the expansive views all around. I felt very comfortable being there with Gunna Dan. I felt free and emboldened to continue with my theme as we made our return journey back to the crossroads at Inagh. And, so I did.

'Under the veneer of respectability, the opposing forces in our parliamentary system are reduced to the childhood catcalls of 'I did' and 'you didn't'. The opposers are ever-castigating the shakers and the makers with the grown-up versions of childhood jibes, such as 'you're a liar', 'you can't be trusted' or 'you're a cheat'. Many of us in the body politic go along with this, and we make and express assumptions that politicians are corrupt, churchmen are evil and those we do not like are criminal. We are still at the infancy of human development. In one way, this is understandable. We are the latest and the newest species on the planet. This means that we are still very new at finding out how to live our lives; our effort to find meaning and reasons in life has only started. This means, too, that we have yet to develop ways to maturely cope with our inevitable frustrations. The emergence of humankind has been the emergence of self-conscious and self-thinking entities. The only learned experiences we have, apart from our own personal experiences, are the efforts, insights and revelations of those who have gone before us. They have handed down humankind's accumulated wisdom, customs, language, literature, music and life-values to us. They have endowed us with their legacies. Our responsibility is to protect, respect and indeed enhance what is now a wide-ranging, multifaceted and eclectic inheritance. It would be woeful of us to continue to destroy what we have and then hand on nothing or, at best, damaged goods to future generations. It would be woeful for all of humankind because then, three times every century (assuming three new generations appear every century), man's indispensable search for spiritual truth would have to start all over again.'

By now we had come to the slope up which we had walked backwards. We viewed again the panorama before us, and as we drew nearer to the crossroads, we commented to each other on the hills and the fields, the roads and the buildings. But this time, Gunna Dan looked down on the graveyard a little away to the left of the church. 'It is the men and women who are buried there and those of their generation who have made Ireland great,' he said.

In a throwaway comment, Gunna Dan then reminded me that I had earlier promised him that I would talk to him about the older people in my home village when I was growing up. Because we were now near the crossroads, we decided to go into the Rambler's Rest. Once we were inside and served coffee, I began to entertain him with a little bit of my home village's history. I began by telling him that the achievements to date in Ireland are extraordinary and remarkable. Even the changes that have taken place since my childhood days are astounding. Gunna Dan was amazed when I told him that in the village of Shanagolden of the 1940s and early 1950s, there had been no running water in any of the houses. Drinking water had only been available from fountains. The fountains often referred to as 'de pumps', were very decorative low metal structures located in judicious positions along the street. They served the needs of the village's households into the early if not the mid 1950s. I remember them well. There was one outside the national school and another outside the church. Then, a little further down from our house was another from which we drew our daily supplies. The others were located further down the street. One event always amazed and intrigued me as a child. In winter, if there was a danger of frost – and there was a terrible one in the early spring of 1947 – all the pumps had to be wrapped in ropes of hay and straw to prevent the water from freezing. But, we preferred another method: Ensuring that the pump knob was turned on all night enabled the water to keep flowing and prevented it from freezing. But, the end result was that we had a fabulous slide of thick ice a good distance along the road away from the pump. Then, in case he was wondering, I told Gunna Dan that because there had been no running water in the houses, all the toilets used the scientifically-proven dry system and, of necessity, were located outdoors.

There was no electricity in the houses, either, I explained. We went to bed by candlelight, and I can recall very vividly the trouble my brother John got into when, because of ravishing hunger, he got into the habit of eating the spare candle. He got caught one night because after eating the candle, he forgot to get rid of the wick. Gunna Dan listened with great interest, and he, in his turn, told me of the similar conditions and difficulties his people had and have, particularly those up in the mountains of Onavistan.

I recounted the conditions under which the servant men and women, employed by the farmers, lived and worked. Invariably they received no pay. Their parents were the ones who secured the employment in the first place, so the parents were the ones who took the meagre pay – generally twice per year. Only the privileged few owned houses, property and valuables. Nobody went on holidays, unless a day trip to the seaside counted as a holiday. The cobbler in the village was always busy because when you got a pair of shoes, you kept them for years, and as they aged with you, they were constantly repaired, patched, soled and re-soled.

The cobbler in our village lived in a very small house, as did a lot of families. There were far too many leaking thatched houses in the village, and I well remember being in a house near us on a rainy day. Galvanised buckets and enamel basins were all over the place to catch the dripping water, which was heavily brown-stained because it had seeped through the aged and rotting straw roof cover.

Gunna Dan was pained to hear that because of the conditions, tuberculosis was rampant and a large number of people had to leave the village to go down to a sanatorium in Glanmire, County Cork for months on end. They were the lucky ones, because the ones who did not make it died. Gunna Dan was really saddened to realise that the lives of so many people were impoverished and diminished. But, and I particularly emphasised this, that despite all of this, the people of the village and of the whole country were remarkable – they were the generation that made Ireland great. They had few resources, little money and many personal afflictions. Yet, they understood sacrifice. This is why they were able to modernise the whole country and improve the living standards for themselves and especially for their children. And better than that, they lifted themselves up with great positive inner strength and creative power. They emerged into new eras with great hope and greater confidence.

And, it was with no little dismay that I told Gunna Dan that the story is much worse today. Despite all the conveniences and comforts of life, despite all the freedoms and all the resources we have, we are an unhappy lot. Crime continues to increase and its viciousness continues to intensify. We regularly read in the newspapers and hear recounted on radio and television so many stories of young people being stabbed during weekends and at night-time when they and their killers are out 'having a good time'. The conduct of people in all spheres of life towards fellow people can be harsh. It is often brutal. One thing I assured Gunna Dan of was that the people of my grandparents' time willingly accepted the discipline of being dignified and noble. Manners mattered. Deportment, etiquette and decorum were learned and practised. Respect for others was a sine qua non.

I then challenged Gunna Dan to tell me if it were possible for the people of this day and age to rise up and chart out a new way forward, a better way, one that would uplift everybody, one that would evoke the strong inner resources of spirit that we surely have and help us all to sidetrack destructive tendencies and in their place give fire and energy to our creative forces. In a very perceptive comment, Gunna Dan told me that he felt – and this he said was from his limited knowledge – the process of individualisation had come too quickly to the people of Ireland, especially the younger generation. With individualisation, the cult of the individual, the social persona of the individual diminishes. The rightful demand of society for allegiance and commitment is ignored. The interdependence between neighbour and neighbour vanishes. Respect of neighbour for neighbour also vanishes. The voluntary contribution of one's time and talents to social, cultural and religious causes does not happen. Instead, we get hostility and violence. Individuals trapped in this cult have a powerful wish to break familial ties of all and every kind. They believe that they own themselves and their choices. Such individuals want to be responsible to no one. Gratification becomes the serious purpose of living. Resources must be freely available. Consumption must be without any obligation. Enough is never enough. Appetites grow and grow. Drink, drugs, sex, abortion and divorce are always on the menu. Social awareness, voluntary commitments, moderation, sacredness and holiness are always off it. The very freedom that is treasured is wantonly wasted. Frustration can only grow, and grow big time. There is no virtue in this kind of individualisation. There is no genuine aspiration. He then turned to me and sadly said, 'It is very difficult, very difficult indeed, for selfish individuals, for self-centred individuals, to empower their inner spirits.'

I was amazed as to how perceptive and how serious Gunna Dan was, but I could not query him at all because, for one thing, we had long finished our coffees, and for another, a lively group of people had come into the bar talking excitedly about some recent event. So, we quietly and quickly left. We stood outside for a while on the footpath. We saluted some passing locals. This was one custom that I had grown to like, if not love a lot in Inagh. Everybody salutes everybody, and everybody acknowledges the presence of the other. They do this with a discrete regard that is lovely to experience. Many are the times when I have heard the men enquiring of each other about the welfare of their wives or the women asking about the wellbeing of each other's children or husbands. Soon, we were left to ourselves and went about parting. Of course, I wanted to meet Gunna Dan soon again, and it did not take us long to decide that we would meet for lunch in the Biddy Early Brewery on the following Tuesday.

Chapter 9

Who Is Who in This World of Ours?

Tuesday was overcast, and all morning it threatened rain. We felt very comfortable being indoors, and we engaged in a lot of chat, particularly on the issues and the events that were of importance locally. It so happened that earlier, on my way to the Biddy Early Brewery, I had called into the Mace supermarket and bought a copy of *The Clare People*. The newspaper helped us find out about local affairs and activities that were planned. We gave a lot of attention to the hurling and football games that were played, and while Gunna Dan read out the reports, I constantly interrupted him with my own comments. When we finished eating our meals, Gunna Dan looked at his little blue book. He noted that the tide had been going out for the last hour and a half or so, and he suggested we go to the coast. I recommended, for a change of seaside scenery, that we could drive out to the White Strand near Milltown Malbay, and this is what we did.

When we arrived at the junction leading into the small car park, we saw that it was chocker-block full. So, I drove onwards and parked further down the road. The beach and surrounds were crowded. The road was empty and quiet. We chose to go walking on the road and felt all the better for it. I loved being there – in the middle, as it were, of the landscape that was to our right and the seascape that was to our left. I couldn't help but tell Gunna Dan about all the life-giving and life-supporting molecules of oxygen dancing, surging, rushing and rolling all over the vast expanse of the Atlantic, billowing onwards and inwards – quadrillions of billions of them, indeed, if not quadrillions of quadrillions. The wonder of it all was that each and every atom and each and every molecule is pure and perfect in its existence, design and structure, and no less so in their activities, be they physical, chemical, bio-chemical or biological. One particular activity bewildered him. It was, as I explained to him, the elastic scattering of light known as Rayleigh scattering[37]. The molecules in the air, being on the one hand so great a number and on the other hand so tiny a size, scatter the various wavelengths of light. Light of smaller wavelengths, particularly blue, is scattered more effectively. This gives us a blue sky during daytime. Without this continuous Rayleigh scattering, I added, the sky instead would be dark all the time and the sun would appear as a white disk in the blackness. No life would be possible, and we would not be here! Gunna Dan was wide-eyed as I told him this, and he was completely bowled over when I added, indeed not for the first time, that each and every atom of oxygen was billions of years old. He laughed heartily when I told him that of all the quadrillions of quadrillions of atoms, not one of them is wonky. And with aplomb I added, 'There's perfection for you.'

Gunna Dan, to be frank, was delighted to hear me go on like this. If he interjected, he did so happily and supportively, never seriously stopping me. I always got the impression that he knew what it was to be attentive and how to give attention. I valued how he could be so mindful about an issue, blissfully ignoring everything else. More than that, he willingly gave importance to me, to what I was saying and to how I said it. I found that his advertence to ideas was strong, focused and deliberate. This was in sharp contrast to what I witnessed all around me. People nowadays live lives full of distraction and noise, so much so that each of us has highly developed the tactic of *switching off*. Our attention spans are constantly compromised because of advertising's invasiveness into our minds. Without knowing it, we are influenced and motivated by the practise of advertising. As a result, our thought processes are dulled. They are compromised. We avoid purposeful thinking about important issues. So, I must confess that I loved how Gunna Dan enabled and empowered me. I particularly appreciated how supportive he always was of me.

I must add, as well, that Gunna Dan was a man possessed of a sturdy independence. He often said that he had always had the wish to know more

---

37 'Rayleigh Scattering.' Last updated 30 May 2010. *Wikipedia: en.wikipedia.org/wiki/ Rayleigh_scattering.*

about science matters. He contended that science reveals various degrees of knowledge and truth in much the same way as literature and music, history and mathematics, folklore and philosophy and, indeed, all the creative arts. It disappointed him that a part of truth and understanding was hidden from him because he knew very little about science and scientific issues. He felt that because he had little or no scientific training, he was prevented from fully appreciating the wonders of the world. Of course, I responded vigorously. I did my best to assure him that his insights were deep, and he did not contradict me when I passionately told him that he had, just like any great scientist, a responsive and inquiring mind, objective and astute.

And so we ambled along on the roadway. By now, we had turned and advanced along a wide sweeping curve of the road. After a short period of quiet, Gunna Dan put this proposal to me. 'Is there,' he asked, 'a proposition that you can present to me that is strong, positive and true, one that will uplift the hearts and minds of every individual in the world? Is there a proposition out there that truly emphasises the uniqueness of every individual in the world?' I knew well that he was being seriously thoughtful, and I understood why. Earlier, when we were driving towards the coast, he had dwelt on the notion that despite poverty, hunger and privation, people in all ages, at all times and in all places have emerged with goodness and greatness. Now, he suddenly revealed to me that he was astounded by the fact that there's no such thing as a wonky molecule of oxygen – that each and every one of them is perfect. Gunna Dan genuinely felt for the lot of every individual in the world. He so wished to hear me say that each and every one of us has significance, that each and every one of us has importance and that each and every one of us matters. He so wished to hear me say as well that each and every one of us is perfect in design, perfect in intent and perfect in purpose. I knew that Gunna Dan, in his insistence, was anxious. I knew I was the cause of that. I knew I had heightened his expectations.

And, of course, he was confident that I was going to respond to his prompt. He knew that I cherished being unencumbered and being away from it all. Yes, he knew that I cherished being free, now that I was retired. And, he knew too that I would not disappoint him. I must say, however, that there was always one thing that disappointed me going through life. I found that people were never bold in talking about their views and experiences of truth and reality. What really bothered me was my own personal realisation from an early age that no one person ever knows what another person is really thinking at any time in life. I had previously noted that influential people, such as the leaders of society, teachers, clergy, newspaper reporters, journalists, television commentators, business people and politicians, have never been able to express the personal ideas that they found to be truthful, inspirational and important. Practically all of them have just reacted to events. They have always demonstrated a benign tolerance towards shady activities and a polite leniency towards unsocial habits and pursuits. Even on those occasions when they have spoken or written on profound issues, supporting materials like quotations and references from others have heavily cloaked their distant ideas. I have never liked this literary dependency. I have never liked the heavy qualifications. I suppose that in my own teaching career I was exactly the same myself, but I still didn't like it. Now that I was in the company of Gunna Dan, I enjoyed a new energy of mind, freedom of spirit and liveliness in thought. There was, I felt, greater clarity in my understandings. Serious notions that had lain undisturbed for some time in my mind, surfaced regularly, and I seriously entertained them all. And so, undaunted, I began.

'What we do not realise, Gunna Dan, is that each of us, each individual in the whole world, can and should deliberately and truthfully say in the inner privacy of mind, *I am the most important person in the world*. We wouldn't dare to say it in public. We hesitate to say it to ourselves in private. Yet, even in privacy we should proclaim explicitly the mantra, *I am the most important person in the world*. When we don't, we miss the importance, the grandeur and the truth of this declaration. We fail to co-ordinate ourselves with the great reality of life and, thus, inhibit the true fulfilment of our destinies. Any mother is the most important mother in the world to her child. Any child is the most important child to his mother and father. Any person is the most important in the world to her lover. Each and every one of us is endowed with importance. It is a truism to declare that there is nobody on Earth who can be more perfect at being you than yourself. Each and every one of us is created in the image and likeness of God[38]. Astoundingly, yet factually, our true nature is the nature of our progenitor. Of all the millions of people born into the world, I am the only one of me. I am unique. I am incomparable. I am special. And always – this will be true. I am always the special creative output of a mysterious and celestial reality.'

38 Genesis 1:26, JB

In the silence that followed, I felt impelled to emphasise my point. 'My friend, none of this information is new. About two thousand years ago, in a wonderful act of divine revelation, Jesus, the Son of God, the second person of the Blessed Trinity, was sent into the world by God the Father to be our saviour and our redeemer. He was a great teacher, miracle worker and healer. He directed his teachings to the hearts and minds of every individual of every age. He explained this very issue succinctly to his apostles: 'He asked them, "What were you arguing about on the road?" They said nothing because they had been arguing which of them was the greatest. So he sat down, called the twelve to him and said, "If anyone wants to be first, he must make himself last of all and servant of all."'[39]

I turned towards Gunna Dan. 'In a nutshell, what I am saying is this: no one person on Earth is more significant than anyone else. There is nobody more important than me in the whole universe. Each of us is endowed with worth and dignity. This status that we have is of divine origin and it is personal for each and every one of us.'

Gunna Dan was overjoyed to hear all of this. It helped him to understand the grandeur of every individual in the world. He so wanted to hear it because it was in sharp contrast to the expression of individualism he saw all around him, an individualism that he had argued with me earlier was not understood. He had forcefully contended that as individuals, we do not understand ourselves. Because of this lack of understanding, we find ourselves using our personal freedoms and individualism to abandon tradition, culture and religion. Our freely chosen individual tastes descend to selecting soap operas to inspire our emotional and mental excitement, the clatter of synthetic music to become our anthems and the contradictory sayings and writings of the myriad opinion-casters as our mantras.

'Should not our personal freedom and our individualism,' he asked poignantly, 'enable us to realise that we are special and unique? Should it not enable us to experience our inherent genius, to grow more thoughtful and to act more knowingly in life?' Then, using a telling phrase, he added, 'Why is it that we have difficulty connecting with the splendour of our own souls? Why is it that there is no grandeur in our thinking?' Such questions flowed freely from Gunna Dan. More and more, I could see that he was responding quickly and perceptively. He was now sure and true in himself. There was no need for him to mull over the issues. And the more we talked, the more we

---

39   Mark 9:34–35, JB

agreed that it is essential for each of us to understand the human condition much more than we do. The upshot of our chat on these issues was that Gunna Dan pressed me to expound further on our individuality.

By then, we had arrived at the gates that led up to Freagh graveyard. We rested there for a while. We could easily hear the sound of tractor engines, and we saw that a few farmers were hauling black plastic-wrapped bales of silage to their farmyards. Shortly afterwards, we were on our way back to the strand. At Gunna Dan's further prompting, I continued.

'Each and every one of us comes into this world alone. In whatever ways we live our lives, we live with this great internal aloneness. Each of us in our internal aloneness is unique and special. It is in this world of aloneness that everything happens. All your powers of insight and intelligence, of discrimination and discretion, of sound judgment and self-confidence are active here. The whole world of music, laughter and fun, of creativity, enlightenment and inspiration, of love, kindness and compassion all belong here – with you, in your inner aloneness. You are centre stage. You are the performing star in a theatre of spiritual energy. You are the most important entity in this spiritual universe. This has been planned for you long before your emergence into self-consciousness. You are at home here. You will always belong here. You are very unfair to yourself when you do not regularly visit your own inner aloneness and spend quality time there. You are very unfair to yourself when you do not perform on this stage. On this stage, you live. On this stage, you grow – from childhood, to young adulthood and on to adulthood. On this stage, you belong totally and fully. There is no place else. When you sing and act, you are superb. When you compose, you are brilliant. When you tune in to divine intelligence, you are angelic. You are perfect! This is bliss. Here, in our inner worlds, the worse singer in the world performs better than Pavarotti or Maria Callas. As a footballer, you are swifter, trickier and more evasive than the greatest player ever. Every man sees himself as Prince Charming and every woman as Princess Beautiful – and rightly so, because in the internal aloneness of your mind glorious things can happen. This is all so understandable. The spirit of the human person is very close to the dynamic of perfection. It is, after all, the state of our creation.'

All of this is full of sound sense, I told Gunna Dan. Our own personal experience supports these truths. I then went on expand on what I had already told him, that in the very first chapter of the first book of the Bible, namely the book of Genesis, written thousands of years ago, we are told that 'God created man in the image of himself'[40]. If this means anything, I asserted, it has to mean that each and every one of us is imbued with divine perfection. Our spiritual capacity is divine. It is infinite. And I argued that this biblical teaching challenges each and every one of us to accept it and its implications. It obliges us to admit and make meaningful to ourselves what our divine origins and our divine destinies are all about.

And then I went further with my argument. I looked straight at Gunna Dan and told him that two thousand years ago, this very same teaching was reinforced for us when the Son of God, Jesus the Messiah, told us 'You must therefore be perfect just as your heavenly Father is perfect.'[41] The remarkable thing here is that Jesus speaks directly to our very beings. At no time does he tell us to strive or try to be perfect. Neither does he tell us to become perfect. His exhortation to each of us is really 'be yourself'. We are told in no uncertain terms that the natural state of our spiritual beings is that of perfection, where all is best to the best possible degree.

Gunna Dan listened intently to everything I was saying and he then continued on the same train of thought. 'Every one of us should wish to get to know and love our true inner selves more and more,' he said. 'We need to appreciate that we are never far from a kindly and understanding God. The reality, Paddy, that you present, is intangible, but it is still real. In the realm of our internal aloneness, all the energies funnelling towards us are strong, positive and sure; they are all full of kindness for us. We will never hear a chastising voice in this pure inner world. Nobody gives out to us. Nobody ever will. Nobody scolds or chides. The great religions of the world teach the message that superlative happiness is our destiny and our lot. Second best is for nobody. Oh! How we need the wit and the will to know it.'

By then, we had come back to where I had parked the car. We felt that before we would go home, we had to walk on the beach. The tide was well out. I couldn't help but kick the many little bundles of scattered seaweed, particularly the bladder wracks and kelps. The walk and the distractions helped us greatly to become more relaxed and easy with ourselves. Gunna Dan was fascinated by the antics of the seagulls. It was only later, on our way back to Inagh, that we began speculating on and pondering many of the issues we had earlier raised. Perhaps because of our tiredness, our comments to each other were few and brief. However, it was with a hint

40   Genesis 1:27, JB
41   Matthew 5:48, JB

of sadness that we accepted that the grandeur of life we had been talking about had not welled up more prominently in human consciousness in this, as I emphasised to Gunna Dan, the start of the twenty-first century.

I loved going on the long walks, but I wasn't too keen on going on too many of them. That is why I welcomed spending our next visit together lingering leisurely on the banks of the river Inagh some days later. We were down by the bridge on the church side of the road. I have always loved rivers and streams, if only to watch and stare and wonder. I told Gunna Dan about the delightful days of my boyhood spent exploring the stream that flowed by our house in the village of Shanagolden. Every summer, my brother John and I, along with the boys from the neighbouring houses, would go on outings up the river that ran alongside the edge of Mulcair's field. Like all boys of the time, we wore short pants. The short legs of the pants could be easily rolled up, and since in summertime we were always barefooted, we were ever-ready to take off for an afternoon's adventure up the river.

For our adventures, we would tie the necks of jam jars with string and in them we would trap pinkeens and sticklebacks. We were well able to counter their darting movements and disappearing tricks. However, catching eels was our speciality, and for this, we used the brown coloured porter bottles available at the time. Collecting the bottles was a gainful exercise for us because the then local publican at the top of the hill opposite Maggie's shop gave us a penny for each one. Even at the ages of ten, eleven and twelve, we knew that the eels would hide under the larger stones during the daytime and that they always faced the current. That was why we always lifted the stones backwards and as gently as possible. Then, we would see an eel lying still on the bed of the river trusting in its own dark camouflage. We would bring the mouth of the brown porter bottle as close as possible to the head of the eel without disturbing it. The hope was that when one of us tickled or even touch its tail, it would shoot forward and hopefully into the bottle. We always greeted success with an almighty shout followed by whoops of glee. At the same time, we would fling the bottle and the head-trapped eel as far as possible into the field. Then, the real fun would start. Who could catch the eel that would, by then, be invariably free from the bottle and wiggling and waggling its way instinctively back to the river? The slippery eel often won its way back, but no matter, we would start our fun all over again. Gunna Dan was astonished when I told him that the very eels we were catching were probably much older than ourselves and that they were born in the Saragossa Sea in the West Indies almost four thousand miles away. He was also astounded to learn that after spending on average fourteen years, if not more, in our rivers in Ireland, the eels then go back across the Atlantic to the waters of their birth to spawn and die.

While we were talking, we spent our time dawdling up and down on the short gravel walk on the river's left bank. I even momentarily thought about going into the river and overturning a suitable stone, but the current was much too fast and the descent down the bank was far from convenient. Instead, we sat down on a nearby seat. The day was pleasant and the lambent breeze was soothing to the face. Gunna Dan then commented that our previous considerations were so noble and exalted, that they were actually somewhat removed from the reality of living that faces people day in day out. He said this as much to himself as to me. Ever since he had spoken to me about philosophical imperatives and his conclusion that therein lies the truth, he had been a changed man. He was much more thoughtful and meditative. He was more at home with the grandness of our ideas. And yet, he remained concerned that life as it lived by most people is so sadly different. I accepted the challenge to respond to his reservations.

'Yes, when we move away from and forget about our true home and instead concentrate solely on living the earthly material life, we live lives of restriction, limitation, complexity, contradiction, pain and sorrow. In fact, we live lives full of frustration. Life seems to have little meaning on its own when we are living in the vale of tears and in the valley of death. In this realm, destructiveness holds sway. Wars and conflicts abound. Mean advantages are taken. False gods of possessions and power are worshipped. Success is based on one-upmanship. Illness and sickness are seen as cruel blows. Inherited diseases and all kinds of syndromes are assumed to be disasters. Tremendous effort is put into maximising comforts in this earthly life. Every effort is made to eliminate what one considers undesirable. Oh! Gunna Dan, I can tell you we have so much to learn. We do not yet know that in truth we do not belong here. We only have short life spans, and while we are here we own nothing. Everything we have is only on temporary loan. Air, water and food pass in and out with rapidity. We do not own, control or manage any of our living processes. Over twenty three thousand times every day, at approximately sixteen breaths a minute, our bodies inhale and expire the molecules of the air. Our breathing happens when we are awake and when we are asleep. It happens independently of our minds and it happens best when we are unaware of it. Another thing is that we are kept totally in the dark about our own metabolisms, about our digestive, circulatory and nervous systems. The fine balance between anabolism and catabolism from childhood to adulthood is not even a mystery to us, as a mystery implies that we know about it but do not understand it. Simply, we – most of us – know nothing about it. And we will spend our whole lives knowing nothing about it. We do not own any of the materials involved in the growth and development of our bodies, so it is just plain silly to ever argue that we own our bodies.'

Passionately, I added, 'every atom in our bodies, of carbon, oxygen or hydrogen, of nitrogen, sulphur or phosphorus, is billions upon billions of years old. These atoms have travelled extensively throughout the planet. And then, by some process or other, they have accumulated and combined to form our tissues and organ systems. And after I am gone, these same atoms in my body this instant will travel around again for billions upon billions of years more, combining and re-combining an unquantifiable number of times, all the while producing other interesting, if not more interesting, living and non-living entities.' Then, with gusto, I added, with my usual hint of provocation, 'You see, the story of evolution is a materialistic story. It is essentially the story of recycling.'

For a moment I thought that my intensity had upset my friend. However, I was relieved when he calmly and seriously told me that he had little or no awareness of this information at all. He had never even thought about it.

'Do you know what?' he asked. 'You are impelling me more and more to accept that true reality cannot be found in the material world or in the world of the body. It has to be in the mind and of the mind. It has to be in the spirit and of the spirit.'

He said this to me after I had continued to explain in more detail how we go through life knowing so little about our bodies. 'This is why,' I said to Gunna Dan, 'that another one of the great questions of life is 'to where do I belong?' The question equally ranks with the other great universal questions of life: 'Who am I? Where did I come from? Where am I going?' And, to emphasise the separateness of humanity from the world we live in, I excitedly continued. 'Rivers would still flow. Tides would still rise and fall. Tornados, hurricanes and storms would still rage their merry ways around the world if we were not here at all. We are very peripheral to the realities of the external world. Our true reality has no foundation on Earth. We are only passing by although many of us take our time about it. The realities of the external world including the world of my body are extremely peripheral, actually unimportant. We have a philosophical imperative to accept this and to accept the consequent issues flowing from it. A major imperative is this: all our limitations in this external world are unimportant, be they lack of food and resources, lack of wealth and health, even the burden of bodily syndromes and defects. All of them belong outside of us. They are only temporarily associated with us. When we pass out of this world and into eternal life we will leave all earthly limitations behind us.'

I paused for a while, but soon I continued.

'In actual fact, Gunna Dan, for practically all of us, we allow the regrets and the baggage of the past to dominate us. We let the false reality of our limitations in this life overpower and overwhelm us. All of us, to some extent, if not to a great extent, are disabled. Some disabilities are more obvious than others. Some of us have inherited syndromes and genetic diseases. Others of us are mentally disadvantaged in various ways. Many of us are deficient in our feelings, in our emotions and in our thinking. Our knowing powers are limited. Our sense organs are limited. Our auditory reach is restricted. Our visual extent is narrow and fallible. And, as far as our sense of smell is concerned, that is very subjective and variable. Everything about us is limited. Our development in the womb was limited. Our fingers and especially our toes are poorly developed. As of now, most people do not know whether they place the right or the left thumb uppermost when they cross their hands in prayer. Ask them into which pocket they put their house or car keys, and the first thing they will do is check. When they cross their arms, they do not know whether the right hand or the left hand is on top. Even at basic level of living, our ability to run is limited and becomes more so with age, as does our ability to see and hear. Our thinking powers are quite important to us because it is in the act of decisive thinking that we find direction and purpose in everything we do. But these powers are also limited, and as we age, they can progressively deteriorate – in some cases, appallingly. Sadly, the limitations of our brains can and do prevent us from seeing the grandeur of this world and of everything in it. Our brains' limitations can prevent us from enjoying the loveliness of life and from seeing the truth of our existence. Our limitations here explain to some degree why, Gunna Dan, your puzzlement grows greater the more you are getting to know us. Put simply, we do not know how to think out our lives with vision and purpose. We confine ourselves predictably to limiting patterns and to dull repetitions. We can let our doubts, and particularly our ignorance, cloud our thinking. This is where we need the most help. Our ignorance, personal and global, is one great frustration, indeed. It keeps us in the dark. It prevents us from appreciating and respecting issues capable of being known. It prevents us from revering the knowledge, wisdom and grace that can uplift us and imbue our lives with great loveliness. We need help. We need an awful lot of help to see the wider picture, the whole picture, and to come into contact with the one great reality of all realities. Our thinking needs to be disturbed. Our minds need to be agitated. There is a greater need now than ever before for all-inclusiveness. All realities must be on the table so that we may see them and relate truthfully to them. We need to be true to ourselves. We need to choose the best in everything. In fact, without any doubt whatsoever, we want the best in everything.'

'And it is with dealing with the issue of doubt that I need a lot of help,' interjected Gunna Dan. 'I know that the main problem is solely a subjective one, but another problem is this: our doubts, to some degree, are always independent of the facts themselves.'

On more than a few occasions, Gunna Dan had raised the issue of doubt and how to cope with it. I knew that this was a concern for him, as it was for me, and that he wished to confront it. Every now and then, he would raise the topic. But we both noticed that each time we ended up talking – often vaguely, it must be admitted – about the topic of certainties. We used to say in jest, 'We exist! We are! Look, we are here!' This time, I decided to respond to his plea. I started talking about René Descartes (1596–1650), a scientist, mathematician and philosopher who lived at a time when the pursuit of knowledge was considered to be in a state of moral and cultural decline. Descartes brought a cold clinical approach to the study of personal knowledge in his *Meditations* (1641), in which he asks if there is any kind of knowledge that can be known with certainty. His adoption of an analytic scientific method in this quest was his major contribution to the study of philosophy. I explained to my friend that what remained intact for Descartes, amid all his doubts, was the fact of the thoughts in his head. He concluded that the reason he was able to think was because of his certain existence – *Cogito ergo sum*.[42]

Descartes was suspicious of the information and knowledge coming from his senses because he knew that our senses could deceive us. He gave prominence to the power of intuition and the process of deduction, and he firmly held the view that everything is capable of being known. Gunna Dan was pleased to hear this, and as he spoke, I found that his comments were insightful and confident. He was not unaware of the philosophers of the past. In fact, I knew that he visited the public library in Ennistymon on a regular basis and spent many a morning browsing its wonderful selection of books.

I then went on to tell him that more than twelve hundred years earlier, Saint Augustine of Hippo (354–430) had grappled with the same problems. The issue of doubt was very pertinent to him because at the time, the sceptics had a very strong influence. They claimed that it was not possible to know anything. Saint Augustine affirmed the existence of the knowing person with his great argument *Si fallor, sum* – 'If I doubt, I exist.' The good man explained in his writings that if we live in doubt and if we deny the testimony of others, then we know not at what place or from whom we have been born.[43]

We had a bit of fun then trying to make out the kind of person a totally doubting person is – such a person never knows how old he is, where he comes from or when or where he was born. He does not know who his mother is, let alone his father, or whether he has brothers, sisters, uncles or aunts. It wasn't long, however, until we turned the argument around and instead spoke about the importance of seeking certainty and recognising it in our minds. We both agreed that if anything is very obvious, and if any idea is discernable and distinct, then we can be sure of its existence. This got us talking about triangles and squares and circles. We acknowledged the certainty of their existence as entities and also as concepts of the mind. We even admired the certainty and simplicity of 2+2=4 and, in our fascination of it, we both agreed that the equation is a lovely example of the perfection of equality. It is total in itself. It needs nothing more for its completion. Indeed, anything extra would be impossible. Slowly but surely, I detected that Gunna Dan was taking the lead as we chatted away. As time went on, it became more and more obvious to me that Gunna Dan was

---

42 Dave Robinson and Judy Groves, *Introducing Philosophy* (London: Icon, 1999), 55.

43 See Saint Augustine's *De Trinitate*, Book XV, Chapter 12.

full of confidence, and this confidence was deeply rooted at many levels. He was lively, brisk and chirpy as he spoke. I even thought to myself that he was like a developed nestling at the edge of the nest, wondering if the time was ripe to fly.

Then, we were suddenly disturbed. A heron flew in overhead and landed leisurely on the river a little upstream from us. Ever so quickly, it anchored itself in the stillness of its own being. It posed like a motionless statuette, still and eerie. Its stillness quietened us. An essence of reverence penetrated and imbued us. We waited as it waited. Even without looking directly at him, I knew that Gunna Dan was beaming delightfully. He was euphoric. An unusually bright radiance emerged from him. When I looked at him his eyes were closed. He was extremely still and extremely silent. For me, without really understanding it, the scene hinted of a sudden connection that Gunna Dan had made with ethereal spiritual existence. I could only but be reverent in his presence. I was certainly tongue-tied.

Eventually, we got up from the seat and walked away from the riverside towards the church car park. Before we parted, Gunna Dan was quiet and content. 'You know what?' he asked. 'When I get home, I'm going to have a good rest, and instead of thinking of useless doubts, I will amuse myself with my certainties.' I could see a roguish glint in his eye as he said this, but I instinctively knew that he was much happier than before.

Chapter 10

The Life of the Mind

I stayed at home the following day and attended to some necessary household work. I had let the work pile up for no particular reason, or if there had been a reason, it was that I was now a man of leisure and didn't feel that I had to do anything. I tidied and cleaned the house. I made great use of the dishwasher and the washing machine. There was nothing left to do but mow the lawn. I was pleased to notice that it was only five minutes to twelve when I brought the mower out from the shed, because the Angelus bell was ringing from the parish church in Inagh just behind me. It always rang five minutes early. I mowed the lawn assiduously and methodically, actually enjoying the rhythm of walking up and down and tolerating the nuisance of emptying the grass cuttings into black plastic bags, later to be brought to the waste-recycling centre at Ballyduff Beg Wood. My last job was to sweep the pathways clean. I normally stare down at the footpath while sweeping the grass remnants onto the lawn, watching every last one of them. Because of this, I am oblivious to anything and everything beyond me. However, on this occasion, out of the corner of my eye I saw Gunna Dan coming in the distance, striding purposefully towards the house and towards me.

'I was over at Keatings' supermarket,' he said, 'and I took the chance you might be in.' He looked at the mower, the plastic bags and the brush in my hand and then declared, as if he wanted the whole world to hear, 'My! But you have been working hard.'

His timing was perfect, and we both went into the house. We made a lovely snack for ourselves of smoked ham and salad with plenty of brown bread and tea. I was glad he called, and it didn't take me long to notice that he had been anxious to meet me. I gathered from his demeanour that he had thought long and hard on the discussions we had the previous day by the riverside. I surmised that he was anxious to update me on his thoughts. In recent times, he often raised the topic of systems and things working in unison and working perfectly. But more often than not, his comments were more like mutterings to himself than explanations to me. We soon sat down at the table and settled into the eating of the meal. Then, casually, Gunna Dan started, and as he did, it was with more of a sense of wonderment than anything else. He marvelled at how, despite all the limitations of our faculties, we could witness and enjoy perfection in its many manifestations. He particularly enjoyed the way it could emerge from anywhere and present itself to our minds for our delight. On earlier occasions when I would discuss perfection, Gunna Dan had been silent and thoughtful, but now he was a different man. He continued talking for some time. He enthused about perfection delightfully, and I was very glad to be there with him. I liked the way he was open and revealing. Much more than that, I especially loved the sensation of seeing a man becoming surer of himself. When we had finished eating the meal, he turned to me.

'Look, Paddy, I want to seriously confront you. We have examined the concept of perfection on many occasions and in many ways. My understanding is much clearer now. The nub of what we have discussed is this: Perfection is all around us. It is expressed everywhere – in the life of plants and animals, in their systems, in their structures and in their functions. The processes of growth, development and reproduction are all essentially perfect in each and every way and in each and every entity. Every physical process on the planet – for example, the purification systems active on the land, in the seas and in the waterways; the hydrological cycle that ensures the constant production of clear, clean water; and the constant synthesis of food – all these, and much more, are perfect in every way.'

I tried to interject, but the man was on a roll. He continued. 'Even our bodies show perfection at work. Look! Paddy, am I to take it that the state of perfection is also a natural and essential energy for our minds, our spirits, our souls and our lives? Does it imbue us totally and fully – as fully as it does everywhere else? Is it not terribly illogical to argue that you will get perfection everywhere – out in the farthest cosmological and universal spaces, throughout all of our planetary system, all over our own global planet, down to the physical, chemical and biological spheres, from the macroscopic to the microscopic, within the bodies of fleas and mice and birds and worms – yet not within the ambit of human experience? Why is it, then, that we cannot acknowledge perfection within our own systems and organs, within our own minds and intellects and within all parts of our beings, even down to the tiniest molecules?'

Again, I tried to interject, but there was no stopping him. With the same flurried passion, he continued. 'Am I missing something here? Am I missing something when I do not admit totally and fully to myself that my mind, my spirit, my soul and my life are as close as can be to the state of perfection, imbued by perfection and energised by perfection? Is perfection not the natural reality of my existence? Of course it is. In fact, I am missing something – and something great – if I do not turn around, stop, close my eyes and say with all the conviction that I can muster, 'Great! This is my life. This is my being. This is my place, my home, my destiny.'

While he was saying this, he had his eyes closed. I felt he was doing his best to focus on the meaning and truth of what he was thinking, of what he was saying and of what he had thought out for himself since we last met. Suddenly, he turned to me and looked me full in the face and declared – for a declaration it was – 'Are we not missing something great when we do not realise the truth that every one of us belongs to the state of perfection and that we are energised by the energy of perfection? Essentially, this is the greatest thing that matters – this is what matters in the life of every man, woman and child ever born into the world, now in the world and ever to come into the world.'

Pausing only for a short time, he, in his unique and excited way, yet very insistently and meaningfully, began repeating himself: 'Every man, woman and child born into the world is destined for eternal glory and happiness.'

His intensity and sincerity kept me in a state of reverence. I found myself thinking, without being able to explain it at all, of Julian of Norwich, who, while seriously ill in May of 1373, received a series of extraordinary revelations telling her that it was in the divine plan that 'all shall be well, and all manner of things shall be well'.[44] It seemed to me that Gunna Dan was echoing the same message, accentuating it by declaring that all will be glorious.

My attention soon turned back to what Gunna Dan was presently discussing. He was tremendously excited about himself and about what he was thinking and saying. I could only understand it somewhat. But, he was soon to disabuse me of any reservations I might have had. We got up from the table and, bringing tea and biscuits with us, went into the living room and sat down.

'There were two issues in particular that impressed, if not stunned me,' he said. 'One was your assertion that there was no such thing as a wonky molecule of oxygen, even though quadrillions of them are about the place, all of them perfect in their design, their structure and their function. The second issue is the life of the mind. When I went home yesterday evening after our spell at the riverside, I began pondering. Time and time again, I mulled over what is for me a clear fact: the mind is constantly being enlivened, enlightened, and yes, illuminated. I realised, perhaps for the first time ever, that the life of my mind was enabling me and empowering me to relate to, and to get to know, so many unknown realities within my human capacity.'

Never was a man more serious. Never was he more intent. And he continued. 'Because of you, Paddy, I'm much more in touch with the reality and truth of perfection, and I have been brought more and more into a great understanding of its fundamental importance in the development and advancement of human life. So you see, Paddy, why it is that I spent a lot of time last night marvelling at the wonder, the power and the life of the mind.'

Gunna Dan stood up, walked over to the far window and looked out onto the pebble-strewn backyard. For a little while, he remained silent. I felt that he needed the time to compose himself and relax. I was actually glad, because I also needed time to let what he had said sink in. I collected the teapot, went out to the kitchen and made a fresh pot of tea. When I returned, I sat into the armchair and waited. Then, ever so slowly, he came back from the window to the couch, and this time, in a lighter mode, he again began to speak.

---

44   Julian of Norwich, 'Chapter 13,' *Revelations of Divine Love*, trans. Elizabeth Spearling (London: Penguin, 2003).

'You know,' he said a little thoughtfully, 'I have spent a lot of time trying to catalogue and list the powers, capabilities and functions of the mind. And I have spent a lot of time admiring the myriad ways that the life of the mind expresses itself.' Then, in a move that took me completely unawares, he asked me if I would list out the powers of mind with him. In no particular order, we slowly began. At first, I began mumbling a few words. Then, simultaneously, we both came out with free will. We laughed at this, but before long we got into a stride, and quickly we were itemising them in couplets: perception and understanding; intelligence and reason; recognition and awareness; knowledge and consciousness; enlightenment and insight; intuition and brightness; memory and retention; judgment and discrimination; imagination and inspiration; ingenuity and wit; creativity and willpower.

In our striving, we repeated ourselves a lot. We drank more tea. We ate more biscuits. However, all the time I knew that Gunna Dan was searching for order and connection, understanding and meaning.

He explained to me that he particularly loved the gift of inspiration. For him, it is a splendid spiritual power, pure, fine and precise, completely independent of reason and logic, instant in its appearance and perfect in its completion. He also loved the power and expanse of the gift of the imagination. 'This is not so much a power that ennobles humanity,' he asserted; 'rather, it is more a power that deifies the spirit of man to a great extent. The gift of the imagination enables us to be creators. It enables us to be creative spiritual beings.'

Then, in a move that alerted me, he directed a question at me. 'What do you think, Paddy, is the significance of free will?' I immediately eased when I realised that he was going to answer it himself. 'A lot of people think that free will means freedom of action. But the very term itself is sourced in the mind and is of the mind. Primarily, free will implies that we choose to anchor our thinking on the important issues of life, and that, Paddy, is something, I'm so happy to say, both of us recognise and accept.'

Surprisingly, I was calm and steady as he was saying this. I can tell you that I absorbed, without distraction, everything he was saying. I welcomed his further explanations of the power of reason. He emphasised to me that our rational powers, along with our free will, are serious ennoblements of mind. They help us to know great and greater realities. He enthused most of all about the power of intuition. This gift, given to everyone in abundance, is a rare blessing for all humankind because it empowers us at crunch moments in life to make choices that are sure and true. He boldly stated this. He emphasised it. It makes no difference as to how disadvantaged or disabled we are. No learning, no language, no speech and no sensations are needed for the full functioning of this great gift. This wonderful faculty of mind enables us to see cosmically and totally. It reveals everything to us, and it does so with knowingness that is exact and immediate, full and direct. The gift of intuition, so freely bestowed on us by God, he stated with conviction, is a transcending power giving us a comprehensive grasp of wholeness and fullness, and because of this, it lifts up our spirits, our inner beings and our true selves to such a degree that we can go outside of time and place and truly into eternity.

When he paused, I began fussing about. I offered Gunna Dan another cup of tea, but he would have none of it. 'Look,' he said. 'There is a great positive determination about everything that is of the mind and of the spirit. The mind is surely a wonder, but what I want to say especially, Paddy, is this: the life of the mind is greater than the mind itself. Let me emphasise it: the life of the mind is superior to the mind itself.'

He left his mug, long emptied of its contents, down at the side table and, re-directing his gaze towards me, he said, 'This is why I wanted to call to see you. I am so excited about this.' And, a little more animatedly, he added, 'I am now convinced that in order to understand the deeper meanings of life, the intellect must have illumination. In fact, and I want to seriously stress this, Paddy, the intellect functions all the time by being illuminated from outside itself by a kindly positive determination, a kindly positive determination that is spiritual and divine in essence, powerful and splendid in action, and yet all the time it is non-coercive and non-threatening.'

He was hopping up and down on the couch. There was no hesitancy, let alone doubt, about his convictions. He was firm and sure. I waited for him to quieten a little, but he was no sooner still than he got up and walked over and back. He stopped by the window and then told me, 'I did not sleep at all last night simply because I have found a new certainty in my life.' His confession, for a split second, amused me, but very quickly, it silenced me.

Standing there in front of me, he collected himself. He became quiet and calm. A reverential and loving aspect now replaced his earlier excitement. His demeanour and countenance glowed brightly, in a very saintly way. Then he said, slowly and convincingly, 'Luminosity in the mind is perfection at work.'

To tell you that I was enraptured is a gross understatement. I now knew that for Gunna Dan, the vibrant life of perfection, in all its majesty and glory, in all its power and essence, was the positive determinative he was referring to, a determinative serving the total being of everyone who comes into life on Earth. Divine Perfection is at work. Divine Perfection is at work all the time. Divine Perfection, the supreme initiation energy, the supreme activation energy, is ever-ready all the time to kick-start each of us, enabling us to propel ourselves to higher levels and to superior realities. This special energy, an energy that comes from outside of us and becomes permanent in us, is pure, fine and discrete. We need to be quiet and still to meet it in our minds and to recognise it for what it is – a divine blessing and a spiritual grace, literally a godsend. This was the great realisation that Gunna Dan was revealing to me. For me, his presentation, for a presentation it was, paralleled significantly with the conviction of Saint Augustine of Hippo, who wrote more than sixteen hundred years ago[45]: 'We derive our light from you [Lord] so that we who were once [in] darkness are light in you.'[46]

I was enthralled by it all, and when I looked on my friend, he was smiling delightfully. I wanted to hug him, and dance and sing, but I was incapable. All during my childhood, we hardly ever celebrated anything, especially the small yet memorable events of life like birthdays and achievements. I always knew this was a deficiency in my life that impelled me into inaction when action was called for. But, in later years, I went out of my way to make up for it. There is one event I especially cherish: I remember calling to a house where the birthday of a litter of cats was being celebrated – cake and candles and drink and all. We sang 'Happy Birthday' over and over again because there were four cats in the litter and four children in the house. I can tell you I loved every minute of that occasion. Now, I felt challenged to do something.

As I stood there alongside my noble and magnificent friend, I suddenly erupted, blurting, 'We must celebrate this very moment.' I went directly out to the kitchen, and from the cabinet I withdrew a bottle of my finest

---

45   Saint Augustine, 'Book IX: Cassiciacum: To Monica's Death,' *The Confessions*, trans. Henry Chadwick (Oxford: Oxford, 2008).
46   See Ephesians 5:8, JB

Spanish sherry and two appropriate glasses. Before Gunna Dan knew it, he was clinking his glass, full to the brim, against mine. I babbled on about saluting life and times and people and places, and I don't know what else I said. I think, though, that I finished up by welcoming the dawning of new and great ideas into our minds and our lives. We both drank from our glasses. There was tremendous relief and succour in the drinking. There was soothing and satisfaction in every quaff.

We enjoyed a splendid afternoon and evening in the house, and when Gunna Dan was leaving, he was lavish in his thanks and appreciation. He even apologised for overstaying his time. I would have none of it. We stood outside for a little time. It had been a long day. We both grew silent, and simultaneously, it seems, we both became aware that there was a noticeable loveliness to the evening light, a loveliness I always associate with the coming to an end of a sunny summer's day. The calmness and the serenity imbued the two of us and, for far longer than a moment, I felt that Gunna Dan was surrounded by splendour and light. As he walked away up the footpath, he promised that he would see me soon again. I continued looking at him, and as I did so, I couldn't help but be amazed as to how easily and lightly he proceeded on his way.

Suddenly, a tiny little pang of lonesomeness hit me. Every previous experience of the feeling saddened me. Normally, I am relaxed and contented in my private aloneness, but this time I felt more lonely than ever. I remember very well how lonesome everybody would be when returning to boarding school after the holidays. Everybody would be crying and sobbing while saying their night prayers before going to bed. Even then, as a child of twelve and onwards, I understood the feeling somewhat. I knew that lonesomeness happens when connections are broken. I knew that it happens when our treasured connections are severed. And, back in those days, I always assumed that the ones who sobbed and whimpered and snivelled the most were the ones who came from the more cosseted and loving homes. Their disconnection was greater, and because of it, they were all the sadder.

I couldn't explain why Gunna Dan's departure made me sad and lonesome. I couldn't understand it. All I could do was to try and ignore it.

Throughout the following day, I thought long and hard on the events that happened in the house, on what was said and done and what was felt and thought. I was slow to admit it, but admit I did: Gunna Dan was a most exceptional person with wonderful insights and inner power. Because of him, I more highly valued the idea of my own power and life. I began accepting into my mind in a very blatant way that the story of our lives on Earth is superbly exciting and personally satisfying. I deliberately entertained the inclination that wonderful energies and entities were out there wafting us along to a glorious destiny. In my efforts to be realistic, I continued thinking that all the limitations that we spoke about, all the negativity and all the doubts were nothing other than grist to the mill. They were nothing other than spurs and prods to make us rise up and look deeper into the whole meaning of life. As Duke Senior in Shakespeare's *As You Like It* puts it, 'sweet are the uses of adversity'.[47] I've always accepted for myself that our adversities, some of them, anyway, may never be eliminated from our lives. I've always accepted for myself that our frustrations can never be fully assuaged. Our wants and desires can never be satisfied. Loyalty to ourselves demands that we spend our lives getting to know and develop our deep inner resources.

I kept on repeating to myself that the greater reality of our lives is in our inner selves. I knew enough to know that down through the ages enlightened men and women have written about this and have lived lives of remarkable dignity and wholesomeness. They wholeheartedly expressed their values and practised their virtues. Fearlessly and often at great hardship to themselves, they lived lives dedicated to this more enduring inner world. When it comes to ourselves, we are challenged to do likewise. There, in the midst of my own thoughts, I reminded myself that each of us is born ignorant and helpless. At birth, none of us knows the alphabet, let alone know how to read. We have but a few years to grow into truth and knowledge. However, we have inherited a rich set of resources that can be found in literature, art, music, science, philosophy and religion. The literature on virtue is expansive and the importance of it in our lives is great. The practise of a virtue is seen as the development of excellence in a person. The practise of virtue is essential to enable and fortify man's natural love for all that is good and holy. Without virtue, none of us can be truly ennobled. We can never be happy and content. All the ancient cultures revered virtue. Their songs and epics inculcated a love and respect for virtue in their peoples, even if in the past the term more narrowly meant manliness, as the name *vir*, the Latin word for 'man', suggests.

Even in pre-Christian times, virtue was understood to be on a par with habitual moral excellence. The Hellenistic philosophers, Socrates, Plato and Aristotle, recognised the four cardinal virtues, and Solomon prayed

---

47   Act 2, Scene 1, Line 12

for them in the book of Wisdom: 'virtues are the fruit of her [Wisdom's] labours, since it is she who teaches temperance and prudence, justice and fortitude.'[48] No wonder he prayed to God to be more virtuous; virtues were necessary and desirable in a conflicted world where so little was prudent, just, brave and temperate. I kept reminding myself that through all the ages, people have had a grand desire to imbue the intellect and the will with the kind of thinking that would enable the natural and the supernatural goodness in people and society to emerge.

I pondered all of this and, in my mind, I began addressing an issue that had long occupied me – namely, what are our values in the world of today? I kept coming to the same conclusion: our values and the values of our parents, children and grandchildren are, for the most part, based on the materialistic world in which we live, and because of this we can be driven to be very individualistic and selfish. This is not surprising. Every one of us has been touched by the slow but persistent de-Christianisation that has emerged in the second half of the twentieth century in Ireland and has spread over every layer of society.

Like it or not, I reminded myself, we all have values. Like it or not, we all absorb our values from all around us. Many of us do so passively, as if by some silent, osmotic process. In the past, people absorbed the respected values of their culture. They learned about them. They appreciated them. They revered them. They practised them. Today, however, we live in the age of televisions, computers and a dizzying host of telecommunication systems. The programmes available for viewing are produced to have global appeal. Because they often have little or no value content, let alone cultural content, they can be successfully sold all over the world. Worse still, a huge number of computer games simulate battles and wars. Shockingly, they are so designed to enable the viewer and the user to interactively engage in the virtual activity of killing, bombing and destroying. Children take to this kind of pastime with alacrity and gusto. Children also take to the Internet with addictive eagerness. Let's face it. The Internet, inter alia, is too full of filth. It is no wonder that I found it easy to concede in my mind that the imparting of values to our children today is a difficult if not a forgotten duty.

Later on in the day, I went out to the back and began hoeing the weeds emerging up through the pebble-strewn yard. The task was easy because the

---

48   Wisdom 8:7; JB; Also see Wisdom 9:1–4, JB.

ground was well drained and the constant, dry sunny weather prevented any significant growth. As I worked, I kept thinking about Gunna Dan and the splendour of the metaphysical journey I was undertaking with him.

My inner being was growing rich with many inspiring insights. My life's mission, I said to myself, has to be self-enrichment. It is everybody's life mission. We need to recognise that our existence in this life is a glorious mission. This is what gives us, for a start, great self-esteem, self-worth and self-respect. This is why each of us must say in our innermost being, *I am the most important person in the world. I am special, and I am unique. I, personally, can and must accept the challenge of living life in the fullness of truth. I must allow for the splendour of perfection to light up my life. It is I who must stand up to myself, take in a deep breath of air and say convincingly to my inner self, 'Let it be done!'* Every one of us in our great aloneness must be able to dance and harmonise with the great power of life that is given to us. The great thing is that we can. We belong to a tremendous inner aloneness where all is perfect, where all is right.

As I continued hoeing, I found it easy to give my complete attention to the job and to maintain a state of definite mindfulness. At times, I could intently and with great clarity hear the distinct scraping sound of the hoe against the pebbles. I saw myself quietly listening to the sounds. I saw myself hoeing. I saw myself looking. I saw myself as I looked at the convergence of hoe, pebbles and weeds. More than that, I could see myself chattering away in my mind. And the biggest surprise of all was that I saw myself looking as if I were far away. And then, slowly, surely and silently, I saw silence itself. I saw it fully and for quite some time. I saw clarity – not the clarity of things and events and peoples. I just saw clarity. I felt freedom. I sensed emancipation. I met solitude. I met all of this and more in the infinite realm of serene aloneness. This was a new emergent experience, often hinted at many times before in my life, even many times in my childhood. Now this experience, this involvement with my serene aloneness, was assured and confident. At the same time, it was mysterious and inscrutable. It was beautiful.

I say that the possibility of my experience was hinted at 'even many times in my childhood' for this reason. It was not uncommon in those days of my childhood to be severely chastised, so much so that I would cry a lot. Sometimes, when left alone, I would see myself crying. I would, if this were possible, stare at myself with my inner eye as I was crying. Then

I would feel silence. The quietness soothed me. It calmed me. I would look, open-mouthed and wide-eyed, all around me. In this discovered silence I would remain very still, part of me afraid to move, but most of me not wanting to move. I wanted to rest in my own sense of personal presence. How long I would rest there I never knew, but sooner or later I would hear the ticking noise of the clock, at first faintly, but then it would seem to get louder and louder, admonishingly so. I always disliked that clock, even though my beloved father treasured it. He would carry it embraced in his fist upstairs to the bedroom every night, and when he would wind it up, the clock, nestled in his strong muscular fist, would swivel one way while the other hand and the winding key would swivel the other way. The act of winding was a musical and rhythmical performance. But still, I so disliked that clock. It brought me out of and away from my serene inner self and into a very noisy and harsh world.

However, in later life I did acknowledge that there are many people out there who have had similar, if not more intense sensations than these, particularly people who have emerged from car accidents and other life-threatening events. The stories of their returns to consciousness can be very personal, if not dramatic. Yet, I am very well aware that in many others cases, the return is uneventful, and, if this is the right word, normal.

Chapter 11

The Gift of Wisdom

It was almost a week later when I met Gunna Dan again, and it was mostly by accident. On Thursdays, *The Clare Champion* comes out for sale, so I strolled up to the local supermarket to get a copy. I had become very interested in the fortunes of the Inagh hurling club – soon to be amalgamated into the Inagh-Kilnamona GAA club. Dates, times and places of the club's games would be in the paper and, if I could at all manage it, I would try and attend some of them. And then I saw him, like a surveyor examining a construction site. The site in question was directly opposite the supermarket, and it was littered with heaps of gravel and excavated tree stumps. Here and there were murky pools of water. All in all, it was a totally unattractive piece of real estate.

He laughed when I suggested he was a property speculator. However, he wasted no time welcoming me. The afternoon was dry and balmy. We were both easy of disposition and because we had no reason against it, we decided to take a stroll out towards Cloonmacken. We were able to relax once we turned off the busy Milltown-Malbay road, and soon we were ambling along in a carefree and leisurely manner. There was no particular structure at all to what we were saying and doing. If I had any agenda at all it was to express to my friend what I surmised the current situation to be. Because Gunna Dan was easy and obliging, I felt able to express myself. He was, of course, very much of a realist as well, and I knew that he would not hesitate to modify my comments as he saw fit.

'We have lost the ability,' I heard myself saying to Gunna Dan, 'to whole-heartedly accept the inner life of our minds and spirits as our important and true reality. This is partly explained by our notions of reality today. Our chosen reality is based mostly on the externals – of the physical world and of the materials in it. It is fashionable to argue that our reality is only what we can see and feel and prove. Yes, everything that we see and feel and can prove is real. However in the present milieu of our lives, nothing is sacred. Scepticism systematically shifts all meaning towards meaninglessness. We poor human beings in this, the morning of the twenty-first century, are seen to have arrived at a cul-de-sac, a *dead end*. The pursuit of truth is replaced by colourful and graphic descriptions of passing events and by the propulsion of all shades of opinions, viewpoints, impressions and theories. All of them, irrespective of quality, are to be considered valid and equal. The whole valueless process is seen to be free and liberating. Yet, ignorance reigns. Worse than that, truth is terribly abused. Selective truth is confined to an extremely small subset of itself. There is a wild appetite out there to control the truth and dominate it. Indeed, very often it is mangled. No longer is it fashionable to revere, serve and respect the truth. And all the better, it seems, if, in the process of mangling the truth, a person's character is ruined, guaranteed strict confidences are shattered or society's cultural and religious inheritances are damaged, if not destroyed.'

We both became silent, and then it suddenly struck me that I was off on a solo run, all on my own. Any other person would be offended that I had made no mention at all to my friend of the deep and serious discussions we had had in the house almost a week earlier. But Gunna Dan was great. Not once did he badger or contradict or interrupt me. Indeed, he was a patient man. He allowed me to say my piece. He listened intently and even, at times, he would encourage me to continue. And I did continue.

'In this dominating modern world, the evidence on every issue must be right before our eyes. Verifiable facts and hard figures are what count. Issues are automatically assumed disproved if they cannot be verified and validated. When the outcome is unpalatable, a massage process takes place and media gurus and handlers get to work. Those who propose other unseeing realities are considered to be religious crackpots, superstitious weirdoes or plain ignorant. We need to understand our realities. Yes, numerous people among us do know this. We have the examples of great writers, poets and musicians. We all have our heroes, be they in sports, academia or the arts. But our era's destructive agenda has all the advantages, and its sole outcome has to be, if unrestrained, inevitable ruin. The constructive agenda, the creative agenda, has a long and hard slog ahead of itself to prevail.'

Gunna Dan was silent as I was saying all of this, but I knew he was listening intently. In fact, I detected a sense of relief from him when I told him that the creative agenda could be much stronger, simply because everyone can be creative and innovative. We can be imaginative and intelligent; insightful and purposeful; and reasonable and rational. Then, with a flourish, I finished: 'Look, Gunna Dan, we both know that purposeful thinking on important issues is what is required.'

Soon we came to the crossroads. The road to the right and up the hill led to Cloonmacken Lake. However, this time we took the road to the left and kept going until we arrived at the monument erected to the memory of Vice Commandant Martin Devitt of the IRA's Mid-Clare Brigade. Martin Devitt was shot dead at the site on 22 February 1920 during the War of Independence, a war that had its origins in the formation of the first independent parliament of Ireland, Dáil Éireann, on 21 January 1919. The first independent parliament adopted the Declaration of Independence and ratified the Easter Proclamation of 1916. We noted the inscriptions and the dedications on the two crosses, one upright and the other prone.

We rested there for a while and began to admire the splendour of the plant kingdom all about us. I had an agreeable enthusiast in my friend. He told me several times that he learned something new on every occasion I spoke to him about the life of plants. The last time we were talking on the topic, I waxed lyrically on how plants transport their soluble foodstuffs and fluids. I explained to him that we have, within our bodies, a closed circulatory system. Our fluids and particles keep circulating round and round in a one-way system of traffic. Plants, on the other hand, have a single open transport system. Water goes up from the ground, and what is leftover and unwanted evaporates into the air from the leaves. This is why, as I explained to Gunna Dan, wet terrain soon dries out if it is planted with trees and shrubs. This is also the reason, and this astounded Gunna Dan, why plants never get cancer. Even if a rogue cancer cell exists in plants, and this is doubtful, the cancer has no opportunity to circulate around the plant. Gunna Dan knew well that plants could survive and live in very cold climates, even in temperatures way below zero. When I told him that this was due to the fact that the cells had anti-freeze within them, without which they would expand and burst, his eyes lit up in wonder. The reason why Gunna Dan loved talking about the trees, shrubs and grasses, their variety, habitats and adaptations was simply because he was amazed at the intelligence that was constantly at work in nature. Then, too, his aesthetic sense enabled him to treasure and admire how green the countryside always is. He deeply loved the colour green. He found it to have both a cooling and warming effect and he was of the view that it promotes harmony and restfulness of mind. He needed no excuse at all to encourage me to chatter away at length. He would say, 'Paddy, aren't the fields lovely? Aren't they like vast stretches of rich green carpets across the landscape?' This time, as he was by my side, he enthused about the bushes, shrubs and trees that weren't too far away in front of us. I felt obliged to respond.

'The majestic trees you see all around you, Gunna Dan, are the climax of the vegetation kingdom. They are the aristocrats of plant life, majestic and grand. They have emerged out of the ground and have grown, developed and prospered with great abundance. Year after year, they produce thousands of leaves. In their lives are a multitude of realities, realities that you yourself, Gunna Dan, told me earlier can emerge from anywhere and present themselves to the mind. One such reality is the material reality of the leaves, which is short-lived. It is ever-changing. And within a few short months, the leaves drop off and die into the ground. However, another and far greater reality can also be recognised, because the life of the tree is greater than the tree itself. In the springtime, the tree's pure and fine power to produce its leaves expresses itself and becomes apparent. This is the internal reality in every tree – its *leafiness* power. Within each tree is the power to produce leaves year after year for hundreds of years. The reality of this superior and enduring power is inspirational and potent, so real and true. When unfettered by external limitations, this power expresses itself fully, abundantly and handsomely in every tree. In its solitary existence and internal aloneness, the tree's creativity is fully flowing, orchestrating all the material entities into a majestic expression of treehood.'

'Gunna Dan, we know this. We admire it. We love it. Landscape artists can enthuse about deciduous forested landscapes, and we all agree with them. But somehow, when it comes to ourselves, and again, Gunna Dan, 'twas you who said it, we miss something. We are unable to see, feel and know the similarly fine internal reality that is inside us, a reality that is certain, yet more enduring, real and authentic. This is sad for many reasons. It is particularly sad because the ancient Greek philosophers, more than twenty-four hundred years ago, expounded profusely on our inner essence and inner reality. They explained how this inner reality is outside of space, outside of this world of ours and outside of time. It is outside of time in the sense that it does not belong to any period of time and has always been present. And it is especially important to appreciate that this inner true and enduring reality is not of or in the mind. It is beyond the mind. The marvellous and majestic thing is that the mind is capable of knowing this reality.[49] The disappointing thing is that when we connect with this idea logically, our minds are still not able to benefit from it. Our thinking lets us down. We remain enfeebled.'

As we walked back towards Inagh, Gunna Dan was very silent. I knew he was thinking seriously about what I had just said. For a while, he said nothing, and I felt that he was pondering a lot. Then he surprised me. He began to recall and to recap all the issues we recently discussed. He started out by saying how he loved the manifestation of perfection that could be witnessed all around us. He spoke about it as if it were a great revelation, but it was obvious to me that he was delighted with the actuality of it. The experience of manifestation enthralled him. 'It is far more wonderful than we could ever realise,' I heard him softly say, as much to himself as to me. I thought that he might not have liked me saying that we remain enfeebled when faced with deeper internal truths. Then, as if to remind me, he began to recall many of the issues and events that we had shared together since we first made each other's acquaintance earlier in the summer, starting from that first swim in the sea in Lahinch. He extracted the pertinent points of all we had said and done. He highlighted the truth experiences we had had. Realistically, yet lovingly, he accepted the turmoil of the human condition and all that goes with it. Still, at the same time, I felt that he was not going to accept this same turmoil lying down. I was confident that he would take it on. There, as I walked side by side with him, my confidence in the man deepened. My reverence for him grew and my spirit danced within myself with a new ease and a stronger assurance. I was happier than ever before.

Gunna Dan began repeating what I had said: 'The marvellous thing is, the mind is capable of knowing this reality.' For a while, I thought he was confused. But then he began explaining to me that the mind knows. He was in repetitive mode. 'The mind knows,' he said many times. He remained silent for a little while. Then he spoke. 'The mind can know the depth and power and significance of a philosophical imperative, and

---

49   See Plato's Theory of Forms (or Ideas).

a second, and a third, and a fourth, and so on. Humankind has arrived here. It arrived here long ago, but it is now slow to go on and move into new and more welcoming territory. We go backwards too often. Is it not time to start doing what we are great at? Can we not explore more space? Can we not climb more mountains? Can we not plunge greater depths? Can we not develop a philome[50] to be a foundation for knowledge and a springboard into new dimensions?' He said this to me in an animated and excited manner, but I knew he was speaking less to me as an individual and more to all of us as members of the one family of humankind.

We arrived in Inagh and moved as if to part, but Gunna Dan hesitated. 'I would love to meet you tomorrow, because I know you will be able to help me establish a way forward. I have been thinking a lot in recent times and I want to share my thoughts with you.' My friend never liked being trapped in vagueness and uncertainty. More than that, I knew he would be positive and decisive, helpful and insightful. With great confidence and anticipation, I heartily agreed.

We planned to meet outside the Mace supermarket and wend our way to the local GAA hurling pitch. This we duly did. As we walked on the roadway towards the hurling pitch the following day, we were silent. The field was splendid and spacious. Slievecallan Mountain was majestic – high and broad and commanding. Because it was still reasonably early in the morning, nobody was about except the two of us. I couldn't but be excited as we stood and looked all around. I proposed that we go walking on the field, and this is what we did.

'There is an issue that bothers me,' Gunna Dan started, as we walked towards the far end of the pitch. 'Every one of us in the world can experience the intangible and the otherworldly from time to time. Every one of us has an innate drive and desire to seek the best and to love perfection. We have spoken about how philosophical imperatives flow from this. I accept that when we are born our bodies know everything and our minds know nothing. Then, as we live, the mind gets to know because it has its powers and qualities, its light and influences. It has its sensations and its energy. And just as importantly, if not more so, it receives divine grace and divine blessing. Our minds enable us to grow into more alive and awake consciousness. But what bothers me is this: in some parts of the world, the terrible struggle to get the basic necessities of food, water and shelter

---

50 *Philome* – a neologism, comparable to *genome*; a *philome* is a catalogue of philosophical imperatives.

can dominate all thinking. In other parts of the world, the terrible greed to get the possessions and baubles of materialism inveigles us into lives of spurious satisfaction. All of us then can be prevented from growing into newer and truer lives. So how can the human spirit progress and advance? What is it that makes us act the way we do?'

The idea of growing into a newer and truer life stimulated me to take up Gunna Dan's train of thought. I also wanted to share with him my understanding of childhood, which seemed relevant to his essential questions. I felt that it was essential to discuss with my friend how important it is to take child-rearing extremely seriously. The unblemished and guileless children of today are the professors, schoolteachers, politicians and scientists of tomorrow. Sadly, some of them will also be the criminals and the destroyers. All of them will be landed with the problems of living life as they will find it. And what they will find is what they will inherit from us. They will be faced with the problems of war, hunger, violence and famine. They will see impoverishment everywhere, even within the minds and hearts and spirits of their forebears. They will grow into adulthood bereft of values and ideals. They will find it difficult to accept the responsibility for protecting civilisation, let alone improving it for the next generation to come.

I knew I was upsetting my friend because he became silent. Yet I persisted, and in doing so, I spoke as much to myself as I did to Gunna Dan. 'Children need to be loved more than ever. They need support. They need guidance. We owe it to ourselves, to them and to the next generation to fortify them and to enable them. It is a crime against all humankind to allow the innocent ignorance of childhood to develop into the culpable crassness of adulthood. We cannot allow our personal prejudices and hang-ups to hinder us from imparting values and ideals. To shirk this responsibility would be 'a disgraceful sort of ignorance'[51] on our part.'

Gunna Dan echoed what I had just told him by repeating some of the phrases that I had uttered. Then, after a short period of silence, he asked, 'Isn't this ignorance the big problem? Do we know how to train and educate children? Do we know how to enable and honour them? Do we know how to love them?' He challenged me to respond. Because I

---

51 Plato 'Apology of Socrates,' *Dialogues of Plato*, trans. by Benjamin Jowett (Cambridge: Cambridge, 2010). The full quote is: 'Is there not here conceit of knowledge which is a disgraceful sort of ignorance?'

knew that he wanted me to continue expressing my views, and despite my growing reservations, I started as follows:

'We know that the infant – the word literally means 'unable to speak' – has the ability to learn and to recall from a very early age. We know, too, that at a basic level the infant can take in information and use it. The infant advances in leaps and bounds the more she experiences things and events. Learning by doing is efficacious in every way. A child quickly develops the art of integrating experiences into reasonable and meaningful coherence. Better than this, the child can quickly integrate memories of successful occurrences into experiential knowledge. This can happen more successfully when the child experiences periods of silence and has time for reflection.'

And in a tone that was quite serious, I emphasised that from an early age children now learn that violence in human relationships is normal and acceptable. They are taught it by the performances of warring parents within the household and by the criminality of aggressive adolescents out in the streets. All the time, they see it on television and on their video players. This can only mean that violence will escalate into the future. Finally I added, 'What chance is there for periods of silence and reflection in the minds of our children today?'

Then Gunna Dan commented that it is important that the child reflectively enjoys every occasion of success. He was saddened to know that there is a lot of noise in the lives of children today. He was fully aware that the grown-up communities of parents, teachers and the adult community in general have their own difficulties and complexes. When children cannot understand the world they are in, they tune out. They lose themselves addictively in television and the Internet. They abandon themselves to noisy electronic and computer games. He was saddened to learn that they spend more and more time on their own, more often than not in bedrooms, away from family and friends.

I continued with my discourse. I wanted to emphasise to Gunna Dan that children and adults should spend more time together and should spend more time talking to each other. I even argued that the adults of this world have the serious obligation to constantly present a value-packed agenda to all children. This needed to be done not only to educate them, but also to dignify them.

'All the learning and personal advancement is made best in the home. Our greatest influences come from our parents, our genetics, our environment, our nature and our nurture. The newborn infant has no fear. The little child has no problem putting a live worm into its mouth and eating it. It is the screaming parent who imparts the meaning and the knowledge of fear into his little head. The parent does this very easily, quickly and intuitively. But just as easily and just as quickly, we can impart love and tolerance.'

We walked more slowly, and the more slowly we walked, the more serious we became. Then we stopped. Gunna Dan started doing something I had never seen him do before. He began wagging his index finger up and down in front of himself as if to emphasise what he was about to say.

'It is important that we love and cherish all children freely and fully. As child development studies show, "Children who are active and angry as infants can be expected to be active and angry as older children, adolescents and adults."[52] Children need love and protection always. This is why the main minder – be it the child's parent or guardian – has a great responsibility. The whole world of the child is totally embraced by the childminder. It is essential that every child, on a continual basis, experience loads and loads of love. Without love, children become completely forlorn. With love, the true meaning of love and of loving relationships is imparted into the very depths of a child's psyche, so much so that it will last throughout his or her life.'

For some time, the two of us tossed these and other related issues around over and over again. And all the time we kept concluding that everybody in the world needs to be ennobled and empowered while journeying through life. Otherwise, we remain unable to tune into, and use, our rational thinking powers. We will not grow to understand more. We will not be able to know more, nor will we be able to know better. Gunna Dan was very quiet and serious within himself. I felt that he was upset. Something was definitely bothering him. Then I knew, by the way he wanted to start walking again, that he was anxious to express his thoughts. He began by asking questions:

'Does our lack of deeper understanding promote a lot of wrongness in the world? Is our inability to know more and to know better a cause of a

---

52 'Child Development: Individual Differences.' Last updated 2 June 2010. *Wikipedia: en.wikipedia.org/wiki/Child_development.*

lot of misfortune in the world? What bothers me a lot is that every one of us can experience the luminosity of philosophical imperatives. But when we do see one of these imperatives and it hits us in the face, the impact of the experience is limited and the synergy it creates seems to dissipate. Its influence on us seems to be shallow. The knowledge we acquire is peripheral.'

'I would consider it a tragedy,' my friend continued, 'if as much as one human being were to go through his or her life here on Earth deprived of the skills necessary to develop and advance his or her true self. Surely all educated people – parents, politicians, doctors and especially teachers – would see this as so? Education cannot be solely about the acquisition of skills and the attainment of knowledge with the aim of gaining advantageous positions in the workplace. Surely all advanced nations should ensure that the personal development of each individual is the chief duty of society?'

During probing questioning like this, I can often become silent. I simply had no answers for practically all the queries Gunna Dan raised, and I so badly wished for them. In fact, I was more tongue-tied than silent. We stopped walking. By this time, we had come back to the wall at the side of the pitch in front of the clubhouse. We leaned on it. Then, after a while, Gunna Dan turned to me and, with no little seriousness, he said, 'It is difficult for humans to be wise.' He repeated the sentiment, though somewhat differently and slowly, as if to give it greater emphasis still: 'Humankind needs to know about the power of wisdom. Each human needs the power of wisdom to help him cope with the challenges of life.'

So, this was it. This is what Gunna Dan was thinking about all along. In one way, his irrefutable statement and the way he said it floored me. It was completely non-judgmental. He pitied the human condition that is so disadvantaged by its many difficulties. The feeling grew in me that the statement called for no ordinary response. I blurted out, 'But nobody in the whole wide world knows what wisdom is, what it means or what it is about!'

Gunna Dan stared at me open-mouthed, but before he could say anything, I began explaining to him that in my teaching career I had a favourite quotation, attributed to Count Axel Oxenstierna, a Swedish statesman who was Chancellor of his country from 1612 to 1654. In a letter to his son in 1648 he wrote, 'Do you not know, my son, with how little wisdom the world is governed?'[53] Gunna Dan tensed when I told him that I always added that the story is no better nowadays.

I knew from my first meeting with Gunna Dan that he had a certain regard and respect for me. I felt it was because he saw me as a non-threatening, indeed harmless, kind of a chap. But now, after this outburst, he began to laugh. He was now seeing a side to me that was bold and daring. He walked all around the place, chuckling to himself. He looked up to the sky and down to the ground. It was some time before he recovered his composure. I then realised that my impulsive reaction had given the impression that I did not recognise the seriousness of Gunna Dan's comment. But it was easy to reassure him. I did not know it then, but he told me afterwards that he was so relieved when he again realised that both of us were on the same wavelength and that I, too, had my own insights on the topic of wisdom. He encouraged me to talk to him on the subject. And so I started.

'Dictionaries will say that wisdom is the quality of being wise, or they might say that wisdom is a body of knowledge. Ask anyone what a wise person is and you probably will get a response along the lines of 'a man or woman who knows a lot'. But these explanations are very shallow. The word itself, however, gives a clue as to its own importance. It is a *–dom* word.'

'Everybody knows,' I continued, and Gunna Dan loved the certainty of my declaration, 'what a kingdom is. It is a place. It is a state. It is ruled by a king. The king influences every activity in the kingdom. Any law passed by parliament is not effective until it is approved by the king and stamped with his seal. The king pays hundreds, if not thousands, of people with the king's money. Letters, stamps, credentials and authorisations all carry the king's logo and monograms. Most importantly of all, every human being belonging to the kingdom is the king's subject.'

Gunna Dan was delighted. I felt that it was not only so much because of my description of a kingdom or because of my earnestness in talking, but rather, and I suspect this, it was also because I was talking about a new philosophical landscape. I then reverted to explaining and developing the meaning of my analogy.

'As with a kingdom, so too, is wisdom a place. It is a country. It is a state. It is a state within our minds. It is a state of our minds. It is a quiet,

---

53   *Quotations: Over 20,000*, ed. John Daintith (London: Bloomsbury, 1996), 285

gentle place, free from all rancour and noise, and when we are there, we become easy within ourselves. The silence and the gentleness still and quieten us. The ambience calms us. We all should go there as often as we can. It is where we belong. And when we go there, we should bring all our limitations, problems, conflicts, regrets, shame and baggage that we carry around with us. The first thing to do on arrival is to throw down the heap and, yes, ignore it. Our first duty is to respect the quietness, the calmness and the loveliness of wisdom. And then we need to allow wisdom to brighten our minds and soothe our spirits.'

The discourse that we shared was animated and lively. I knew that Gunna Dan was thrilled with the analogy of visiting another landscape. 'Paddy,' he said as he looked straight into my eyes, 'you have set the scene so wonderfully for me, I feel as if I am there already.' We got up and walked towards the sheltered stand on the far side of the playing pitch. As we walked, we could see the church in the distance.

Gunna Dan and I had developed the habit of going to the eight o'clock Mass on Saturday evenings. And every now and then, we would talk about religion and particularly about Jesus, the Son of God. Gunna Dan was especially keen to know more and more about God's gift of his only son, Jesus, for the salvation and redemption of humankind. Ever since he first attended the Eucharistic sacrifice of the mass in the church in Inagh his veneration and homage for Jesus the Messiah had grown immeasurably. He was sensitive enough to admit to me that in every way, he found God's gift of his son Jesus to be a stupendously significant fact of life. There was no doubt in Gunna Dan's mind. God was very much alive in the world. God was very much active in the world. And I was all the more aware of his confidence when he spoke to me about perfection and wisdom, truth and illumination.

Then Gunna Dan began to reveal to me his own insights and understanding. He spoke about how every one of us is born to be self-conscious. We were born to become more and more aware of our true inner selves and inner aloneness. 'These are our birth duties,' he argued. 'Our inner aloneness is a place apart, a place that is still and silent.' And as he was saying this to me, he turned towards me and with emphasis added that our inner aloneness is 'a place apart that allows wisdom, one of the great gifts of perfection, to emerge and to disclose itself to us, and in the process, to illuminate our minds and spirits. In our inner aloneness, wisdom will gently encourage us to be true to ourselves, to never accept second best, but rather to boldly and daringly choose what is best in our personal circumstances. The influence and gentle power of wisdom will help us to realise that we belong – as does all of creation, certainly – to only one true world, one true realm, and this is the realm of perfection. Wisdom in all its loveliness will entice us more and more to accept its empowering message into our lives, and the more we accept it, the more we will love it.'

I continued to listen to him intently and noted his seriousness as he argued that in order to be dutiful to ourselves, we need to come into a serious relationship with the greater capacities of our spirits. We need to acknowledge the presence of the positive determinations always working with us and for us. We need to encounter them.

I understood what he was saying. One of the things I loved about Gunna Dan was his great respect for the human condition, the human struggle and the human person. Despite all the wrongness and wrongdoing going on in the world, he always respected and revered man's powers of reason, intelligence and insight. He never doubted but that every one of us, even in our selfishness, always clamours for what is best in our circumstances. He readily admitted to himself that each person's mind can give great and wonderful direction to that person's life, and that each person's mind can know that the most perfect, the most true and the most noble is what our spirits want. He would often say to me reflectively what he first said to me on our walk back from the Martin Devitt monument to Inagh: 'The mind is capable of knowing this reality,' he would say, and then he would add, with his usual repetition, 'The mind is able to know it.' He would insist that the mind, in its freedom and its spirituality, is capable of knowing anything. Gunna Dan's understanding was clear – the highest fulfilment for each of us is the knowledge of the utmost truth. He even went further – the highest fulfilment for each of us is union with the supreme truth.

Once we arrived at the far side of the pitch, we immediately turned around and walked back towards the clubhouse. As we did so, I realised that Gunna Dan was delightfully influencing my mind and expanding it, bringing it on a journey from the good, through the better and onto the best. He was very excited, and very excitedly he continued speaking.

'This is it. Wisdom tells us loudly and clearly that what is best in any situation is the only true choice to be made. Despite all our limitations, disabilities and disadvantages, only the possible best matters in the circumstances we find ourselves.' Then with tremendous gravity in his voice, he added, 'Paddy, perfection is never a severe taskmaster. Perfection is satisfied when we, on our part, do our possible best. Immediately, our frustrations are diminished and numbed. We begin to live more and live better. We become happier. We are in tune and in harmony with the inner truth in ourselves.'

After only a little pause, Gunna Dan turned to me and, still animated, said, 'This is only part of the story, you know. The real magic is that the same approach and the same standard is the divine plan for all of humankind. Only the superlative best is intended for us. Only the superlative best is willed for us. Only the superlative best is wanted for us.' Then, as if he knew, he added, 'This is the only way whereby God's plan for each and every one of us can be expressed.'

I then knew why it was that Gunna Dan was so anxious to meet me. He had clarified in his own mind what he felt and knew to be the destiny of every one of us. He had also clarified for himself that while we try to seek the best in everything, divine intelligence, the supreme determinative, is there with us at all times to help us on our way. He wanted to share this with me. I supported him fully in all his efforts. 'You know what, Paddy?' he asked, interrupting my thoughts. 'We need to recognise and accept this. We need to recognise there is meaning to our insights. When we see and appreciate this, no matter to what degree, an obligation is imposed on us – an imperative is handed to us – and that is to acknowledge that second best is never, and never will be, on the agenda as far as our destinies are concerned. Let me not mince words: the destiny awaiting each and every one of is supreme bliss.'

As he was saying this to me, I became absorbed by the idea that he had earlier postulated, of developing a philome of philosophical imperatives. In my wistful and wishful mind, I dreamt that a body of literature existed that contained a long list of acceptable and previously agreed-upon imperatives. I so wanted this foundation for intellectual activity to exist. I so wanted children of every age to inherit riches and resources that would be self-sustaining. I wanted the best of the past and present to be easily available and accessible. In fact, I wanted more. I wanted there to be a global recognition and acceptance of a core of philosophical and spiritual imperatives. However, very quickly, I found myself attending to what Gunna Dan was saying.

'We need our space. We need to nurture our inner space. Outside our inner space, we are totally lost. We need our inner space most when we are overburdened and overwhelmed. And in this respect, Paddy, I want to thank you for letting me know all about the invitation that Jesus, the Son of God, so graciously, so benignly and so courteously gives to every one of us. "Come to me, all you who labour and are overburdened and I will give you rest. Shoulder my yoke and learn from me, for I am gentle and humble in heart, and you will find rest for your souls."[54] Paddy, this was pure magic to me the very first time I heard it, and it still is. The challenge of the invitation is a daring yet delightful one. We are invited to go beyond our human selves, beyond our frailties and our frustrations, and even beyond our troubles and our woes. When we do, we will find sure and certain rest.'

I immediately expanded on the theme and told my friend that Jesus was no stranger to wretched inflictions and 'great distress'.[55] It was he who carried a woeful burden with him into the garden of Gethsemane. This burden is often described as a burden made up of the world's ills. Jesus is described as 'the one that takes away the sin of the world'.[56] It is not possible for any human being to take on a burden or have a burden greater than his. His sorrow was such that he sweated blood. Now, at this time of all times in his ministry, he knew that he needed to enter his inner space. There he went, and as he was going, he said to his sleepy companions, 'Stay here while I pray.'[57]

'Of course, Gunna Dan,' I said with conviction, 'I now know what this means. He went into the world of inner aloneness. There he saturated his mind, spirit and being with the reality of perfection and with the superlative best. Here he experienced a transfiguration that was luminous. No wonder he spent several hours there. All the time, while he was praying, he was in heaven. When he returned to the land of limitations, he was fortified. He was renewed. He was absolute. He was free. He was now a man on a mission. He knew with crystal clarity what he had to do and he was going to do it.'

By now we had left the pitch. We walked back towards the Milltown-Malbay Inagh road. We passed the houses and went down the watery

---

54 Matthew 11:28–30, JB
55 Matthew 26:37, JB
56 John 1:29, JB
57 Mark 14:33, JB

roadway to meet the main road. Then onwards we walked towards the supermarket and the church. Gunna Dan expressed his wish to visit the church, and I went with him. At this time, however, I got the distinct impression that he wanted to spend time in communion with God in his inner being. More than that, I knew that it was a great satisfaction to Gunna Dan's affections to be making encounters with the person Jesus and with the event of Christianity itself, encounters that were giving his life a new horizon and a decisive direction.[58]

---

58   See Pope Benedict XVI, 'Deus Caritas Est – Encyclical Letter,' *The Holy See: www. vatican.va/holy_father/benedict_xvi/encyclicals/documents/hf_ben-xvi_enc_20051225_deus-caritas-est_en.html* (25 December 2005).

Chapter 12

Kindness in Our Lives
and in Our Times

W
hen I was apart from Gunna Dan, I spent quite a lot of time thinking about what he said and, more often in recent times, about how he said things. By now I was convinced that he had, as it were, upped the tempo, and he was bringing me onwards and upwards into new levels of thinking and being. Don't get me wrong on this; it isn't as if I was an unwilling companion. But when I was away from the man, I felt a discomfort, and yes, even though I am loath to admit it, a lingering lonesomeness. I knew that I wanted to spend more and more time with him. I knew, too, that I should relax more and be easier with myself. I knew that I should lighten up. I spent some time thinking about all of this. Later in the day, I realised that it had been a long while since we had gone for a swim or were out for a drink or a meal. I decided that I would suggest to my friend that the two of us would have a recreational day out to the beach in Lahinch.

We greatly enjoyed the journey to the seaside town. We were only out on the road a little bit when Gunna Dan said to me, 'Paddy, you mentioned Solomon to me the other day, and I am under the impression that quite a lot of people have heard of Solomon, the wise man.' He emphasised the fact that he was a wise man. This started me thinking. Perhaps my friend remembered what I had previously declared – namely, that nobody nowadays knows the meaning of wisdom.

I regaled my friend with the teaching I had in school of the story of the two mothers, and he laughed when I told him that my childhood impression of Solomon was very much fixed on the baby being cut in two rather than on the wisdom of the man himself.[59]

As we drove along, I began telling my friend that the story of Solomon in the Scriptures always interested me. I was particularly taken by the way Solomon explained how wisdom, sent to him by God, helped him to acquire knowledge.

> It was he who gave me true knowledge of all that is, who taught me the structure of the world and the properties of the elements, the beginning, end and middle of the times, the alternation of the solstices and the succession of the seasons, the revolution of the year and the positions of the stars, the natures of animals and the instincts of wild beasts, the powers of spirits and the mental processes of men, the varieties of plants and the medical properties of roots. All that is hidden, all that is plain, I have come to know, instructed by Wisdom who designed them all.[60]

Then, in lightness of heart, I speculated to Gunna Dan that Solomon must have been an adult student in some college of further education of his time, almost twenty-one hundred years ago.

Notwithstanding the company of jellyfish, we enjoyed the swim to no end. It was particularly satisfying for me. The waves were energetic and frequent. They vigorously massaged and pummelled me, and they induced a continuous, dynamic and physical response in me. I jumped and ducked and dived. Gunna Dan was equally brave, equally energetic. He met the bigger waves head on. He loved submerging under them and would stay out of sight for what was, in my opinion, a great length of time.

After the swim, we moved as if to jog or start a brisk walk. I thought better of it and raced Gunna Dan back to the rocks, to the towels and our clothes. When the tide is out, the whole place is very spacious. The heaps of rocks at the dunes' edge, presumably to prevent sea and wave erosion, make for grit-free, elevated dressing areas. The golden sand is compact, and because of its firmness, it is clean and smooth. We took our time changing back into our clothes. Once we had our kit bags on our shoulders, we headed back to the promenade and went straight to Joe's Restaurant.

---

59 1 Kings 3:16–28, JB
60 Wisdom 7:17–21, JB

While we were sitting at the table, we congratulated ourselves on our daring and on our achievements. I had a chicken panini; Gunna Dan had a Caesar salad. We spoke a lot on the importance of exercise and the benefits of the sea air. Once we concentrated on the eating, the talking stopped. We couldn't but help overhear some surfers behind us excitedly talking and engaging in jocular and lively banter. As we were finishing the meal, we could distinctly hear them talking about a great festive occasion organised for them on the following Saturday up in Fanore beach, namely baptism by immersion, and how joyous it was that they were now becoming born again Christians. In the silence between the two of us, I could not but wonder at the first and physical birth of the body into this world of ours and then on the later re-birthing of our minds and spirits into other newer worlds awaiting us. I kept admitting to myself that in one way or another, all of us wish to live lives full of hope and aspiration and that, when all is said and done, each of us is in constant need of resurgence, renewal and perhaps re-birthing. I even went so far as to acknowledge to myself that re-birthing is an evolutionary process culminating in our passing out of this life and into the next. However, I was not able to ponder for long. More people, adults and children, were coming into the café. The noise levels were rising, and because we had finished eating, we paid the bill and left.

The journey home was carefree and uneventful. As we were nearing Inagh, I drew Gunna Dan's attention to the ewe and her lamb all alone in the triangular field that sloped downwards towards the bend on the road. Then a little further on, Gunna Dan pointed out the tall netting at the back of the goalposts on the village side of the GAA pitch. They were quite imposing in the distance.

I felt that Gunna Dan wanted to say something to me before we would come to the end of the journey. Sure enough, he did. 'One thing I can tell you is this, Paddy. The walk we had on that pitch was a very fruitful and a very productive one. It was great for me to talk out with you my understanding of wisdom. It is my serious wish to make it a more important influence in my life. That talk we had was so encouraging to me. But, do you know,' and he turned sideways towards me, 'this is only the start of the story? Wisdom will always support and help everybody, "since her radiance never sleeps."[61] Its light and power will enable us to always see what is best in all our circumstances. Wisdom will never ask

---

61   Wisdom 7:10, JB

us to do the impossible. It will never chastise us. It will never give out. It will always be gentle with us.' He sat quietly in the seat. He folded his arms. He closed his eyes, and very profoundly, he added, 'It is absolutely impossible for wisdom to do this because, in essence, wisdom is divine kindness, and divine kindness is always uncritical and unconditional.' Then he was quiet.

Sometimes the road can be very busy with traffic in all directions. This time, however, we were the only ones on the road. Because we had the road to ourselves, I was able to ponder on what my friend was saying as he was saying it. What first struck me as tremendously wonderful was the aura of serene silence about us. I can tell you I was thrilled to be with him. He comforted my mind and heightened my spirit. I must say I was very happy. We had enjoyed our afternoon of ease and relaxation. And now, alongside me, Gunna Dan was giving me the wonderful benefit of his considered thinking. And, as always, his affirmations were perceptive and astute, but more than that, I appreciated that he continued to speak with ever-greater confidence, if not greater authority, every time we met.

We arrived in Inagh. I parked the car and we got out, but as we stood in the church car park, Gunna Dan turned towards me deliberately. He looked into my eyes, and with the greatest conviction, he said, 'If we could only accept the imperative of divine kindness – that divine kindness will always turn the other cheek, it will always go the extra mile with us, it will always give us that needy coat, it will always be there for us and, no matter what happens, it will bring each and every one of us home to itself.'

I had grown to appreciate and admire Gunna Dan's sure-footedness at he went about revealing his insights. And the fact that he was again talking about everyone on the planet clearly emphasised the magnanimous and cosmic nature of his mind and spirit. He was less bothered now than he was earlier. He became quieter and, I thought, much more content. We were in no hurry to part. We walked around a little bit. I was surprised to realise that very soon afterwards, we grew silent. After a lovely period of quiet, I said to Gunna Dan, 'Do you know what? I have a difficulty. It is this. I know that nobody in the world understands the meaning of kindness!'

He never heard me. He never heard me, because he was in a trance. When I looked at him, I saw a man of tremendous composure. He had his eyes closed. A warm breeze fluffed his linen suit. The suit's golden colour was all the more splendid because of the day's sunlight. In fact, the light was remarkable. It clarified everything all around us. The colours of flowers and leaves and grass were accentuated. I loved being there. I looked all around me. I loved being there with this man. I noticed I was walking much more slowly, and I almost thought that Gunna Dan was gliding.

After a little while, I repeated my daring statement. But this time, I modified it to the effect that it was first necessary for everyone to understand kindness in order to appreciate the blessings of wisdom.

Then, as a matter of fact, Gunna Dan answered, 'Yes, kindness is the great gift from wisdom for all of humankind. We need to know this. We need to understand this.'

There and then, without the slightest hesitation, I said to my friend, 'Let's meet tomorrow down at Cloonmacken Lake. We will have lots to discuss.'

I always like going to Cloonmacken Lake. I find it restful, calming and spacious. Arriving there is like arriving at a true destination. From then on, you are not going anywhere. You become suspended, as it were, between time and eternity. Then, all you can do is just stop, look, stare, take in the view of the surrounding areas and relax. This is what I did and what I like to do. Because we met in the early morning, nobody was about. Everything was quiet and still. The sun shone gently. A lot of the animals were stretched out in the fields, chewing the cud. Even the fields themselves, I felt, were lying contented on the broad and open landscape. We soon sat down at the lower table, the one nearer the lake, and Gunna Dan addressed me immediately.

'Look, Paddy, you amazed me when you told me in the car park yesterday that nobody knows the meaning of kindness. I had not allowed for this at all, but, knowing you, I have concluded that it is your wish to explore the topic.'

I then went on to tell my friend that nobody has ever explained the concepts of wisdom or kindness to me. It was not done in the home, in school or in church. I told him that I had the hunch that these topics are not raised at all to any degree in the lives of most people nowadays. I particularly told him that television programmes, particularly the soaps, are noteworthy for their lack of any kindness. Episodes all the time present the lives and times of people in domestic, school and work situations. Rarely, if ever, is there a kind act depicted.

'Oh, yes, we all have a vague notion what the words mean but that's about it,' I said to Gunna Dan. 'Dictionaries will tell us that kindness is the quality of being kind or that kindness is a kind act[62]. This is actually meaningless and unhelpful. It is meaningless in that it does not tell us what kindness is. It is unhelpful in that we still don't understand the term, the concept or the idea.'

I even went so far as to tell Gunna Dan that the word kindness should be replaced with a new word 'kinddom'. Of course, the convention of pronunciation would cause a little problem, but this new word, like other –*dom* words, would immediately carry with it the significance of quality and the importance of state – two factors that would have to be explored to explain the word. But, as I told my friend sitting there beside me, I was going to take a different way altogether to explain myself.

I started by telling him that it is impossible for any one of us to be kind unless we first enter into the realm of kindness – or kinddom. This is a state of total independence – free from prejudice, malice or mean spiritedness. It is the state of personal largesse, of nobility and grandeur. And being in this realm enables us to be fully ready for action. The required action is that we bestow kindness, not because people deserve it, but rather because people need it. Kindness is not solely a human act. It is the wisdom of divine intelligence working in us. The only standards that count are those of divine intelligence, the standards that we have known all along – namely, that nothing matters except what is best for you, what is best for me and what is best for everybody.

And continuing, I told Gunna Dan that Jesus, the Son of God, explained and expanded on the teaching of kindness when he told us,

> Love your enemies, do good to those who hate you, bless those who curse you, pray for those who treat you badly. To the man who slaps you on one cheek, present the other cheek too; to the man who takes your cloak from you, do not refuse your tunic. Give to everyone who asks you, and do not ask for your property back from the man who robs you. Treat others as you would like them to treat you. If you love those who love you, what thanks can you expect? Even sinners do that much. And if you lend to those from whom you hope to receive, what thanks can you expect? Even

---

62 'Kindness,' *Concise Oxford Dictionary*, 9th ed., (New York: Oxford, 1995), 747. Or consult any dictionary!

sinners lend to sinners to get back the same amount. Instead, love your enemies and do good, and lend without any hope of return. You will have a great reward, and you will be sons of the Most High, for he himself is kind to the ungrateful and the wicked.[63]

Gunna Dan was bowled over by the implications of this teaching. It opened a vista for him – as he told me so sincerely – into the reality of the infinite. 'It is not possible,' he said, 'to over-exaggerate the importance of kindness. It is not possible to over-exaggerate the immensity and lavishness of kindness. This teaching is *absolutely* glorious. Divine intelligence is infinite kindness itself and it includes, enfolds and enraptures every man, woman and child in the whole universe.' And, with increasing excitement, he continued. 'Divine intelligence loves, forgives and forgets. It blesses and rewards. It gives to everyone. It gives the best, the grandest, the noblest and the greatest. It gives, not because we deserve it. It gives because we need it. Divine intelligence has no enemies, never had and never could have. Nobody on Earth ever loses the favour of God's goodness. All of us are loved to an infinite degree.'

Gunna Dan, in his excitement, repeated himself over and over again. Several times he said, 'This is powerful' and 'This is marvellous.' He said it more to himself than to me, as if he was already deep in pensive mode. He woozily hopped up and down on the seat and then got up and walked to the lake water's edge. It took some time for him to become easy and calm. I remained sitting and looking. When he joined me at the table, he was serenely beaming. Both of us then spent some time looking out over the lake in silence. After a while, he just said, 'It is great to be here.'

I don't know how long we stayed silently sitting. The quietness between us was a wonderful experience. It helped me to regain my own independence of reflection, and I engaged in reveries of otherworldly thoughts, ideas and feelings, of hopes and expectations, of what is and of what is to come. In my introversion, I became unaware of Gunna Dan alongside me. Then I had the strange feeling that he was not alongside me at all. I could not help but acknowledge that a little pang of lonesomeness surfaced within me. It was ever so slight, but nonetheless its presence disquieted me.

A car drove in the gateway to the lake and parked down towards the end of the gravel area. An old man got out along with his wife or possibly his daughter. From the back seat of the car, a young girl of about seven or

---

63   Luke 6 27–35, JB

eight years of age struggled outwards. She had a bag of what turned out to be bread with her. The ducks seemed to know the girl, because even before she got out, they flocked to the concrete paving in anticipation of her visit. By this time, Gunna Dan and I had stood up and walked apart a little. The girl then happily began feeding the ducks, all the time talking to them.

We engaged for a little while in amiable conversation with the couple, and then set about going. But before we did so, Gunna Dan surprised me. Effortlessly and easily, he engaged the attention of the girl. He began talking to her and helping her to break up the bigger pieces of bread. He was quick to recognise from the outset that the girl had special needs. He was in no hurry. He lingered there with her, all the time chatting and listening. Before we left, Gunna Dan asked her for a hug. She seized him strongly, smiled brightly and clasped him warmly. I knew there and then while Gunna Dan was embracing her that he was blessing the girl with the full kindness of divine intelligence. I knew that at the same time he was praying that she would be ever enfolded and enraptured in divine love. I knew as well that Gunna Dan, being the all-inclusive man that he was, was also blessing her mother, father and brother, her grandparents and all her extended relations who were not even with her that day. I knew, too, that he was mindful of the whole community of disadvantaged people everywhere and of their helpers and carers who vocationally look after them.

Chapter 13

Considerations on Oneself

I have always accepted that it is very much a part of every person's true nature to respect life and people and, importantly, to acknowledge the common dependence all of us have on divine intelligence. More and more, I had grown to recognise that Gunna Dan's sense of respect, indeed reverence, for all of us on Earth was far greater altogether. And at that lakeside, it became much more than that for me. I saw close-up that Gunna Dan actually shone with shimmering light. I still saw it as he got into the car for the return journey to Inagh. The smile on his face was one of lovely benediction. I could not but be touched by it. I could not but be blessed by it, and I told my friend sitting alongside me as much, but he was loath to listen to my compliments. I drove slowly back to the village, all the time in silence, and all the time in wonderment. As he was leaving me, he thanked me sincerely for being with him and he surprised me with the earnestness of his wish to see me soon again. So I told him straight out that every now and then I love going out to Seafield and walking on the beach there, a beach that is situated a little distance southwest of Quilty village.

It had been a while since I visited Seafield, and Gunna Dan had never been there. He jumped at the opportunity when I asked him to come with me. A couple of days later, the two of us went there. I like Seafield's beach because it is a contrast to that of Lahinch. It is more rugged, more apart and perhaps even more natural. When we arrived, we took our time going down the sloping walkway onto the beach. We took in the views and were struck by the apparent nearness of Mutton Island. Broken pieces of seaweed, particularly wracks and kelps, were scattered here and there.

The raucous cries of the seagulls were clear and loud. It did not take long for us to get into a stride, and soon we were off on a steady walk. It was Gunna Dan who starting talking first.

'Look, Paddy, I am always amused when you come out with what could be called outlandish statements and arguments. At first I assumed you just wanted to be provocative, and later I felt that they were actually the quaint insights of your mind and personality, but now I have accepted that, to you, they are meaningful and true. Since we last met, I have thought an awful lot about the magnificence of kindness. Its luminosity shines brightly in me all the time. I am brought more and more into the real world of my inner being. I see things differently. I see things gloriously different. And yet, when you said that nobody in the world understands kindness, I politely passed it over. Yes, I did hear you. And ever since you made that bold statement of yours, it has haunted me. It haunts me now more than ever. All the time, I keep repeating to myself, 'What if! *What* if nobody knows the meaning of kindness? What if! *What* if nobody understands the grandeur and splendour of this wonderful virtue?'

I listened intently to what he was saying. His solicitude for every individual on the planet kept emerging. It appeared to me that it occupied a lot of his thinking and his meditative processes. By now, I had come to realise that he would never abandon his growing sense of responsibility towards all of us.

'We all need to respond to the challenge of kindness,' he continued. 'We all have a mission. Kindness must be a feature of our lives. We must adopt it. We must have it. We must take it on. We need to live it. And as we live it we must bestow it. There is one thing I need to emphasise, Paddy, particularly to and for myself – the great insistent logic of this virtue is – I must bestow kindness because of need and not because of merit. And the first person on whom I bestow it must be my own good self. There is this great duty that we all owe to our own personal selves: we must be kind and tolerant to our own selves.'

Nothing was going to stop Gunna Dan from emphasising his thoughts, and on my encouragement he continued: 'Kindness obliges us to uncritically and totally accept ourselves as we are. But, in this, many of us have a major problem. We do not know our own worth and value. We do not appreciate our own self-worth. Yet we all want to be important. And in our need, we create a problem for ourselves. We think that our personal value and eminence come solely from ourselves. However, our worth, our value and our dignity paradoxically do not come from within us at all. Everything comes to us from outside. The source of our great worth comes from what divine intelligence knows of us. It knows that we are made in its own image and likeness. Divine intelligence, by bestowing unconditional kindness on us, endows everyone in the world with self-worth and dignity. This is why all peoples everywhere are supremely valuable.'

Gunna Dan abruptly turned towards me and, in a more troubled way, he said, 'Our thinking needs to be agitated here. We base our self-esteem and self-worth on others. We spend a lot of time wondering what other people think of us. We seek their approval all the time. We second-guess them on how we look. We speculate on the supposed thoughts they have of our perceived blunders, and we keep wondering all the time if they are watching us. We do it ourselves. We begrudge. It is far better for us to spend our time thinking about truer situations and truer realities. God made each and every one of in his own image and likeness. The destiny he has for us in the next life is supreme happiness. The great gift he has for us in this life is unconditional kindness. We must tenaciously think about this more and more. We must acknowledge the implications of what we think. And then we must accept them. For a start, we must accept ourselves uncritically.'

Slowly and pensively, Gunna Dan continued. 'The first great duty that each one of us must accept is this: we must be kind to ourselves. We must grow to understand what it is to be unconditionally and uncritically kind. We must accept the challenge to be truly and fully kind to ourselves and to others; all of us must.'

We walked along the beach in silence for some time. The beach at Seafield is much noisier than the one at Lahinch. For one thing, the gulls continuously squawk. For another, the waves can thunder as they crash into the rocky outcrops scattered here and there along the beach. The noise, however, did not interfere with our deliberations, and before long, Gunna Dan had started explaining himself again:

'We all have our own persecutors and enemies. They are to be found in the stockpile of the regrets and wrongs of life, in the well-remembered and well-nourished hates from the past, in all the baggage of our limitations, in pain, sickness and deficiencies. Even in our attached tragedies. All of this baggage belongs to the external finite world of limitations. This is the very place where we do not belong. We belong to another world – that of the infinite and the supreme. The finite world is – for all real purposes – non-existent and non-consequential. The finite world is constantly diminishing. In time, it diminishes into nothingness. Nothingness and nihilism can only make sense (if they make sense at all) within the diminishing and contracting world of the finite. They could not make sense anywhere else. The infinite world is an expansive world of superlative glory.'

Then Gunna Dan emphasised what he was saying. 'The first great response to living in this finite world, a finite world of limitation and frustration, needs to be this: Be kind to yourself. Never have regrets. Never criticise. Never criticise yourself. Never criticise others. Criticising is a waste of time. It does no good. If you allow for so-called *good criticism*, then you must allow for a whole host of attached features. Your so-called good criticism must be completely free of your own baggage, bias and hang-ups. You must be free of dogmatic notions such as 'I am right' and 'you are wrong'. You must be free of the messages that say 'I know the truth, and you do not.' All these positions are antagonistic. All these positions generate hostility. They cause frustration. But there is a deep reason why you should never criticise yourself or others, which is, every one of us unconsciously suffers from an innate frustration and sense of guilt simply because our latent wished-for state of perfection is not yet fulfilled. This is why we are readily and hastily critical. This is the human condition. This is the sin of the world. No human is free. In a phrase, there is no such thing as good criticism. It cannot exist.'

'The good-minded person will instead focus on helpfulness. His mindset is then fully infused with friendliness and kindliness. His subservient and subordinate approach will loudly proclaim that he is there to give assistance as it is required and in a way that is comforting and kind to the receiver. The truly helpful person is always able to cope gently with the sheep stuck in the briars. The truly helpful person knows what it is to be kind.'

We stopped in our tracks in order to cope with an accumulation of brown wracks that were tossed on top of, and all around, a cluster of craggy rocks. Remnants of different types of seaweed, green, brown and purple, were strewn all over the place, so much so that I found the terrain to be dangerous and slippery. It was not possible to walk around the heaps of seaweed and, because of this, it was necessary to give attention to one's footing. I took my time. I wanted to take my time anyway. I was letting all that I had heard sink into my mind. Gunna Dan was also taking his time, but he had less difficulty coping. In fact, he seemed to enjoy the activity of crunching his way along the shingle beach and in next to no time, he was ahead of me. When I saw him there in front of me, I suddenly found myself intently looking at him. Feelings of gratitude and happiness welled up in me.

I can tell you I just loved being there with him. I always like being in the company of friends who are more fun and more daring than I, and I love being with people who express their insights freely and fully. All alone on the beach at Seafield, I was thrilled while listening to what Gunna Dan was saying. I admired his forthrightness. I agreed with everything he said. But what hit home with me were his strong assertions on the frustration of perfection in our lives. It seemed to pain him that we can be so hurtful to ourselves and to others. Then, turning to me, he made what I can only describe as a plea:

'Would not a little solidarity with our fellow travellers on the road of life and a little empathy for their human condition help us to be more tolerant, more forgiving and more forgetful? Could we not be a little easier? Yes, it is all very fine to help the poor sheep stuck in the briars and brambles. Criticising the dumb animal for getting there in the first place is useless. Even with your tender, loving care, even with great delicacy, the same sheep will embed itself further into the mess and thwart your noble efforts to rescue it. Good criticism does not exist, and it cannot be invented.'

'There are so many other ways to do better. Maintaining regrets is an act of great unkindness to yourself. Never punish yourself. Comfort yourself. Everyone should know that divine kindness is a *fire brigade* virtue. It rushes to save you when you are on fire with anger and regrets. It drenches you with coolness and calmness, with ease and contentment. Again, let me say it: kindness is always there for us, but not because we deserve it. It is there for us because we need it, and often in our lives we need it badly. The thirsty person needs water. The hungry person needs food. The one without clothing needs clothes, and the one in prison needs visiting and help. Kindness wants you to recognise its presence in your life. Kindness, the wonderful gift that comes from wisdom, demands that you abandon all negativity and that you abandon it totally. Our baggage is made up of external realities, which are, by definition, apart from us. They are outside of us. They are not us. We are apart from them. There is only one thing to do in response to them – dump your baggage, abandon it and ignore it. Again, and I want to repeat it, we belong elsewhere. Always remember that it is only the best of everything that is wanted for you and, indeed, destined for you.'

Then he grew silent. Tremendously silent.

In one way, he was saying all of this as if he were talking only to me. Yet, because of the way he would look sometimes at me but more often than not, way out into the distance, I felt, as if by some magical or angelic means, that he was speaking to the hearts and minds of everybody. I particularly felt that he had come to be an angel for everyone. My feeling was reinforced when he would stop and peer intently way out into the spaciousness of the open sea. When he spoke, he spoke urgently and passionately. He, more than anything else, accepted the imperatives that flowed from his understanding. He thought about them. He reflected on them. And he accepted them. There were no half measures.

By this time, we had arrived at the far end of the beach. The sand became soft and soggy. It even hinted of danger. In fact, it reminded me of tragedy. You see, we had passed Carricknola on our way outwards and would pass it again on our way back. The name literally means 'the rock of Nuala'. On this rocky promontory, in ancient times, a woman by the name of Fionnuala horrendously lost her life in the pursuit of love. Then, much later, in September 1588, many ships of the Spanish Armada foundered off the coast of Clare, close to where we now were. Hundreds of sailors drowned, and those who survived the sea were executed on land. I couldn't but think of this, and in the silence that existed between us, I even brooded on it. But, I was not allowed to wallow in my morbid thoughts for long. Gunna Dan, too, had noticed the increasing sogginess of the underfoot conditions. We turned back and soon were striding confidently back to where we had started our journey.

It was Gunna Dan who spoke first. He told me that he was now spending a lot of time thinking more and more on wisdom. 'It is a wonderful gift,' he enthused. 'Wisdom serves. Wisdom always serves in the present moment. Wisdom is always available in the now. It totally and fully serves you, blesses you and helps you in the newness of the present moment. Forget the past. Abandon the memories that haunt and hurt you. Do not worry about the past. Do not worry about the future, either. The future does not exist. The only time that exists is the now. The only time that matters is the eternal present. This is where we live. Wisdom is there to help, to support and to serve. To be wise, no study is needed. No certificates, diplomas or degrees are required. With wisdom, failure is impossible. The concept of winners and losers does not even arise. In the serene realm of my aloneness, I compete with nobody.'

He paused. Then, with emphasis, he continued. 'Wisdom simply cannot engage in the blame game. Wisdom never criticises. The response from wisdom is to always turn the other cheek and to walk the extra mile. In essence, wisdom is true kindness.'

'It is essential here for me to be emphatic. It is impossible for any struggling, burdened, hassled, harassed, stumbling or bumbling human being to be blameworthy or to be a failure. This is not in the plan. It never was. It never will be.'

Gunna Dan then turned to me. 'We all play the blame game. We are so critical of others and ourselves. Every individual has shortcomings. This is part of our humanity. Respect for our humanity demands that we tolerate quite a lot in our lives, in others and in ourselves. Doing the best for ourselves in the circumstances we find ourselves in does not mean that we have to win. Very often there is no glory in winning.'

He paused for a while. Sometimes he would pause to let certain points of view sink in. Other times, I felt he would pause to reorganise his thoughts. This time, I felt he was doing both. I remained silent with him. Then he spoke.

'We all need to respond to the divine gift of wisdom. And this is not difficult; we just need to ensure that our efforts are wholesome. The only difficulty here is that few people understand the meaning of wholesome actions. Wholesomeness means that with an easy mind, you make the best use of whatever is available. Indeed, this in itself may be very paltry. But, no matter; all that is required is that you put the best possible effort in what you do. Wholesomeness is fullness of effort. The outcomes are very much secondary. In fact, the outcomes are completely independent of success and failure. Success and failure belong to the external fleeting realities of the outer world. Only those who live in the darkness of this world give them importance.'

'All of us are finite physical creatures. Nobody is designed to be the fastest runner in the world, the second fastest or the third fastest. Nobody is designed to be the winner at everything. The concept is ridiculous. This might explain why we loudly boast when we win *something*! Any person can run. If you are of a certain weight, height and limb length, and if you naturally have a slow resting heart rate and a higher red blood cell count, you will run longer, farther and quicker than anyone else who is not so well endowed. This assumes, of course, that you put in fullness of effort. Another athlete with a faster resting heart beat will run faster and better over shorter distances. A disabled person, on the other hand, may make very little progress but still put forth a wholesome effort. As long as you give 100 percent, your effort is full and this fullness, independent of success and failure, is akin to perfection.'

'There is no such thing as the 'also ran' in this life. Remember this: the glorification of the winner is a shallow and hollow activity. Instead, the more worthy glorification is that of the whole-hearted effort we make when we try our best. Every effort should be acknowledged. We need to praise children more in our homes and in our schools. We need to support them in all their efforts and do so genuinely and lovingly. Children understand adults, and they can quickly get to know adults' motives and attitudes. No school should have an enrolment greater than four hundred learners, and then the school should only be permitted to run if the ratio of enlightened frontline educators to learners in the school is at most 20:1. Then the approval, the acknowledgement and support of every learner's wholesome effort can take place. Better still, an environment can now exist where wholesomeness is encouraged and expected.'

'The actions of every single person in the world can always be wholesome. Fullness of effort is all that is required. Fullness of effort never varies. Fullness is fullness. The size and shape of the container is irrelevant, be it a cup, a thimble, a bucket, a water tank or even yourself. When each is full, it is full, and this fullness is completely independent of every limitation. The experience of fullness and wholesomeness is to be found in your own inner aloneness. When you find it, it will stay with you forever.'

By this time, we had returned to the car and set out for home. There was no stopping Gunna Dan. He was gushing and bubbling. It was not until I took a right turn off the Quilty road and onto a quieter road just before Spanish Point that I could relax. I drove more slowly. Then, I was able to give more attention to my friend. He enthused about how close all of us are to infinite goodness, to the infinite life of supreme bliss, about how divine kindness uplifts and sustains us. He was inspired. He repeated for me that we are far closer to infinite goodness than we could ever imagine. He was sure of this. I listened to him delightfully. The mystery of life, of living, of birth and growth, of growth and death, the cycle of times and the march of events fascinated him wonderfully. He discoursed up and down, over and back. Then he amazed me when, deliberately turning towards me, he said, 'You know, Paddy, the whole mystery and scenario of life can be seen as one fantastic giant cryptic crossword, full of surprises, ever-permitting us to experience intuitively delightful bursts of insight and inspiration.'

He laughed heartily when he saw my open-mouthed silent response and expression. But I knew that my friend, Gunna Dan, cherished every little insight that blessed him. I knew, too, that because of his understandings, he was all the time becoming happier, more content and more self-assured.

Later at home that night, I reflected on all of the day's events, on what we said and what we did. The analogy to the cryptic crossword strengthened in me. I felt that Gunna Dan had by now looked at all four quarters, and things were beginning to fall into place for him. He kept emphasising to me that the clues to life were all around us. He analogously spoke of the expert crossword compiler as one who gives clues and hints, and even answers, abundantly. He was at pains to say that it is always the clear, purposeful intention of the excellent compiler that the puzzle is solved. All these thoughts kept tossing around in my head. I surmised that it is the self-made busyness of life and the regime of work that prevents us from meeting with and recognising spiritual visitations when they come into our lives. I reminded myself of what Gunna Dan told me about inspiration – a splendid spiritual power, pure and fine. I recalled his enthusiasm for the gift of intuition, a divine gift that we all possess – an ennobling gift, an empowering gift, one that enables us to achieve a comprehensive grasp of truth and wholesomeness.

Then, I began to give more attention to the puzzles that I imagined were going on in my friend's head. There, in the middle of the night, I began to realise that for Gunna Dan, kindness and wholesomeness were the linchpins to the understanding and realisation of perfection and wisdom in our minds and in our lives. I kept thinking about all of this for a long time. Slowly but surely, I realised that there was another linchpin of great importance to Gunna Dan. He revealed it to me when I dropped him off at the car park in Inagh. He came over to the driver's side window, leaned in and said, 'There's another significant issue we need to explore, Paddy, and it is this: man must love his fellow man.'

I was not at all surprised that he said this. Through all our time together, Gunna Dan never forgot that he was like everybody else, a member of the one family of humankind, where all of us are brothers and sisters, and within which we owe great loyalty and love to each other and to the purpose of our lives and our living. Time and time again, his mind and spirit revealed a dimension of inclusiveness that was majestic. I had myself thought that Gunna Dan was the kind of being who could not be happy in heaven unless everyone else was there with him.

And yet, throughout all of that night I was haunted by a host of contradictory ideas and notions. I couldn't clarify for myself why I was uneasy, but uneasy I was. I began over and over again telling myself that Gunna Dan was very sure about all he said and felt and thought. He was endowed with light and ease, with delight and even giddiness. And yet again, I was still uneasy. Slowly, I began to admit to myself that my lack of enthusiasm stemmed directly from a keen awareness of life's harshness. I was different to my friend. I kept reading in the newspapers about crime and murder, stabbing and robberies. The newspapers, television and radio constantly carried stories of wars and starvation throughout the world. The stories in the local and national newspapers were equally depressing. During the small hours of that night, I decided that I would dump onto Gunna Dan my pot pourri of negativity, literally a 'rotten pot' of all the wrongs that happen and continue to happen in this world of ours. It was only when I roused up sufficient determination in my mind to do this that I fell asleep.

Chapter 14

Counteracting the Dark Side of Life

A few days later, I went to the library in Ennistymon. I generally spend a little time there every now and then. I also use the computers therein to receive and send e-mail messages. On my way out, I met Gunna Dan coming in. He readily agreed to change his mind and change his plans. We both walked up the tree-lined avenue to the Fall's Hotel for coffee. Before Gunna Dan could settle into a stride, I began unburdening myself. I told him how I had been anguished by an invasion of disturbing circling thoughts and wild maddening feelings. I emphasised to him that I was actually angry at the state of the world that we were living in. I was angry at the failure of the leaders of society to give honest and true leadership. I told him forthrightly that by failing to manage the political and economic affairs of the nations, they had greatly added to the anguish and pain of millions in the world. I also told him that their failure to promote diplomacy, restraint and dialogue had led to the growth of hostilities, war, destitution and degradation.

Gunna Dan listened to me attentively. I actually did not stop complaining until we were seated at the table. I paused to ask the waiter for toasted sandwiches and tea. Normally I dislike myself for being such a moan. Part of me wanted to apologise. In reality, however, I was betwixt and between and did not know what to do. Slowly I realised that I had confidence in my friend, so I was going to avail myself of it. To tell you the truth, I was really pleased that I had offloaded my thoughts onto him.

I felt that a monkey was now off my back. I was even more pleased when Gunna Dan told me that everything I was saying was so understandable.

'*Failure* and its opposite component, *success*, belong to the outer world of external reality,' he said, 'an external reality that is superficial and extremely short-lived. When we confine our living to this external place, we are completely and totally in the dark. Then the blame game runs wild. Punishment becomes part of the adults' lives. Success is praised even when this success is achieved at another's expense. The consequences of failure on people can be brutal. Cheating, lying, thieving and destruction all take place in order to ensure the perpetrators' success. False notions of what is right and wrong dominate. And because we are totally in the dark, the leaders of our societies are also in the dark. They have to be in the dark. All our chosen realities are of the dark. Our external realities belong in the dark. With them we stay in the dark. Here, there is no luminosity. Here, there is no wisdom. Here, there is no kindness. Terrible mistakes are consequently made. Without knowing it, leaders of society do not know what is right from wrong. How can they? They do not know the difference between the good, the bad and the indifferent. They have no awareness at all of the bad, the worse and the worst. And knowing the distinction between the good, the better and the best has no chance at all. Worse still, in those moments when they are most certain that they are most right, those are the exact same moments when it is impossible for them to be more wrong. Many awful deeds have been inflicted in the name of righteousness.'

I was delighted that Gunna Dan was addressing the issues that bothered me. More than that, I was very pleased that he revealed an incisive understanding of humankind's condition. I needed to hear this. I needed to assuage, if not dissolve, my own negativity. But what I cherished most was that Gunna Dan was focused on what I was calling the 'dark' side of life. I was comforted that he was now doing this – so much so, in fact, that I felt bold enough to offload my angst onto him.

'Gunna Dan, the living out of our lives in this outer darkness can be pure hell. Over the centuries, holocausts and genocides have taken place, in the Americas, in parts of Europe, in the Far East and in Africa. Man's inhumanity to man continues to this day, unabated. Whole peoples are subjected to killing, torture and starvation. Men, women and children are helplessly entangled in a vortex of savagery and brutality. The people who ensnare them believe themselves to be right. Spokespersons for the warring factions, including the leaders of powerful nations, can go in front of television cameras and claim that their actions are just, noble, right and true. The people who suffer know that the whole thing is wrong. Worse still, they know that there is nobody out there who can hear their screams of *Stop! Stop! Stop!*

Gunna Dan was saddened by the tone of the conversation. Instead of stopping me, however, he expanded on the theme. He spoke more about global problems. He repeated more to himself than to me that when we live our lives in the outer darkness of external reality, we cannot but create hells for ourselves. He turned and looked at me and said, 'Divine intelligence has given importance and uniqueness to each individual. It wants each of us to recognise that we have importance. Divine intelligence wants everyone to know that the real reason that we are here is that we are on a journey that takes us into the light, into what is best and into what is perfect. There is a philosophical imperative for us to recognise this. The first step is to allow the luminosity of perfection to brighten our minds, our beings and our spirits. We need to allow the luminosity of perfection to animate our human energies. When every individual in society takes on this journey and takes on the responsibility to be true to oneself, then and only then will society emerge from darkness and put a commencement to the dawn of Aquarius. It is an imperative that each of us responds with a resounding *yes* to this journey.'

I never saw a man more serious in my life. I began to realise more and more that Gunna Dan was greatly pained by the predicaments and sufferings of each individual person. This seemed to trouble him more than anything else. He argued with me that nothing dramatic can take place and no new insights can emerge when individuals unthinkingly trust in their materialistic societies and place their faith in whatever it is that these societies offer.

Gunna Dan then continued. 'It takes character, strength and courage to be able to stand on your own two feet and, in the face of the jibe, the mean act, the nasty scheming, the cunning and the conniving, to respond with kindness. Perhaps a good way to respond is with nothing other than your inner silence, perhaps also with a prayer … for yourself and others. But however you respond, surely you will always do so with restraint and with a view that there is always a third, more dignified option. More and more as you go through life, you grow to realise and accept that you belong to a much grander cosmic perspective and to a nobler scheme of things.

More and more you know that wisdom is by your side. You are endowed with heavenly power. You are a giant of a person. You have grandeur and finesse. That's why, Paddy, I want to encourage you to have steeliness of character and strength of will. Every one of us must explicitly develop this in ourselves. We need to be strong because another great challenge that faces each of us is the great challenge to love our neighbour.'

As Gunna Dan said this, I recalled his parting words to me at the car park in Inagh, and I began to realise that this was now another significant component that Gunna Dan wanted to concentrate on. He had intimated it long before this. However, I did not get much time to linger on my own thoughts, because he soon continued.

'Love is real, and it is essential to know it, because love gives fullness to a person's relationship with all of life – with the world we live in, our fellow human beings, our own deep selves and the divine intelligence that has put us here. Developing a loving nature within ourselves is an essential duty in life. We can never be true to ourselves otherwise.'

Then, with decisiveness, he cut to the chase and declared, echoing the Pauline philosophy 'Love is kind'[64] and, going even further, he added, 'and divine love is supremely kind.'

There was one thing that I had grown to realise about Gunna Dan. He had a great love for each and every member of the family of humankind. He often used the phrase 'all of mankind, including all who ever were, all who are and all who ever will be', a concept that is expressed in the old County Clare prayer, *Beannacht Ar Chách*, which concludes with '*beannachtaí ó Rí na grást le gach anam a bhí, a bheidh ní 'tá*', meaning '*blessings from the King of grace, on every soul who was, who will be and who is*'.[65] He saw clearly that the one great family of humankind was on an onward march – indeed, on more than one occasion he said it was on an onward expansion – to a loving, fulfilling and exciting destiny. He also saw that many of us flounder terribly on the journey. However this never diminished his reverence for the human condition. I now knew that he held this reverence because of our divine origins. He assumed that while our predicaments were serious hindrances to ourselves, the self-conscious experience of human identity, was essentially a thoroughly optimistic

---

64   Corinthians 13:4, JB
65   Diarmuid Ó Laoghaire, S.J., *Ár bPaidreacha Dúchais,*. (Baile Átha Cliath: Foilseacháin Ábhair Spiorsdálta, 1975), 233

event. And with time this reverence grew stronger because his entrustment in the divine was developing considerably. His whole bearing, attitude, thinking and, indeed, his message again reminded me of the teaching the Lord God gave to Julian of Norwich when he said to her in one of many showings, 'What is impossible to you is not impossible to me. I shall keep my word in all things and I shall make all things well.'[66] It was as if Gunna Dan deeply understood God's plan for each one of us.

Then he surprised me by telling me that he found it difficult to discuss and to explain the topic of love. What bothered him was the fact that humans have tremendous difficulty loving themselves in a positive, uplifting way. He felt that all of us must first understand that we are obliged to hold ourselves in the highest regard. This he contended earnestly and forcefully.

'Self-love,' he argued, 'belongs to the same category as self-respect, self-esteem, self-contentment and self-confidence.' He looked straight into my eyes. 'You must have regard for yourself and your own well-being. You must acknowledge your own importance. You must respect the great mystery of life. You must salute, indeed revere, the mystery of your own existence. You will not be able to do any of this unless a fundamental emotion is expressed. You must accept yourself as you are and love yourself properly, with true kindness and tolerance. Each one of us needs to stop and be still at moments in our lives. We need to wake up a little more. Actually, we need to wake up a good bit more. We need to itemise our thinking and the important facts pertinent to our existence here on Earth.'

I was almost overpowered. I knew that normally he did not impose forceful obligations on anyone. But now I detected that he was somewhat zealously exasperated. 'I want everybody to acknowledge, to accept and especially to love his or her personal integral worthiness,' he continued. 'Please do not accept what I say as pious talk. Let me remind you that nobody in the whole of the universe is ever second best – or third or fourth. There is nothing higher than your spirit in the natural order of things. Only divine intelligence, divine light is higher than your spirit in the supernatural order of things. Being higher than you, divine intelligence wishes to bless and love you. Each of us is supremely important. Each of us is uniquely lovable. And let me state it loudly and clearly: there is nobody

---

66   Julian of Norwich, 'Chapter 32,' *Revelations of Divine Love.*

on Earth or in the whole of the cosmos more lovable and more important than you are.'

I knew immediately and instinctively that my friend was talking directly to the heart and mind of each and every individual in the whole wide world. He repeated the statement, and then he continued.

'Nobody can challenge this. I want to emphasise this: nobody on Earth can stand up and truly declare that he or she is more lovable and more important than you – or than anyone else for that matter. You are the most lovable and most special in all of creation. This is meant to be. This was planned for you. The greatest among us is the least. The least among us is the greatest. These words have meaning. These words always had meaning. Only the superlative best is being expressed in you and for you at this very moment. These arguments have great implications. These arguments come with wonderful philosophical imperatives. Our real world is the world of the superlative best. When all is superlative, then all is the same. All is gloriously the same. All is peacefully the same. True peace envelops and radiates from this world of sameness. There is no hierarchy. All is quiet, true and silent. It is so understandable that divine intelligence is serenely silent and kind, supremely uncritical and loving. Our real home is here. We belong to the serene, silent, supreme aloneness of divine kindness. We have to see ourselves in the light of this truth. There is no other way. Only then can we treat ourselves much more lovingly and tolerantly. What follows from this is also important. We must treat our neighbour lovingly and tolerantly, as well.'

I had grown to understand Gunna Dan more. I knew what he meant. He had realised for some time now that all of us, that is, all of humankind – all who ever were and have now passed on, all of us present on Earth today and all who ever will come – belong to the one family of divine goodness and divine love. This is the only family that is. And Gunna Dan was certain that divine goodness and divine life saturates us all with love, perfection, wisdom and kindness. He was certain that God's love for each individual person is total and unconditional. Gunna Dan often claimed to me that our lack of awareness of God's divine love was our greatest disability. This ignorance prevents us from being loving and caring people. It prevents us from going the extra mile. It stops us from being broad-minded and generous people. It certainly prevents us from being happy. Worse still, it prevents us from being able to be happy.

I had noticed for some time now that when Gunna Dan was talking to me about God and God's divine intelligence and divine love, he would start shuffling around a little until he became more settled, more anchored. Then he would get into a trance-like state. Even though he would be looking all around him, I felt that he was also looking way beyond this world and that in some way or other, he was seriously connecting with an esoteric life now unknown to me. I looked more closely at him. We were sitting at a table overlooking the river. Through the expansive windows, he was taking in the whole vista before him and admiring it. We could actually see treetops below us. Beyond them, the froth and the bubbles on the surface of the cascading waters were dancing, sometimes giddily upwards, and then again giddily downwards. We could not miss noticing the ruined church on the distant hill. We both commented on the modern parish church situated on the Lahinch Road. We could see a good stretch of the town itself, and further beyond, we could see the fields and more houses. I looked at Gunna Dan. He was very relaxed. He was content in himself. He was always happy to dwell in his inner world. And then a tinge of lonesomeness made its presence felt within me again. This surprised me because I was sitting there next to him. Oh! How I wished to be more connected to him! Then Gunna Dan began speaking to me. He reminded me of the earlier comments we had made, and he began to talk to me about our inability to be happy. He then turned to me and said that it is so important that we love our neighbour. Our neighbour, he strongly asserted, also enjoys the favour of God unconditionally.

We spent a long time that day in the hotel's Dylan Thomas bar. The area is large and spacious, and we sat in the far corner of the room looking out at the cascading river in the distance. We were oblivious to the noise and chatter. Children ran around happily, and you didn't have to be a rocket scientist to know that the swim they had in the leisure centre invigorated them greatly. Gunna Dan decided that he would forego his visit to the library and would return with me to Inagh instead. I always liked his company in the car while I was driving. Normally I like the light, casual and carefree talk we always have with each other in the car. Normally when driving, I would not engage in any deep discussion. However, on that occasion I confessed to Gunna Dan that my mind was in turmoil. The way I said it distressed the poor man. It came out a little wrong. Eventually I was able to get across to him that I was often thinking about all the wrongs going on in the world and that I would be cross about it in my mind. I confessed that I would be cross in my mind about loads of things, about things happening locally and nationally as much as globally. I complained to him in particular about the billions and billions of dollars and euros being spent on the armaments industry throughout the world and about the inability of human society to wake up and do anything about it. All this time, Gunna Dan listened to me very calmly. He consoled me greatly when he told me, as we were parting, that he wanted me to share all this negativity with him. He assured me that there was no hurry at all and that we would come to it in due course. He readily admitted to me that we all have a strong need to address the frustrations of our minds and spirits, and, in what I could only regard as a matter-of-fact attitude, he added that 'we are all the better for it when we do'.

Just before we bid adieu to each other, I told Gunna Dan that I was going up to spend some time in the village of Kilfenora the following day and that he was welcome to come with me. He jumped at the opportunity. It had been a long time since I had been there, and I was anxious to see again the ancient high crosses and the wonderful monastic site situated in the village. One other thing I wanted to do as well was to call into the Burren Centre and read and learn all about the Burren limestone landscape, a landscape of tremendous appeal to scientists and botanists; to archaeologists and historians; to geologists and folklorists; and indeed to everyone with a sense of imagination and wonder.

Chapter 15

Hallowed Grounds, Holy Places

We left early the following morning. We drove into Ennistymon and from there took the northwest route out of the town towards the village of Kilfenora. The journey was uneventful. We chatted amiably and casually and, as I often do, I kept chattering away about the things I was seeing and noticing. Gunna Dan would always comment on the countryside. The greenness of the vegetation was always a wonder to him. When we arrived in the village, we decided that we would first go into the Burren Centre. It was opened, and there weren't too many people about. When you go into the centre, you get an impressive introduction to the visual delights and ancient mysteries of this unique spot in Ireland. A twelve-minute video called *A Walk Through Time* took us back thousands of years. We were both astounded to learn that the dolmens and burial tombs are more ancient than the pyramids of Egypt and that bears and wolves shared the then totally different landscape with our ancestors.

The presentation describing the Burren landscape was breathtaking. The geological panorama that we looked at was austere, and yet, hiding in this limestone wonderland were astonishing habitats for distinct species of flora, and to a lesser extent, fauna. We could not be but wide-eyed at the great variety of species of plants and rare flowers thriving therein, many of them more suited to mountainsides, others more at home at the seaside and still others belonging to the lowlands. It was astounding for us to learn that alpine, Mediterranean, Arctic and native plants grow side by side. To say that Gunna Dan and I were astounded is a great understatement. Gunna

Dan was unrestrained as he raved gleefully about what he witnessed and saw on the video. Despite the starkness of the karst landscape, despite the silvery greyness of the limestone scenery, he saw a magical place that was full of light and colour and energy. 'The light is enlightening,' he told me earnestly and with great emphasis. He was even dancing as he said it. 'The colours are tremendously vibrant, and the energies exuding from the place are powerful and uplifting.' As I listened to him I saw that he was a man inspired. More than that, he was tremendously vibrant and energised. Suffice it to say that as we walked away from the centre, and on Gunna Dan's insistence, we promised ourselves that in the very near future we would spend a day exploring the area around the hill of Mullaghmore.

We strolled out into the spacious square of Kilfenora village. The broad expanse was empty except for a few parked cars and one bus. I always like to visit the monastic sites around Ireland. All of them were at one time great centres of study, learning and piety. I never doubted but that the monks and the scholars of those times sanctified the countryside and that anyone visiting these sacred places could not but be blessed and comforted. We decided to walk towards the cathedral, a small building that was built on the site of a monastery founded by Saint Fachtna in the sixth century. The cathedral dates to the very early 1200s, but not surprisingly, it has undergone many changes, changes that can be dated century by century up to modern times.

Gunna Dan was bowled over when I told him that the people living in Ireland in the olden times, at the beginning of the Christian era, about fifteen hundred years ago, made three significant contributions to the history of the creative arts in Europe: namely, the sculptures of Celtic high crosses, which we were now about to admire; the production of illuminated books and manuscripts, including the Book of Kells; and the creation of delicate ornamental works of gold, silver and copper filigree used in the production of chalices and patens for church services. I couldn't but help tell Gunna Dan that one of the finest examples of metalwork from about twelve hundred years ago is the Ardagh Chalice, a chalice that was found almost intact in a field near the village in 1868. Then I further couldn't help but tell him that the village of Ardagh in County Limerick is only six miles from my home village of Shanagolden. And, I added that the Ardagh Chalice is now attractively featured as a centrepiece in the National Museum on Kildare Street in Dublin.

We walked around the place slowly, stopping every now and then, enabling us all the better to examine and reflect. From the outside, the cathedral building was drab, but no matter; I still admired the imposing east window with its three linear divisions, all symmetrically constructed to funnel and direct the early morning sunlight into the deepest interior. The distinctive attraction of Kilfenora and its real glory, however, is in the high crosses. The two of us loved the imposing reconstructed thirteen-foot high Doorty Cross, a cross that was re-assembled from scattered fragments and re-erected by the Board of Works in the 1950s. We could make out the figure at the top of the cross, which is supposed to be a bishop, perhaps Saint Peter. Underneath this figure are two smaller figures, one holding an Irish-type crosier and the other with a T-shaped crosier.[67]

I explained to Gunna Dan that the carvings on the crosses were important visual entities in times long ago when there were few paintings and fewer books. The people could then read the stories of the scriptures from the crosses. I told my friend that throughout the olden times, the favourite stories for depiction always included Adam and Eve in the Garden of Eden, the crucifixion and the resurrection. For quite some time, we slowly and easily ambled about the place. We conversed when it suited and remained silent when it pleased. Then my friend called me. Surprisingly, he invited me to sit down on a wall that was near us and not far from the roofless chancel. We were only sitting down a short while when he told me that there was one story in particular from the scriptures on his mind, that it had been on his mind for some time, and that he would like to talk to me about it.

Without ado, he began talking about the parable of the good Samaritan.[68] When he did, I must say that I was not in the least bit surprised. I readily recalled to mind that day in Lahinch when he helped the poor man who fell on his way to the washrooms. At that time, I had acknowledged to myself that he was, in a very special way, a Good Samaritan to the poor chap. Furthermore, I knew that he enjoyed reading and discussing the contents of the New Testament with me. I was well aware from our conversations that Gunna Dan revered and admired Jesus greatly. He particularly appreciated the strength, poise and grace of our Saviour. He found Jesus' strength of authority and his decisiveness,

---

67   Anne Korff and Jeff O'Connell, *The Burren, Kilfenora The City of the Crosses, A Rambler's Map & Guide* (Dooris, Ireland: Tir Eolas, 1988).

68   Luke 10:29–37, JB

particularly his decisiveness of will,[69] astounding. He noted with great regard that Jesus never went out to argue, threaten, harangue or admonish. He loved the way that Jesus would empower, allowing truth and grace to well up within the minds and spirits of his listeners so that they could have their own personal responses to his teachings. What Gunna Dan found particularly admirable was that Jesus' life on Earth was one long, uninterrupted series of acts of love for his fellow man culminating in the ultimate sacrifice, the laying down of his life for the redemption and salvation of everyone who comes onto Earth. Everything about Jesus was a beautiful wonder for Gunna Dan.[70]

Gunna Dan loved the parables in particular. He found them treasure troves full of wisdom and love. In them he found that the unimportant, neglected and downtrodden were exalted. None more so than the unnamed man who went on a hazardous fifteen-and-a-half-mile journey from Jerusalem to Jericho. We discussed how this man fell among robbers who stripped him, beat him up and left him for dead. He then had no identity whatsoever, since two cultural identifiers were taken away from him; namely, the type of clothes he wore and, because of his unconscious state, the manner of his speech and accent. Jesus presented this victimised man to his listeners. They presumed that the victim was, like themselves, Jewish. They were horrified that one of their own would be so severely assaulted as to be left with no status and no dignity whatsoever.

Gunna Dan then explained that one of the reasons why he had a tremendous regard for Jesus was because he always spoke with great authority and assurance, an authority and an assurance that was not of this world, an authority and assurance that came directly from God the Father. And yet too, Gunna Dan appreciated the fact that Jesus always wants to be supportive of the outcast and and the downtrodden. In a short time to come, Jesus would become an outcast himself.

With the acquiescence of Gunna Dan, I began talking about the parable. As the people listened to Jesus tell the story, they heard Jesus say that a priest who passed by the man had walked on the other side of the road. They knew immediately that the priest was only concerned about

---

69 For example, Matthew 5:48, JB, when Jesus says, 'You must therefore be perfect just as your heavenly Father is perfect.'

70 Anthony Maas, "The Character of Jesus Christ," *The Catholic Encyclopedia*, 2d ed., vol. 8 (New York: Robert Appleton Company, 1910) at *New Advent: www.newadvent.org/cathen/08382a.htm.*

himself. He did not want to be defiled by going near a dead body. The legal implications would be severe on his house and his family. The priest would risk becoming unclean, and the process of becoming clean again was costly and time-consuming. Then a Levite also passed on the other side. The Levite would have been an assistant to a priest at the temple and would have similar reasons for avoiding the stricken man. But when the Samaritan[71] arrived on the scene, he felt compassion for the victim. He bandaged the man's wounds, put him on his donkey, brought him to an inn and took care of him.

The details in Jesus' story were not lost on Gunna Dan. He explained to me that the pouring of the oil and wine (which the Good Samaritan did when bandaging the man's wounds) was indicative of God's anointing of the downtrodden. This is the clear teaching that everyone enjoys God's unconditional kindness and love. It is the clear teaching that the downtrodden and, in particular the so-called failures in life will always enjoy the uncritical helpfulness of divine goodness. The Samaritan's payment of the two denarii to the innkeeper and his commitment to pay more on his return symbolised the necessary purchase of freedom. The Jewish listeners would have known that the wounded man would have been arrested and put into jail if he could not pay the debt of his stay at the innkeeper's.

Gunna Dan was inspired during the telling of the story, and what pleased him greatly was that at no time does Jesus directly answer the question, 'Who is your neighbour?' What he does instead is to ask the question, 'Which of these three, do you think, proved himself a neighbour to the man who fell into the brigands' hands?'[72] Gunna Dan was quite forthright as he continued.

'There is a reason why this question was asked. It is because the Son of God, Jesus, wants each of us to think for ourselves, but it is more than just that. He is telling us that we need to think about issues. He is telling us that we have a personal responsibility to seek enlightenment and truth. In other words, our duty in life, if any, is to think. He is telling us that truth is there to be discovered and found. He is telling us that personal participation in the process of thinking is required. The type of thinking that is required is that type of personal and purposeful thinking that leads to decisive choices

71 For historical reasons, Jews and Samaritans did not get on with each other. See John 4:9, JB, and 2 Kings 17:24, JB, et seq.
72 Luke 10:36, JB

and self-confident responses. It is often assumed that there are people out there who know all the answers and who have the authority to tell us what to think. This is not so. The experts themselves – if they claim that status – must accept their own personal responsibility towards life and think things out for themselves genuinely and truthfully.'

Gunna Dan paused, but soon he began explaining to me that what he found remarkable in particular about the Gospels is that on many occasions, someone in the stories is posed with questions and then asked to think for himself or herself. In the example of the parable of the good Samaritan, we have a question of the highest degree, a question that is evocative and effective. It appeals to our senses, our feelings, our decency, our minds and our spirits. The question evokes and provokes personal cognitive responses. The beauty of such potent questioning is that it induces the very enlightenment we seek. It induces truthful and knowledgeable responses within us, but it does even more than that. It expands our minds to such an extent that we can glimpse the divine mind at work. Here we are asked by a wonderful educator to think deeply and feel strongly about everybody, particularly the outcast and the downtrodden. We are challenged to come to a true understanding of what unconditional kindness means and what uncritical helpfulness means. We are challenged to be decisive in our thinking and in our responses. There are no two ways about it. Thinking is a serious fundamental duty for all peoples and individuals everywhere. The duty to think cannot be underestimated. This explains why the unidentified author of the devotional classic, *The Cloud of Unknowing*, written almost seven hundred years ago, claims that those who wish to contemplate God, whether beginners or experienced, 'cannot pray unless they think first'.[73]

I had grown to notice that Gunna Dan was now more assertive in his views. Here in Kilfenora, in view of the high crosses and ancient ecclesiastical buildings, he spoke solemnly, and I got the clear impression that he was speaking with greater certainty about the next life. It was as if he knew, as if he enjoyed intimate insights into the divine plan and wanted to tell all of us loudly that we were the beneficiaries of total unconditional kindness and love. We got up and decided to walk further downwards towards the more distant high cross, the West Cross.

73 Anonymous, 'Chapter 35,' *The Cloud of Unknowing*, ed. Clifton Wolters (Middlesex,England: Penguin, 1976).

As we strolled through the field, Gunna Dan began to emphasise to me that our respect and our regard for our fellow men and women on Earth must be wholesome and unconditional. It is an imperative that they be wholesome and unconditional. And it is an imperative that we must adopt the Golden Rule as our main principle for living with each other. He emphasised that this rule must not be seen as a consequential one or be looked upon as a duty. He emphasised to me that the Golden Rule simply means that in our actions and in our thoughts we must love our neighbour and the stranger; that in our minds we always wish both well and will never do anything that would hurt and pain them.

He stopped walking and, in what was now a habit of his, looked directly at me and said, 'The adoption of the Golden Rule in our lives promotes true God-like kindness. It brings God-like kindness into our lives. It brings us all closer to the power of divine wisdom.' He turned to renew the journey through the field, and I turned with him and walked with him. And, as if in an afterthought, he added, 'The practise of the Golden Rule dilutes and dissolves the frustrations of this life.'

I had to admit that the Golden Rule did not feature that much in my personal education in the national or secondary schools. It definitely did not at either university I attended. Yet, I fully agreed with Gunna Dan that this crystal clear and powerful teaching is a fundamental moral ethic. It is a succinct and wonderful guiding tenet that inspires right action and best behaviour in the relationships between fellow human beings. Both of us, as we continued talking, recognised that over twenty-five hundred years ago, this very tenet was promulgated in a way pertinent to our lives and times here in Ireland. The phrase 'You must love your neighbour as yourself'[74] appears in the book of Leviticus as the words of God spoken directly to Moses. And again later on we get, 'If a stranger lives with you in your land, do not molest him. You must count him as one of your own countrymen and love him as yourself.'[75] Gunna Dan went on to tell me that there are many expressions of this same Golden Rule throughout the New Testament. As I listened to him, I realised more clearly that Gunna Dan was increasingly absorbing the implications of the Scriptures. He then told me that the dialogue between Jesus and the lawyer in the book of Luke was powerfully instructive. To inherit eternal life, the lawyer quoted from the Law, 'You must love the Lord your God with all your heart, with

74   Leviticus 19:18, JB
75   Leviticus 19:33–34, JB

all your soul, with all your strength and with all your mind, and your neighbour as yourself.' And Jesus told him that he had answered right: 'Do this and life is yours.'[76]

It was then late afternoon. We returned to the village and, with a sense of thoughtful expectancy, went into Linane's pub. We sat down at a table in the inner room, ordered, and soon were served a fine plateful of toasted sandwiches and a big pot of tea. The place was surprisingly busy. A man and a woman, presumably parents, were occupied in the task of writing copious quantities of postcards. They kept checking the names and addresses of people, presumably the recipients, with each other. Three children, in all likelihood, theirs, were playing, happily running about the place. When one of them jumped over my outstretched legs, they all did. They enjoyed my bemused look greatly. Both Gunna Dan and I relaxed in their company.

When we left the pub, we checked that we had sufficient supplies of water with us in the car. We had got into the habit of bringing plastic bottles of water with us everywhere. We set off on the Corrofin Road, a road that would take us onwards towards Leamaneh Castle and Killnaboy. We had no sooner started than Gunna Dan began to swig from his bottle of water. After his first gulp, he began praising the country of Ireland and how it was blessed and endowed with the splendid gifts of nature. And then he started itemising these blessings: sunshine and rain; clear, clean water; abundant and verdant growth; the temperateness of the climate; the variety of the weather; the wonderful ever-changing vistas of the sky, and so on. Then he took another swig of water from the bottle and gasped as he finished, 'Where would we be without it?'

I couldn't but start enthusing about the properties of water. I told my friend that I was totally staggered when I had learnt in my student days at university that the compound water is, of all compounds in the universe, truly unique and special. It is totally different from all the related hydride compounds, which are all gases at room temperature. Water is uniquely liquid. The unusual liquidity of water is in itself uniquely secured in that water resists freezing and vaporisation. And yet more uniquely again, when water freezes, its solid state, namely ice, floats on its liquid form. This bizarre conduct ensures that various plants and animals can survive

---

76 Luke 10:25–28, JB

extremely well in lakes, rivers and streams when these waterways are frozen over.

Gunna Dan was mesmerised by my discourse. He was also amazed at the way I was enthusing about it all. But I kept going. And, in a manner that he loved, I dogmatically stated that no life could ever evolve, let alone survive, if the reverse occurred – which normally happens for other hydride substances. If the solid ice were to sink to the bottom of seas, lakes and rivers, plants and animals could never survive, and worse still, the ice would never melt because heat rises upwards and could not travel downwards to melt it.

Gunna Dan dearly loved all of this. But, I had a serious intent. I wanted to tell him that the appreciation I've always had for the wonder of water has always brought me into the world of the mystical and the spiritual. One thing is certain, I told him: water has been created to be different and special. The uniqueness of water has enabled life to evolve and develop. And just as seriously and without any apology I declared that in my view all scientists agree that the existence of liquid water at standard conditions of temperature and pressure is quite unusual. It is different, exceptional.

Not long afterwards, Leamaneh Castle emerged into view, which changed our agenda and diverted our attention. Turlough Donn O'Brien, one of the last kings of the ancient kingdom of Thomond, built this castle in 1480. Eighty-five years later, in 1565, during the Elizabethan conquest, the whole area was delimited and fixed into a county by Sir Henry Sidney (1529–1586), who was twice Lord Deputy of Ireland, from 1565 to 1571 and from 1575 to 1578. It was he who gave the name Clare to the new county. Some sources state that the name comes from the Norman de Clare family who had earlier been given the region in 1275, following the Norman Conquest. However, there was also a local place name, *An Clár*, meaning a board or table, at the site of an important crossing over the River Fergus outside the town of Ennis. The site is now known as the village of Clarecastle. *An Clár* seems a likelier origin for the modern name of the county.[77]

I was able to park at a safe spot not far from the crossroads. We got out, which enabled us to better see Leamaneh Castle, an imposing five-

---

77 'County Clare (*An Clár*)', *Irish Ancestors*. Last updated 2010. *Irish Times: www. irishtimes.com/ancestor/browse/counties/munster/index_cl.htm.*

storey ruined building with its many transom and mullioned windows. Gunna Dan was saddened when I told him that the whole country had a huge number of ruins and that from these ruins could be read the history of cruel times and cruel events. Not soon afterwards, Gunna Dan began giving attention to the bilingual signposts at the crossroads. We spent time reading, translating and interpreting them. All in all, this was a very absorbing activity as much for Gunna Dan as it was for me.

The rest of the journey home was uneventful. After passing through Corrofin, we took the road towards Mauricesmills. We kept chatting away and did not notice the time passing until we were back in Inagh. Just before Gunna Dan got out of the car to leave, I told him that I was going into Ennis the following Saturday to do some shopping. I was as pleased as could be when he said he would come with me.

Chapter 16

Towards a Global Ethic

G unna Dan called to the house on that Saturday morning at ten
o'clock, as we had arranged. He had a few shopping bags with
him and a folder, as if he were going to meet someone important.
We set off without delay, and once we were settled into the journey,
Gunna Dan remarked that nowadays there is no difference between one
day of the week and another. People seem to work all seven days of the
week, he contended. He probably made this remark because several large
trucks laden with sand, gravel and concrete blocks had passed us by on
the road.

Before I knew it, I was telling my friend about the Saturdays of my
childhood in Shanagolden. They were a tyranny. Immediately upon getting
up and coming down the stairs, and long before we had breakfast, we,
the children of the family, were obliged to gulp down a mug of a black,
dank bog-water-like concoction made from the infusion of senna leaves,
an infusion that was left to brew overnight. Gulping was the only tactic
available to us in the face of this compulsion from our parents. The stuff
was vile, obnoxious, repulsive and nasty. But worse, it inflicted a terrible
purgative onslaught on our poor little insides, and for the rest of the day,
we were at the mercy of our overactive and painful bowels.

Then, after the breakfast during winter and summer, we had to bring
the wooden table and all the timber chairs out to the backyard. Either my
brother John or I had to get buckets of water, and with a scrubbing brush
and a box of bleaching powder, we had to scrub everything everywhere.

We had to work hard and thoroughly, because at inspection time, woe betide us if any one area of a chair or the table were not covered in sudsy lather. After this initial inspection, the great rinsing started, and again woe betide us if on the second inspection a speck of sudsy lather was noticed anywhere. If my brother John was scrubbing outside, then I was scrubbing inside on the then bare kitchen floor. I had to go down on my knees, and using another scrubbing brush and another box of bleaching powder, I had to wash the concrete floor section by section according to the precise, slavish ritual of 'wet, powder and scrub' followed by two rinses and two wipes. The inspection process inside the house was a constant and integral part of the practice.

Gunna Dan would keep looking at me with sideway glances as if I were not for real, but he did not doubt me. He was silent when I told him that in the winters we suffered terribly, not surprisingly, from chilblains. Chilblains were purplish red swellings along our fingers, and in my case, as I remember only too well, also along the outer edge of the earlobes. They were constantly itchy and painful. I couldn't help but scratch them until they tingled, and the augmenting tingling spurred me on to scratch them all the more.

As if in reflective mood, I continued telling my friend that life at that time was harsh for everybody. People in general were harsh on themselves and on each other. He was astonished when I told him that phrases like 'child-friendly' and 'child-centred' did not even exist. The concepts had not yet emerged into the consciousness of most men or women.

Sitting alongside me in the car, Gunna Dan took all of this in. He became equally if not more reflective. When he began talking to me, I knew he was talking seriously. His tone and affect reminded me of the walk we had taken in the field in Kilfenora when we both readily acknowledged the importance of the Golden Rule for every man, woman and child in the world. And immediately I was able to recall his words to me at the time: the Golden Rule, he'd said, 'brings God-like kindness into our lives'. There in the car and with folded arms, he began to explain to me that down through the ages, mutual respect for one's fellow men and women was held as a fundamental basis for right living.

'Many of the ancient Greek philosophers spoke about it and taught it,' he explained. 'Thales of Miletus, a pre-Socratic philosopher and one of the seven sages of Greece, is quoted as saying, "Avoid doing what you would blame others for doing." From the sayings of Sextus the Pythagorean we get, "What you do not want to happen to you, do not do it yourself either."[78] I would venture to say that most people do not realise that many of the great religions of the world besides Christianity – Judaism, Islam, Hinduism and Buddhism, to name but a few – proclaim the same teaching.'

Then he concluded in what I guessed was a sad tone, 'This all embracing teaching is universally taught in some way or other throughout the whole world and has been for millennia. But somehow or other, something is missing, something is greatly missing.'

However, for some reason both of us became sombre as we spoke about the current state of world affairs. I have always felt as I told my friend alongside me, that we have ignored, if not lost the wisdom of the past. We have lost the benefits of the great minds of those who went before us. Worse, I have felt that we, as individuals, societies and nations, have purposefully disregarded that which was historically found to be good and noble and true. There are too many victims on Earth today. It is one thing to be a victim of a natural disaster. The peoples of the world can and do respond readily and helpfully to these. Another thing altogether is to be a victim of your fellow man's inhumanity. Whole communities throughout the world are starving because starvation is imposed on them. There are too many societies in the world whose peoples are being killed, maimed or tortured. So-called civilised countries see nothing wrong with the development of sophisticated killing machinery. Worse still, the leaders of our so-called modern society purvey these abominable goods to the places of conflict, furthering the awfulness of man's inhumanity to man. And the peoples of the world can do nothing about this. As individuals, we are totally inept and unable. Yet, as individuals, we have the right – should have the right – to live in a much better global organisation. But, as it is, we live in a macabre, dreadful world. What chance then can individuals have of developing their potential, of knowing and realising their divine origins and divine destinies? What chance is there for the global establishment of the ancient universal precept 'Love thy neighbour as thyself'?[79]

Gunna Dan was very patient with me as I expressed my views. He understood me more than I realised. The positive man he was, he argued

---

78 'The Golden Rule.' Last updated 6 June 2010. *Wikipedia: http://en.wikipedia.org/wiki/ The_Golden_Rule*
79 Leviticus 19:18, JB

that the very presence of so many ills in the world emphasised the need for the global acceptance of the ethic of the Golden Rule. I seriously agreed with him and, in fact, I was very thankful to him for this more positive perspective.

We stopped our talking as we approached the outskirts of Ennis and began making plans. I drove to the far side of town and parked the car in the car park of the Temple Gate Hotel, not far from the St. Francis Credit Union building. I told Gunna Dan that I first wanted to go to a clothes shop and then to an electrical retail store. If I had plenty of time afterwards, I would also call into one of the many attractive bookstores in the town. Then I added that what I would love most of all would be to meet him for lunch at the hotel at around half past two. This pleased him greatly, and we set about to part – but before we did so, he patted his folder with the knuckles of his hand and asked, 'Is it okay if I leave this here until we come back?'

It was actually close to three o'clock when I arrived back at the car park. Gunna Dan was there before me, and he was not at all bothered by my delay. We put all the bags, bits and pieces into the boot at the back of the car. Gunna Dan collected his folder, and we made our way into the hotel's bar, the Preacher's Pub. We saw a vacant table in an elevated corner, and we made straight for it. We were in an area that was opposite to where we first met on that eventful day at the start of June, but other than an 'over there, wasn't it?' from my smiling friend, the event was ignored. We examined the menu and marvelled at the extent and the variety on offer. Eventually I ordered a New Yorker steak burger, and he, a chicken snitzchel. It was the garlic and parsley butter that appealed to him. What also appealed to us was that the meal would be served with French fries and crispy, fresh salad. We had been out all day and were both much hungrier than we would care to admit. We confined our drinks to bottled still water, and once the orders were taken, we settled in for a pleasant respite from the shopping and walking.

We sat in silence at first, but soon Gunna Dan asked me if I knew anything about the 'Declaration Toward a Global Ethic' that was presented at the 1993 Parliament of the World's Religions. When I replied that I was completely unaware of it, he began telling me all about it. The date was 4 September 1993, and the place was Chicago, Illinois, in the United States of America. The 'Declaration Toward a Global Ethic' was signed by 143 leaders of all the major religions of the world.[80] Gunna Dan went on to explain to me that at this parliament, the religious leaders acknowledged the wrongs of this world. All the signatories declared respect for the community of living beings, people, animals and plants, and for the preservation of Earth, including its air, water and soil. They recognised that humankind is one family and stated that we must not live for ourselves alone but should also serve others, never forgetting the children, the aged, the poor, the suffering, the disabled, the refugees and the lonely.

We concentrated on the food when it arrived at the table, and both of us relished what we received. As we munched away, Gunna Dan was confident about the progress that can be made and that actually is made in human affairs. However, as time passed, I became gloomier and admitted as much to my friend. He remembered that he had promised to share the gloominess with me and supported me as I complained about the state of world affairs. Since 1993, I explained, little or no progress has been made. Indeed, it would not be difficult to argue that the global situation has become much worse since then. I argued that every one of us must give importance to the external world we live in, but this is the very world wherein a huge amount of money is constantly being spent equipping numerous armies all over the world. This is a terrible indication that human beings on Earth are living in darkness. A great number of people in many countries are conscripted into armies that are engaged solely in horribly destructive campaigns. Many of these campaigns engage in the slaughter of our fellow men, women and children, and cause starvation and famine for those who survive.

For a little while, we sat in silence that was only interrupted when the waitress asked us if everything was all right. Gunna Dan couldn't help but notice that many of the waitresses working in the pub seemed to come from distant countries. He commented that it was obvious that in this instance all of them were working diligently and in good cooperation with each other. 'We are all the same, with the same needs and with the same hopes,' he said, as if to emphasise his argument that great progress is being made all the time. But, alas, I wasn't very enthusiastic about his comments. Instead I brusquely reverted to the theme on armies and their preponderance throughout the globe. I couldn't help myself as I unburdened my views.

---

80 *Global Ethic Foundation: http://www.weltethos.org/dat-english/03-declaration.htm*

'No woman should ever be in any army at any level anywhere,' I started. 'Armies deal in death. This is against every essence of womanhood. Every molecule in a woman's body is a life-producing molecule. So, too, are all her chemicals, systems, organs, tissues and blood. And this is only at the level of the external material world. She is explicitly fashioned as part of the divine, celestial and cosmic scheme of things to give, enhance and support life. Her whole being, mind, body and spirit are complementary and augmenting. No man knows this. He rarely knows any of the stages in the biological cycles and rhythms of woman. He is not meant to know. And he only knows if a woman tells him, and then superficially, only at a shallow mental level. This terrible ignorance of the feminine – which exists simultaneously at the personal, societal and cosmic levels – is an essential reason why the world's consciousness about womanhood needs to develop more strongly, purposefully and effectively. The world needs this development now more than ever before. The world needs a more expressive womanhood that will influence and guide all human activity. The world needs more like-mindedness in this, as is the case in many other issues. From the perspective of the divine, there is no hierarchy between men and women. "God created man in the image of himself, in the image of God he created him, male and female he created them. God blessed them, saying to them 'be fruitful, multiply, fill the earth and conquer it. Be masters of the fish of the sea, the birds of heaven and all living animals on the earth."[81] The God-given responsibility of men and women together, being masters on Earth, needs to be more fully accepted and more fully addressed. If a hierarchical system prevails in human life and living, then some kind of advanced dual non-hierarchical partnership system should go along with it. Men need this much more than they realise.'

Just then, two priests came in. They went over to the blackboard and examined it. Eventually they got the attention of a passing waitress and ordered soup and sandwiches. They went over to the far corner of the room, sat at a vacant table and engaged in quiet conversation. Gunna Dan remarked on the seriousness of their countenances and wondered why this should be so. I remarked, however, that there was another serious issue on my mind, namely the assigning of clerics to positions of rank in the army. I couldn't help but make the comment, and I continued.

'No priest or cleric should ever be a member of the armed forces or travel with them on the road to conflict,' I said. 'Each cleric must be able

81 Genesis 1:27–28, JB

to answer the question 'where do I belong?' and then confront his or her answer. A definite relationship has to exist between the professed religious person and God, as he or she perceives God to be. The professed religious people in our world have to be with God always. With God they share in a great communion of saints and angels along with all of peoples of this earth. No priest can start offering the sacrifice of the Eucharist without realising that he is in august company. Just read or say the Confiteor. In this confessional prayer, the priest calls on all of his brothers and sisters who are alive with him in this life, all of them without exception. He calls on the Blessed Virgin Mary, all the angels and all the saints who are in heaven. Later, everybody who ever lived on Earth is remembered and prayed for.'

Gunna Dan interrupted me to tell me that it is this universality that gladdens him every time he visits church for the celebration of the Eucharist at Mass. I was more than pleased with this interruption because it encouraged me to continue, and continue I did.

'A professed religious person does not belong to the fleeting external world of earthly life. He is more removed, indeed far removed from it than most others. Worldly issues such as owning property, wealth accumulation, the pursuit of a career and, especially, the taking on of possessive and selfish relationships are not on his agenda. They cannot be. He is, at all times, at the centre of a spiritual cosmic world. He assuredly must be far removed from the pleasures and baseness of this world. And, he certainly does not belong to any military army.'

I paused, but only for a short spell. I wanted Gunna Dan to share my gloominess of mind. I knew he was more receptive to me at this time, and because of this, I again felt encouraged to continue.

'Armies achieve nothing. The management of an army system has to concentrate all its abilities, skills and intelligence on improving its killing power, advancing its torture and punishment techniques and inflicting damage and destruction. Military units all over the world train in peacetime as if they were at war. It is the serious duty of the leadership within armies to provide battlefield conditions during peacetime for this training. The whole point of military exercises is to produce soldiers who are proficient in the skills required for the battlefield (whatever these may be) and to produce soldiers who are aggressive and fit for fighting. This is what peacetime means in those countries where the military presence is strong. The concept of peace means nothing other than that there is no war. The implication in this suggestion is severe. Everybody in the army must always prepare for war. And what can a cleric or priest do when he or she is in the army? Kneel down with his fellow killing comrades and pray for the souls of those about to be killed? In this world of ours, as it is today, all is in darkness. In this world it is now impossible for the leaders of society, of nations and races to see what is right from what is wrong. And in the dark, it is the lunatics who are in charge of the asylum.'

Gunna Dan cringed. Yet his response was quite firm and sure. He even supported my saying of what I said. He agreed that the horrors of this world need to be recognised. He repeated his earlier argument that what I was saying emphasised the necessity for the 'Declaration Toward a Global Ethic' and for its renewed adoption throughout the world. He stressed that the declaration includes a commitment to a culture of non-violence, respect, justice and peace. Further, it declares that human beings shall not oppress, injure, torture or kill other human beings, forsaking violence as a means of settling differences. Then Gunna Dan reached out for the folder that he brought in with him and took out of it a fifteen-page document that he told me he downloaded from the Internet. He began reading out a section from it:

'There is a principle which is found and has persisted in many religious and ethical traditions of humankind for thousands of years: What you do not wish done to yourself, do not do to others. Or in positive terms: What you wish done to yourself, do to others! This should be the irrevocable, unconditional norm for all areas of life, for families and communities, for races, nations, and religions.'[82]

Gunna Dan was earnest as he spoke, and he was at pains explaining to me that he wished that the consciousness of individuals, societies and nations would be greatly raised. He so wanted the leaders of the world to accept and support the Global Ethic, an ethic inherently acceptable and badly needed. He especially wanted that as many individuals as possible would sanctify their lives by purposefully incorporating the principles of the Global Ethic into their minds.

I must admit that Gunna Dan was much more optimistic about this raising of consciousness than I was. He then went on to tell me about

---

82 'Text of the Declaration,' *Declaration Toward a Global Ethic, Global Ethic Foundation:* *www.weltethos.org/dat-english/03-declaration.htm.*

the letter His Holiness, the late Pope John Paul II sent to all the heads of state and government of the world, dated 24 February 2002. The Pope's letter referred to the 'Decalogue of Assisi for Peace'.[83] The Decalogue was proclaimed a month previously (24 January 2002) by more than two hundred leaders of the world's major religions, including the Pope himself, when they met in the town of Assisi in Italy. His Holiness was convinced that the ten propositions in the Decalogue would inspire political and social action from within all the governments. Gunna Dan then reached back again to get his folder, and from it he withdrew a copy of the letter of His Holiness and a copy of the Decalogue. Over a cup of coffee, he and I noted the contents of each proposition. Indeed, we discussed them and at times argued over them. Gunna Dan was brilliant in his explanations, and for a moment I even crazily thought that he could have been involved in drawing them up. What pleased the two of us no end was the undertaking made in the second item, which reads, 'We commit ourselves to educating people to mutual respect and esteem, in order to help bring about a peaceful and fraternal coexistence between people of different ethnic groups, cultures and religions.'

I was pleased because this item addresses the wider dimension of what education is all about. Gunna Dan was actually more deeply pleased because he felt that in the hearts and minds of individuals everywhere, there is a great hunger for the nourishment of the spirit. And very deliberately, he argued that this hunger of the spirit needs to be addressed. He reminded me that all frustration arises from within us simply because, despite our desire for fulfilment and wholesomeness, an emptiness prevails in our lives. He explained to me that the lack of completeness and wholesomeness is a feature of any and every imperfection. And then forcefully he concluded, 'Humankind needs to understand that here and now, in this very present moment, our deliverance and emancipation lie in aspiration and transcendence.'

Our return journey home to Inagh was a pleasant, optimistic one. For one thing, my friend lifted my spirits. He was much more positive than I was. He even said to me very seriously that everybody in life is on an onward march to glory despite all the diversions on the way. But he also spoke to me of his own wants and needs, and of his hunger for what is

---

83 'Letter of John Paul II to All the Heads of State and Government of the World and Decalogue of Assisi for Peace.' 24 February 2002. *The Vatican: www.vatican.va/holy_father/john_paul_ii/letters/2002/documents/hf_jp-ii_let_20020304_capi-stato_en.html.*

really true. He emphasised to me how he considered himself so fortunate to have anchored himself in Ireland and particularly in County Clare. However, while he was speaking, I was admitting to myself that it is I who is the fortunate one. I knew this very clearly. I realised for some time that I was in the company of a special visitor in my life. He amazed me by how he was so knowledgeable of world efforts to promote the rights of every person in the world. He was strong. He was consistent. He was sure. He uplifted me.

I do not like admitting this, but when he left me I again became very lonesome. This was a feeling that was growing and strengthening in me all the time, which saddened me greatly. Gunna Dan was becoming more ethereal. He was speaking more and more to me about the transcendent state. It seemed to me that he was becoming more anxious for it himself. It began to dawn on me that he was leaving me, and to be blunt about it, I did not want him to go. I wanted him to be near me all the time. I tried to rationalise as to why I was heaping all the ills and wrongs of the world onto the altar of his mind and spirit. I kept concluding that I was somehow unknowingly afraid. That what I was doing was nothing short of making a great, global scream. My whole inner being was crying out, 'Don't go! Stay with us and help us! Help us out of this mess!'

Chapter 17

Ascending the Heights

The following morning, I got up early. I had planned to take the lawn mower to Milltown-Malbay to get the engine serviced. The pull rope had frayed badly, and I was afraid it would break. I took the mower out to the front of the house and parked it behind the car. I covered the boot with plenty of newspapers, and as I was about to lift the mower, I saw Gunna Dan in the distance. I couldn't mistake him. He had this lovely striding gait; if you were to watch it long enough, you might think he was moving to some musical tune. He heard my story of the mower and, the good man that he was, he helped me lift it into the car and secure it.

He called to the house because he had left his sunglasses behind in the car. When he retrieved them from the glove compartment, I asked him to join me for breakfast. He was delighted to do so, and what pleased me no end was the fact that he was thrilled to see me. For my part, I was appreciative of the fact that every time he came into my company, he exuded contentment and gladness. He always honoured me. We went inside, and before long we were sitting down at the table enjoying tea, toast and marmalade. His demeanour was light-hearted, and I was, in fact, very happy that he had called to see me. Indeed, he was at pains to soothe me, as he showed by the way he started talking to me.

'I have great hopes for all individuals in the whole wide world,' he said, and as he was saying this, I began to realise that this was his way of dealing with all the negativity I offloaded onto him the previous day. I knew in hindsight that I had painted a very dark picture of the external reality in which we live. He was kind to me and agreed that it had needed to be said. It did not overwhelm him. He had a much wider perspective than I had, and he seemed to know more. He seemed too, to be able to give full attention to every detail we had discussed. I had noticed that he was at all times tolerant and easy within himself, calm and sure. As I listened to him I assumed with a certainty that surprised me that he had made a much more tangible connection with the spiritual and the divine than heretofore.

He then spoke to me with supportive assurance. 'You see, as we grow in the understanding of the real things of life, and as we absorb the truths that are presented to us and revealed to us, we also grow in confidence in ourselves and in our thinking. It is essential that we all engage in purposeful thinking because purposeful thinking enables us quickly and assuredly to make decisive positive choices. Our actions then are true and wholesome. We soon grow to have tremendous confidence in everything we do.'

Then he continued, this time a little more seriously. 'Self-confidence is essential. Most of us do not possess a strong sense of self-confidence. There is a reason for this. None of us can have genuine self-confidence unless we are confident in ourselves and with ourselves in the quietness of our inner aloneness. If you worry about what other people think of you, or about how you look, or whether you will be a success or a failure, then you block yourself from ever growing in confidence. Indeed, you are spending your time concerned about the baubles and trappings of the external world. It is when you are in your own inner aloneness that you can truly address the issue. And the very first way to go about it is to recognise your certainties. It is only in your inner aloneness that you can be comfortable with your own certainties. Certainty inspires confidence. I'll put it to you another way. You are a very strong, self-confident person when you can draw up a list of your positive certainties – the longer the list, the more confident and sure you are. It is important that you do not unthinkingly declare a certainty for yourself that is handed down to you or, worse still, imposed on you. Some of us find it easy to accept statements or issues presented by others as certain. But it is much more mature to come to your certainties as a result of thinking more and thinking better in order to know more and know better. All our philosophical imperatives help us. When we have considered and absorbed them, our certainties become a reflection of what we feel and think and know. We enjoy this mental and emotional state. It affects our whole being. We look smarter. We feel better. We smile more. We are much more sociable. And, we have this quiet, sure independence.'

I can tell you that I loved listening to him. I was delighted because he lifted my spirits greatly. As I sat there near him, I knew he was echoing an issue that was important to him; namely, that it is essential to love oneself. He was going further. I felt that he was also stating that it is important that each of us be brave and daring as we go about living out our lives.

Soon afterwards, however, he re-directed my thinking by asking me if we would travel up to Mullaghmore Mountain in the near future. He reminded me that he greatly enjoyed the visit we had to the Burren Centre in Kilfenora and since then, he had been expectantly waiting. There and then, we planned to go on the following Thursday. Gunna Dan got up to go after finishing his breakfast. He apologised for delaying me and wished me well in getting the mower fixed. But as he was leaving, he gleefully told me that he was looking forward to a terrific day out in the wonderful, wild and open expanse of the Burren.

We left early on that Thursday morning to go to Mullaghmore Mountain. We travelled via Mauricesmills, and from there we drove onto Corrofin village. I like travelling on this road because it is a scenic route. You are surrounded on all sides by the hills of Clare. Sometimes they are close together, but when they are farther apart, you can see broad expanses of grassy fields separated by irregular hedgerows. When the road is high on the landscape, you can see for miles all around you, and at every twist and turn, the valleys below you are ever-changing in shape and depth and texture. We crossed the bridge over the river Fergus and drove into Corrofin village. From there, we took the right turn for the Gort road, and soon we were out into the open countryside again. Gunna Dan remarked on the abundance of hazel trees, shrubs and bushes.

I then told him that in the beginning of October 1995, I went down from Dublin to Shanagolden to visit my parents for a weekend. But instead of taking my usual route back to Dublin, I decided that I would go back to Tarbert in County Kerry, take the ferry and cross over the River Shannon to Killimer in County Clare. I drove through the county in the direction of Gort, because from there I would quickly be able to get onto the Galway road to Dublin. Gunna Dan was bemused by all of this. I had to spend some time explaining to him that the Clare senior hurling team had just won the All-Ireland Hurling Senior Championship – their first in eighty-one years of trying – and that the remarkable achievement of the hurlers had electrified everybody in the county, if not the whole country. And I told my friend that I had a wonderful journey that day. The towns and villages were decorated with flags, streamers and bunting. People waved happily as I passed. After driving through Corrofin, I became reluctant to leave the county, so I decided to park by the roadside on the very road we were now travelling and to go for a walk. To my surprise, I found that the bushes were laden with hazelnuts, and before long, I had collected a bagful of them and brought them home to Dublin with me. I enjoyed eating some of the nuts. I couldn't help but tell Gunna Dan all about how the seeds are full of carbohydrates, proteins, fats and minerals, and how these foodstuffs are packed into the internal seed leaves called cotyledons. This fascinated him greatly. Because of this, I went on to explain that the seed is essentially a living womb carrying within it the plant of the future and the necessary nourishment and nutrients to sustain its present and, to some extent, future life.

I finished with a flourish by telling him how the seed leaves, the cotyledons, are the first entities to surface in the developing plant. They live their lives in splendid largesse, dispensing their nutrients to make the new roots, shoots, stems and true leaves of the emergent plant. Once they have given up their goodness, once they have fulfilled their function in life, they perish and die. The thriving sprouted plant then glories in its own new world.

On occasions like these, Gunna Dan would become very silent, and I must say I always loved those moments when I could almost see him reflecting and pondering. I would often wonder what he was thinking. I often wondered about the man and about his life, his experiences and understandings. But these moments could not last for long. Invariably, I would start off talking again. And so it was that I soon began telling him that this escapade in the Burren of County Clare reminded me of my childhood. I told him that back in the early to mid 1950s, my brother John, my sister Bernie, the neighbours' children and I, on an autumn afternoon, would take off trotting to Ballylin forest near Creeves Cross in Shanagolden to collect chestnuts and hazelnuts. Our joy was great when we would return home with pocketfuls of trophies gathered in the wood, and our joy was all the more complete when we would show them off to our classmates in school the next day.

My friend was quite curious as to what I did with the remaining hazelnuts I brought home with me to Dublin, and he was somewhat taken aback when I told him that later, during the month of November of that memorable year for County Clare hurling, I scattered them – there must have been thirty-five to forty of them – on a bare patch in my back garden and forgot all about them. To my great surprise, practically all the nuts germinated the following spring, the seed leaves emerging first. Some years later, I transplanted most of them into the grounds of Pearse College in Crumlin, Dublin. Back in 1985, I had established an arboretum in the college. At that time, I was very keen to promote the concept of the urban forest, and I wanted to do my little bit in expanding the green forested areas of Dublin. Over the years, we planted a significant range and variety of trees and shrubs on the college grounds, and to this very day, the 'All-Ireland winning Clare hurling hazel trees' are thriving therein.

Gunna Dan loved listening to all the reminiscences I brought up. And every time, he would ask questions of me and make comments. It was clear to me that he enjoyed all my stories and events, my descriptions and explanations. I even felt that he would love to have been with us in time to share in the adventures of our boyhood days and to be with us in our growth and development. As I drove along on that sunny day towards Mullaghmore, he was very happy. In fact, I had never seen him as happy before and, because of this, I was extremely content and greatly at ease. Soon we took a left turn and drove some way up a narrow road. When we saw a clearance on the widened part of the roadway, I pulled in and parked the car. We got out and climbed over a little dry stone wall and then found ourselves standing in the Burren. We said nothing at all, so concentrated were we on looking all around us. We could see craggy rocks and slabs and boulders of various sizes and shapes everywhere. Their surfaces could be lumpy and bumpy like a grotesque rash on the landscape's skin. The natural carbonic acid of the rainfall had gouged out holes of varying depths into the limestone. The vista before us was a weathered and shattered one, full of fissures, nooks and crevices. And as we continued looking, we were able to see a wonderful world of novel vegetation, plants small and big and flowers colourful and delicate. We began walking ever so slowly among them, every now and then stooping down to better see, scrutinise and admire.

I can tell you that there in the heart of the Burren, my senses flourished – sight and sound and smell and touch and taste. I listened and I heard.

And I heard a sweet silence pervading everything all around me. I became aware that my deeper senses were acknowledging the relics of times past, when megalithic herdsmen had roamed the landscape and lived out their lives in communion with the elemental forces. I could not but admire their craftsmanship and ingenuity as I gazed on stone tombs and cairns that were thousands of years old.

Gunna Dan was by then squatting between some limestone slabs and examining the vegetation thriving in the fissures and clefts. The little micro-gardens of unique plant species thrilled him. There, in the one spot before his very eyes, were a variety of plants, some of them characteristic of alpine areas, others of arctic climes and others again of temperate zones of the world.

A lot of the time, we did not talk at all. We didn't need to. In fact, at times we couldn't. We couldn't because we were intent on soaking in the magical sensation of the place and were so quietly carefree. I enjoyed a tremendous quietness of mind and spirit. The on-going internal chatter stopped. I moved easily and effortlessly from spot to spot. I even felt that I was gliding. Gunna Dan was very boyish in the way he moved and hopped. For a man of his age, he was very lively and whimsical. And he, too, was absorbed in his own thoughts – or perhaps, in his own silence.

I often ponder on the world of silence. I have had a love for the experience of it even in childhood. I would, as it were, run there ever so often to distance myself from the world of noise, hurt and abrasiveness. I always knew that this world was much more comforting and supportive. I always knew that the silent state is a friendly and warming place, way beyond the terrible clatter and clutter of life around us. In this silent state, there is no imperfection whatsoever. There couldn't be. From within this state, your spiritual being is directed and impelled towards the source of your very life, your true nature, your real identity. And your true happiness is found when you give in to this impulsion and let go.

I have always felt, and I have always admitted it to myself, that friendly people, kind people, indeed, holy people are enabled to be such because they live lives more often in their worlds of silence than in the outside world of noise. To me, Gunna Dan was one such person. I was able to look at him more closely here in the Burren and I must admit that I was so thankful that I had gotten to meet and know him.

We began moving forwards. We weren't actually climbing upwards. We were, more or less, sidling along sideways in an upward manner. We gave attention, interest and curiosity to every little thing that came our way. Then, after some length of time, we decided to rest on a sizeable clint near us. It was comfortable as slabs of limestone go, but it was especially convenient for viewing the features all around us. In front of us were numerous grassy patches, the vegetation was diverse, the flowers were abundant, the insects, particularly the bees, were humming and we were happy. We were easy. We admitted as such to each other. We looked all around us. By this time we were close to Mullaghmore Mountain. We noted how in some places the horizontal limestone layers of the mountain were stretched out somewhat. In other places the limestone appeared squeezed and squashed. It surely was a fabulous panoramic display. We spent time identifying key landmarks in the distance. We even vied with each other in the activity. We couldn't but admire the grandeur of the spaciousness all around us. And then we grew silent.

Suddenly, I saw it. I was taken completely by surprise. What appeared to be a giant bumblebee ran unsteadily across to a boulder not far in front of us. It stopped. Then, nervously and frenetically, it began eating something. Its long nose quivered constantly. Gunna Dan saw it, too, and whisperingly enquired as to what it was. It was a pygmy shrew, the smallest mammal in Ireland, with most individuals weighing in at about three and a half grams, less than half the weight of a fifty cent coin – or a euro coin or a two euro coin, for that matter. All these coins weigh the same at eight grams. Gunna Dan kept asking me questions. I kept whispering my replies. The pygmy shrew kept on quivering in its quest for food. Then it turned and came back towards us. It was oblivious to our presence. In our full view, it kept foraging. We were able to have a good long look at its head and snout and body and tail. I particularly admired the lovely chocolate-brown colour of the dense fur-like body hair.

Then Gunna Dan amazed me. He slid ever so quietly off the limestone slab. Silently and slowly, he stooped. And then he slipped his fingers underneath the grassy leaves and underneath the body of the pygmy shrew. Before I knew what was really happening, the little thing was snugly hunched in a little ball in the palm of his hand. Gunna Dan was radiant. The heat of his hand warmed the little fellow. The softness of his hand comforted it. The concentration of his mind stilled it.

Then I had a lovely realisation. All three of us – Gunna Dan, the pygmy shrew and I – were in some way now existing beautifully in a state of blessedness. The colours and the light all around me strengthened and intensified. Gunna Dan – in his golden linen suit and deep white shirt – was unbelievably lustrous. An aura radiated from him and enveloped him, the shrew and me. An emanation of deep purple and lilac hues quivered all around. My mind was stilled and my inner being was uplifted. The light and the silence saturated us. Bliss flourished, and I was very happy.

I do not know how long we remained suspended in wonder. All I know is that eventually Gunna Dan lowered his hand ever so slightly and the pygmy shrew skedaddled off into the taller grasses on our right. I whispered ever so gently to my beloved friend that it was great to be here with him, that it was a wonderful experience, about how it was my first time ever to see a pygmy shrew, about how I had read all about them, about how I had always marvelled at their size and weight, about how all the living processes of life functioned so effortlessly and perfectly in so small a body and with so little biomass, about how I was bowled over by the fact that the life of the little shrew is immeasurably greater than the shrew itself and about how happy I was to see one so close up. I kept babbling on about how perfect they were in their structures, functions and metabolisms. And then I began telling my dear friend how blessed I was to be with him and to know him. But when I looked at Gunna Dan, I realised that he didn't hear me at all. He was still ecstatic. He had his arms folded. His legs were crossed. His eyes were closed. He was completely absorbed in a world of silence and light. I could feel and sense that he was way beyond my own horizons. He was completely transformed. He was transfigured.

How long we spent there, I did not know. Neither did I care. For one glorious moment, I was carried out of myself and transported heavenwards. My whole being was boosted. The experience was so sustaining and satisfying. It was complete. It was total. It was full – so much so, that I was unaware of all bodily sensations and unaware of my senses. I was an elated man when we started to make our way back to the car. Then I began to think of our earlier visit to the Burren Centre in Kilfenora village and how we were told that we would be transported back to ancient times and how we would come across the mysteries of our forebears' civilization and culture and how thousands of years ago they left their mark on the landscape in the form of dolmens, cairns and burial chambers. And this, indeed, was the mindset I had had as I drove towards the place earlier that morning.

Now, on my way down from the mountain, I was totally mesmerised and enthralled by what I had seen, felt and witnessed. And it wasn't the past that astounded me. It certainly was not. Rather, it was the sure, certain glimpse I got of a future delightfully serene, all-saturating and all-illuminating. And it was more than that. I so wanted, there and then, to tell Gunna Dan so much – about how I felt, about my wonder and delight, about how thankful I was to have met him that first day on the beach in Lahinch and later in the Preacher's Pub in Ennis. And, too, I wanted to ask Gunna Dan so much – about himself, about his feelings and his experiences. But every time I looked at him, he was so self-composed, his eyes were almost closed, and as he stepped from rock to slab to boulder, I all the time felt that he was going to trip or fall, so unconnected was he still from this earthly life.

Unbeknownst to myself at first, I found myself chaperoning him down the hillside, which I did as if Gunna Dan were the most precious entity in the whole of the universe. To me, he surely was. I kept looking back at him as I progressed, and all the time, he was smilingly tranquil and languidly placid. And as I kept looking at him, I knew ever so well that for a deliberate and purposeful period of time, he had surrendered himself fully and totally to an unworldly grasp of the transcendent, and I also knew that he was extremely loath to leave it.

Chapter 18

Listening and Learning

I helped Gunna Dan over the wall and onto the road near where I had parked the car, and soon we were on our way. I drove through a few side roads until we came to the hilly village of Carron, a village that is situated smack right in the middle of the Burren. I parked outside Cassidy's Pub and restaurant and suggested to Gunna Dan that we both needed a cool drink, a little something to eat and the chance to relax, rest and talk. To this, he heartily agreed.

We sat at a table by a spacious back window, and all around us we could see far out into the distance. The rugged terrain loomed before us in the distance. To our right, we could see the bowl-like expanse of a dry turlough, the largest turlough, or disappearing lake, in Western Europe. I ordered mineral drinks, and we examined the menu. When our time came, both of us ordered the Craggy Garden salad. And then we tried to relax.

However, for a long time I, unlike Gunna Dan, could not relax at all. He just sat there quietly. He was composed and content. He seemed to be taking in the surrounding views and, as far as I could make out, most of the time he was focussing his gaze on the distant hills. To be honest, I did not know what to do or what to say. My mind was buzzing. What pleased me greatly, however, was the realisation that the rapture of the phenomenon on Mullaghmore Mountain was caught and claimed by my mind, spirit and soul, and I was happy to assume, for assume it I did, that from now on my experience at the mountain would remain, to some degree, a constant for me in my life. More and more, I began to relax. More and more, I became easy with myself, unbothered and untroubled. I looked around more. I became more in tune with what was happening around me.

Slowly but surely, I began to give attention to the four ladies seated at a table at the upper end of the dining room. Earlier, they had saluted us heartily on our way in, and now they were engaged in lively and loud conversations. It soon became obvious to me after unwittingly overhearing them that the two elder ladies were widows from Birmingham, England, returning to County Clare for their summer holidays. It was apparent, too, that the two younger ladies were from Dublin and likewise holidaying in the area. Both Gunna Dan and I could not help hearing and observing them. The gist of their excited talk was that all four of them found out for the first time in their lives that they were related through the Clancy and O'Shaughnessy families that had once lived in the areas of western Clare and south of County Galway. They were astounded by this startling coincidence. They could not get over the fact that somehow all four of them ended up in an isolated place in the heart of the Burren and unbelievably discovered that not only were they related to each other, but they also knew many of the kinsfolk in both families. The joy and vivacity of the occasion for all four ladies was palpable. Gunna Dan and I observed and enjoyed it, but neither of us said a word.

Then, after some moments, Gunna Dan stirred in his chair. He sat up and rested his arms on the table and said quietly to me, yet with conviction, 'Paddy, there is no such thing as coincidence.' He looked at me with what I at first thought was an impish smile. His demeanour was surely delightful, if not a little roguish. Then it dawned on me that his manner and bearing were much more knowing, much more serious. He let me ponder and dwell on what he said for what seemed some length of time. For a long time, I thought that my friend was tired, very tired. Slowly it began to dawn on me that he was earnest, indeed anxious. He had never been as anxious as this before. A strange feeling came over me. I felt that he wanted to impart solemn insights to me, but it was more than that. I felt that he wanted me to understand him better, perhaps to understand his message and his purpose much more deeply.

He then continued. 'In this life of ours, we separate everything. We dissect everything. We cut up everything into little jigsaw pieces. We disconnect everything. We sunder. Then, when we are in the middle of chaos and see connections, we are amazed.'

Gunna Dan shifted a little more in his chair. He became a little more serious and continued. 'All the major issues impinging on our lives are simple. Even the material world is made from simple elemental entities. Only four of them – carbon, hydrogen, oxygen and nitrogen – make up 96 percent of the human body, and if we add in two more – calcium and phosphorus – the percentage goes up to 99 percent.[84]' Then he repeated, as if to emphasise it for me, 'Everything in life is simple, all life is simple; if we could only but see it.'

'Any complexity that there is exists only because simple issues are made complicated. Nothing can be complex independent of simplicity; complexity is made from simplicity. Simple laws govern the world and humankind. In fact, Paddy, you are the one who emphasised this very issue for me. It was you who told me earlier about Saint Augustine, who wrote, 'How simple is the love of God and one's neighbour!'[85] Also, Paddy, illuminating truth is a fine power available to all of humankind to guide all of us in the living out of our lives. This illumination is simple, singular and one. It is pure and indivisible; silent and serene.'

He paused and looked around a little. As he did so, I began to realise that never before did I see my friend so sure, so true and so full of knowingness. All was now quiet and so he continued, somewhat solemnly. 'Paddy, there is only one religion – namely, that you love God and that you love your neighbour. This simple message has been revealed and presented to us throughout the ages and splendidly made known to us again by Jesus, the Son of God, the second person of the Blessed Trinity. This powerful teaching tells us loudly and clearly that we are all connected in one family with God in his divine love, wisdom and kindness. The simplicity of this message of love, given to us by God himself, insists that we love and respect our neighbour; in fact, that we love and respect everybody.'

His outstretched fingers started to gently tap on the edge of the table. After a few moments he stopped tapping and declared, and a declaration

---

84   'Abundance of the Chemical Elements.' Last updated 6 June 2010. *Wikipedia: en.wikipedia.org/wiki/Abundance_of_the_chemical_elements.*
85   Saint Augustine, 'Book XIII: Finding the Church in Genesis I,' *The Confessions.*

it was, 'All virtue, all goodness and all merit are encapsulated in one word – kindness. In the book of Wisdom itself, we read that the virtuous person must be kindly to all people[86]. The practice of unconditional kindness towards ourselves and our fellow travellers in life endows us all with sanctification and holiness. It is impossible to exaggerate the significance of this divine gift. It is impossible to overstate the necessity for kindness in our lives. We need its penetrating power. It is at this present moment, at the start of the twenty-first century, that humankind needs to adopt kindness as the great global virtue. Humankind needs to make kindness meaningful in the living out of human life here on Earth.'

He waited again for another few moments, and I waited in silence. Then he continued. 'Another thing, Paddy: spiritual life, the life of the spirit, is simple and pure. It is quiet and gentle. It is light and easy. It is restful and soothing. It is full and complete. It is strong. It is silent. It is powerfully and splendidly silent.'

At this he grew very quiet, much more so than before. Then, after a little time, he stirred just a little in his seat. He looked directly at me and said, 'The essence of spiritual life is found in the act of loving *the best the best*. The human soul, created in the likeness of God, is satisfied with nothing else.' He inhaled a deep breath as if his whole body needed the extra air, and he continued ever so seriously. 'Loving the best the best is the realistic actuality of human life and human living.'

I then knew that, in revealing himself to me, Gunna Dan was also enlightening me. I realised that in an extraordinary way he was presenting me with gifts for my mind, my spirit, my soul and my very being. I was solemnly silenced and staggered by it all.

He paused again and looked out the window. I knew that what he said made perfect sense to him. He paused long enough to allow himself to meditate on what he had said and to relate to it. We both remained silent. I sipped my drink. I must say that I found Gunna Dan's revelations at one level very comforting, but at another level I found them formidable. I treasured the privilege of knowing how he was thinking and what he was thinking. And I had no doubt but that his thoughts were majestic and sublime. I felt like a child on the shoulders of a giant, a child who could now see more and farther out into the distance.

---

86   Wisdom 12:19, JB

Not long afterwards, the waitress came with the salads and we settled down and began eating. It was obvious to me that both of us needed the meal. Our energies, particularly our nervous energies, had been exhausted by the day's wonderful events. We ate for some time in contented silence.

Once Gunna Dan had finished eating his meal, he again began talking. 'There is only one science. It is the science that has to know everything and the science that strives to understand everything. But, of course, that is the very science that is not wanted. The science that is wanted by the world is the science that divides, disconnects and compartmentalises subsets of knowledge. What we have instead is a choosy science, a reduction of the extent of science itself and, worse still, a reduction of the extent of reason. Within this sphere, we get hundreds of separated subjects and disciplines in the universities, schools and laboratories. When scientists wanted to develop methods to capture intrinsic human traits to convert them into vectors of numbers to create templates for future comparisons, they gave a new name, biometrics, to their study, further sub-dividing an already fragmented body of knowledge. And on and on it goes. Before long, the sub-divisions will be in the thousands.'

He paused. And after a little time, he continued. 'There is only one philosophy. It is that philosophy that illuminates the mind enabling it to see perfection at work. It is that philosophy that endows us with luminosity to see perfection at work everywhere – in life, in ourselves, in others and in everything. This is the wonder of the self-conscious mind. Gifted with grace and blessings, it can, from within its own finite ambit, know itself. It can know its own existence. And, it can especially know the existence of the infinite world within and beyond.'

'Paddy, all life is connected. Everything is connected. It is understandable that we are amazed when we come across and experience coinciding events. This amazement comes about because we do not understand the insignificance of the finite world in which we live. We all truly belong to the world of the infinite. Every man, woman and child in all our forms and stages, even the child who never makes it, fully belongs to the infinite world. We belonged to it before we were born. Let me put it to you this way. The finite world consisting of all the galaxies, stars, solar systems, planets, satellites and everything else, of which there are trillions, is much smaller than the tiny speck of a breadcrumb here on the side plate in front of me on the table, in comparison to infinity. What's more, the infinite world is ever-expanding, while the finite world is ever-diminishing.'

Gunna Dan paused for quite some time. By this time, I had finished eating my meal. And still, for a little while more, we remained silent. Then he surprised me by saying, 'The finite material world in which we all live is our cotyledon.'

He began to remind me of the discourse I had given him on germinating seeds, of how the seed leaves, called cotyledons, are packed full of nutrients and how upon germination, the stored foodstuffs are used to make the new roots, shoots and the upper parts of the new plant. Once the new plant is established in its new world, the once life-giving and life-sustaining cotyledons shrivel and shrink, degenerate and die. I remembered the discussion well.

'This is our finite world,' continued Gunna Dan. 'With the passage of time, our finite world continues to diminish at an even more rapid rate. The verve and vigour of youth weakens. Our desires and feelings and appetites constantly change, and with change, the finite world experiences an ever-increasing deterioration. The faculties of our minds and bodies become compromised. Infirmity and mortality loom on the horizon. Attachments and possessions lose their attraction. We realise more and more that we own nothing here on Earth. We own absolutely nothing. The cotyledon that had been so necessary soon degenerates and shrivels into nothingness. Similarly, when our bodies shrivel and die, our spirits will flourish in the essence of divine kindness. It is then that the true selves of each and every one of us will enjoy, to the full, the gifts and bliss of heaven.'

Then he startled me. 'Look, Paddy, I want to be more explicit. The full disclosure of the human story and the full expression of human life cannot happen until humankind relates purposefully to fullness and wholesomeness; until we admit fully into our minds the reality of perfection; until we cope meaningfully and tolerantly with the frustrations of our existence; until we become correctly uncritical of ourselves and our fellow humans; until we endow unconditional kindness on all those around us and until, in the thinking of all of this, in the doing of all of this and in the very being of all of this, we transcend this finite and limited world.'

Gunna Dan breathed heavily. He paused. He rested. He relaxed. I felt that he was exhausted and that he needed the respite. Then it struck me, and forcibly. I was sitting there with a man imbued and saturated in a life of otherworldliness. It was clear to me that not only did he know and understand liberation of the spirit, but also he seemed to experience an ongoing connection with the transcendent and with the divine. Yet, at the same time, he revealed an anxiousness, a great want to be connected to every man, woman and child in the world. He wanted everybody to be on his journey with him.

Still, as I looked at him, there was no tension in him, no stress. His compass seemed to be all-embracing and infinite. He could have come from anywhere. He could have gone anywhere. But the one thing I knew, for which I will always be deeply thankful, is that he had come into my life. And he came into my life so quickly, so easily and so quietly. I looked at the man again. He was restful. His eyes were closed. His arms were folded. There and then, I calmly admitted to myself that just as quickly, just as easily and just as quietly, he would leave me.

The two of us were joyful as we made our way back to the car for the return journey to Inagh. At the same time, we were tired. I even felt that Gunna Dan was exhausted. The trip home was almost in complete silence. It was as if divine silence entered Gunna Dan's mind and spirit in order to soothe and alleviate him after what was for both of us a roller coaster of a day. We both experienced the silence in our own ways and in our own time. We needed to. I badly wanted to prolong my own sense of knowingness and to perceive again the sensations of the day. Then, too, I had to give extra attention to driving because I found that my responses to the task were not coming freely and automatically. Yet, this did not stop me from thinking all the time about my friend in the car beside me. I began musing on his manifestation in my life, and I kept acknowledging to myself that the man came purposefully because he was on a mission. His mission was simple. He wanted to tell me and to tell everybody that the story of life is a magnificent and glorious one, far more glorious and far more magnificent than the human mind can grasp.

We came home the way we went: back to Kilfenora, onwards to Ennistymon and then out the Ennis road that would take us to Inagh. Gunna Dan soon realised that in a short while we would reach our journey's end. He began thanking me for looking after him throughout the day. He would not allow me at all to minimise the importance of what I had done for him. He insistently thanked me for understanding him. He was very appreciative. He even turned towards me to emphasise it and said, 'When I was still, you were still; when I was in wonder, you were in wonder. You harmonised with me, and in our harmony I was free. I was fully free, and because of this, I became unlimited in my being and in my spirit. Your presence and support enabled me completely.' Then, at which I could only marvel, he added, 'I saw, I felt and I lived again, but this time more specially than ever, the permanence and majesty of transcendent life.' And he finished by telling me forthrightly that this transcendent life exists for everybody.

His earnestness silenced me, but it also warmed and comforted me no end. Then he amazed me when he told me that to a greater extent than I had heretofore experienced, I, too, would experience the gift of being unlimited and spiritually free. We drove into the church car park in Inagh, and with surprising alacrity, Gunna Dan hopped out. His parting words to me were, 'I'll meet you down at Cloonmacken Lake on Sunday morning at about half past nine, and afterwards we can get the eleven fifteen Mass in the local church. Okay!' He was very precise about it. He was very insistent, as if he had planned it way in advance.

Chapter 19

The Totality of It All

I surprised myself with how practical and pragmatic I became when he left me. I began making plans in my mind as to what I would do between then and Sunday. For one thing, I could spend all of Saturday cleaning the house. I realised that I needed to take the accumulated rubbish up to the Ballyduffbeg Central Waste Management recycling centre. There was another consideration on my mind. On Sunday afternoon, my godchild Clara, her brother Cormac and their Mamó[87] Eileen were coming to visit me in Inagh. And then, too, I needed time and space to relax and reflect, to ponder and to wonder at all the events that had spectacularly happened in so brief a period in my life. My dimensions and perspectives had now widened and deepened. Even though I was coping, I felt polarised. One part of me was ethereal. I wanted to be, and I did spend a lot of my time, pensively alone, loving the quiet moments and the light of the summer days. Another part of me was trying its best to be pragmatic and functional, and in this I had not been succeeding very well. The house was in a mess. It was essential for me to wash all the cups, saucers and plates that I had abandoned carelessly in the kitchen sink. The floors, and particularly the windowsills, were cluttered. Outside, I wanted to hoe the weeds that were now thriving at the back of the house. I particularly wished to mow the lawn and clip the briars. So, I welcomed

---

87 Mamó is Gaeilge or Irish for Granny, according to the Irish-English dictionary (*An Roinn Oideachais*), *Gearrfhoclóir Gaeilge-Béarla*, (Dublin: Irish Department of Education, 1981).

this opportunity, and I determined that I would transform the place and have it spick and span by the time my visitors would arrive.

When I got home after dropping Gunna Dan off at the car park, it was late. I went to bed early, expecting a long night's sleep. Instead, during all of that night I pondered a lot on the day's events. Actually, I pondered a lot on Gunna Dan. I was full of mixed emotions, feelings and thoughts. Overall, I was happy. Overall, I was confident. I was happy because the dimensions of my life were expanded and stretched, and what I had witnessed and experienced elated me. I now knew that my friend Gunna Dan was living life in an infinite world of the eternal present, and he was telling me that from his infinite perspective, everything was sublime and supreme. When he spoke to me, walked with me, cared for me, helped me and supported me, he did so from his world – even though I always had thought and assumed he was living in mine.

I was confident because now I knew more, understood more, believed more, accepted more and realised more. In fact, I was in awe – delightfully so. I now knew that even though my finite world would continue to shrink and even though my life processes would wind down, Gunna Dan would always be there for me and would never be far away from me. I knew with a certainty that he would be just ahead of me. A great feeling of ease and rest and contentment came over me. There, alone in the middle of the dark night, I knew I would be lonesome no more.

Gunna Dan had shared with me his wondrous numinous experience on Mullaghmore Mountain. He enabled and empowered me to vibrate and co-ordinate with great mystical energies. As a consequence, I had experienced a much greater sense of self-conscious existence. This sense had been full and total. It had been tranquil and pure. I felt the certain sensation that the experience had been loving and totally lovable. It had been boundless. I had been saturated to the extent that I entered a state way beyond thought and feeling and emotion – indeed, beyond everything.

What was also assuring and comforting was the fact that Gunna Dan entrusted himself fully, totally and unconditionally to the reality of otherworldliness. He entrusted every one of us to the quintessential truth. He entrusted himself and everybody to the reality of all realities, a reality he started out so purposefully to seek and later so assuredly experienced. I now knew that he was living on a plane of splendour and wonder. More and more, I saw that he was gladdened, brightened and elevated. This state was so natural to him. It was so normal.

Even at the table in Cassidy's Pub in Carron, I had realised that Gunna Dan was lifting me up to higher levels. He wasn't just talking or speaking to me. He was strongly telling me – my whole psyche and my whole being – that my existence and the existence of every human being were of astounding, never-ending existential importance. 'There is no such thing as coincidence,' he had said. This insistent assertion kept surfacing in my mind. The way he had let me ponder on it and linger over it had been intentional and insistent. He had been telling me loudly and clearly that our self-conscious existence here on Earth is of deliberate design and of deliberate purpose. He had also been telling me that all the individuals in the one family of humankind are destined for eternal glory and happiness.

Sunday morning was clear, bright and sunny. The minute I left the house, the flickering breeze fluffed the floppy coat sleeves of my linen suit. The air was dry and light. I was in high spirits as I set out for Cloonmacken Lake on that expectant morning. Gunna Dan had arrived before me and was sitting at the upper table with his back to the lakeside. Even from a distance, I could see that he was ebullient.

As I was approaching him, he said delightfully, if not jocosely, 'This is the first day of my new life.' His greeting was loud, clear and penetrating, and I accepted it in a matter-of-fact way because in my mind, every morning we wake up hale and hearty is indeed the start of a new life. He spread-eagled his legs and stretched his hands out wide as if he were embracing the whole of County Clare, if not indeed the whole world. Enthusiastically, loudly and clearly, he addressed me.

'I cannot but bless you, Paddy, and bless all the people of County Clare and all the peoples of the world. Life is a great privilege. Oh, the wonder of it! Oh the glory of it! One thing is sure, Paddy; it cannot be fully grasped by the mind. It cannot be fully felt by the heart or experienced by our very beings; so great, so vast and so infinite is the majesty of it all. And yet, Paddy, every one of us can sense it. Every one of us can get to know it to some degree. We are aware of this already. There have been and will continue to be innumerable peoples who experience deep, fruitful insights into our glorious destiny. There have been so many in the very ancient past and we are fortunate that today we have the legacy of their writings and their wisdom.'

And there, sitting at the table by Cloonmacken Lake, my friend Gunna Dan regaled me. He particularly relished talking about the Holy Scriptures and the prophets of old. In a remarkable admission to me, he told me how my earlier comments and views on the prophet Isaiah influenced him. From his own study of the Scriptures, Gunna Dan knew that in Isaiah's time, the people suffered tremendous injustices. For a long number of years, they were the helpless victims of wars, famines and oppression. He appreciated how Isaiah kept on teaching that all wrongs would eventually be righted and that spiritual awareness and consciousness would prevail. Gunna Dan spoke at length to me about all of this. It was quite clear to me that he was empathising with suffering peoples throughout all the ages and throughout all time. Then, in a remarkable outpouring, his freewheeling spirit began to recite,

> On this mountain,
> Yahweh Sabaoth will prepare for all peoples
> a banquet of rich food, a banquet of fine wines,
> of food rich and juicy, of fine strained wines.
> On this mountain he will remove
> the mourning veil covering all peoples,
> and the shroud enwrapping all nations,
> he will destroy Death for ever.
> The Lord Yahweh will wipe away
> the tears from every cheek;
> he will take away his people's shame
> everywhere on earth,
> for Yahweh has said so.
> That day, it will be said: See, this is our God
> in whom we hoped for salvation;
> Yahweh is the one in whom we hoped.
> We exult and we rejoice
> that he has saved us;
> for the hand of Yahweh
> rests on this mountain.[88]

---

88   Isaiah 25:6–10, JB

He concluded his recitation of the messianic banquet with a flourish, and added, 'This is truly powerful. This is remarkable. Just imagine – a banquet 'for all peoples'! This is so wonderful. And the Lord will 'wipe away the tears from every cheek'. This is so splendid. Let the whole world know this, let the whole world be assured of this –the fullness of divine kindness will be our only judgment experience. I love it. I love it. I love it.'

Gunna Dan was effusive. 'Look, Paddy, humankind seriously needs to know and love this. In fact, humankind already knows it to some extent. Almost twenty-eight hundred years ago, the prophet Isaiah wrote all of this and more. He wrote it with certainty and with clarity. It was written by an inspired mind that was blessed with universal kindness, unconditional kindness that is ageless and timeless. Then, eight hundred years later, the Son of God, Jesus himself accentuated this future celebration of man's deliverance. He did so particularly when he took his place at the table for the Last Supper and told his apostles, 'I have longed to eat this Passover with you before I suffer; because I tell you, I shall not eat it again until it is fulfilled in the Kingdom of God.' Shortly afterwards he added, 'From now on, I tell you, I shall not drink wine until the Kingdom of God comes.'[89]

'Paddy, this is the wonderful fulfilment for all the prodigal people of this world of ours. Paddy, this is the glorious destiny for everyone. This certainty is there for every man, woman and child privileged to be born into the world. And from this certainty emerges the greatest and most underrated philosophical imperative of all time and for all time. It is even a spiritual imperative, and it is this: every one of us has a compulsive duty to be happy!'

Gunna Dan was enthused, and his enthusiasm was infectious. He was delightfully happy, and I knew there and then that in front of me was a contented man in every sense of the word. He was content to the extent that his mind, body, spirit and soul were not in the need for anything more. He was fully free. He was excited to be on a spiritual journey to the top of this mountain and excited that all of us were there with him and climbing it with him. His vigour was eloquent, and fully confirmed that he had already started on this journey. He was totally participative and fully entrusting. There was not any doubt, unease or sense of risk for Gunna Dan. As I sat opposite him at that table, I became aware, as if I didn't already know it, that he was totally enlightened. I even developed

---

89   Luke 22:15–18, JB

the thought that Gunna Dan was an eternal spirit who was never meant to die.

I easily pondered on all of this as I sat there at the table with Gunna Dan. I was aware that while I was looking at him, his whole being was assuring me, energising me and comforting me all at the same time. I explicitly and deliberately accepted into my mind the notion that his whole spiritual being was telling me that the universe is supportive and sustaining. What surprised me was how relaxed and easy and contented I was. What surprised me more was that I was so consciously wide-awake like I never had been before. And what surprised me most of all was my certain realisation that with Gunna Dan I was spiritually elevated and spiritually free.

We stood up and, each of us in our own way, walked towards the water's edge. Just as we got there, the chapel bell was tolling, announcing that the Sunday Mass would be starting in ten minutes. 'Come on,' said Gunna Dan in a boyish, joyful and eager way. 'Come on,' he said again. 'Let's go and climb our mountains.' We turned energetically and, in so doing, scattered the ducks that had assembled at the table we earlier vacated. Feathers flew everywhere. This was as much to our surprise as it was to the ducks. I was even more surprised when I realised that ducks do not lose their feathers that easily. Incredibly, some of the feathers were floating lightly upwards, others were hovering in mid-air as if wondering whether to go up or down, some rested on the table and others landed on the seats. The dancing and resting feathers were a delight to watch. Gunna Dan noted it all with total amusement.

No wonder he was excited as we left the lake. He was excited and exhilarated all the way back to church. I even felt that he was on cloud seven of the seventh heaven, and particularly so as we walked up the centre aisle, took our place in an empty pew midway in the church and knelt down.

The celebrant at the Mass was the very venerable Father Hogan, a man of about eighty-five years of age, if not more. Because of the shortage of priests in the Kilalloe diocese, the older, retired priests were pressed to remain on and continue administering to the spiritual needs of the people of the parish. In practically all cases, they also were pressed to support the temporal, cultural and sporting activities of the surrounding areas. Father Hogan was not a slow man in his saying of the Mass, which I felt was because he was surefooted and earnest as he went about offering up the sacrifice of the Mass.

Gunna Dan and I greatly enjoyed going to Mass, and afterwards we would discuss our understandings and impressions. On one occasion, he pestered me to explain how it is that the priest is the minister of divine worship on behalf of all humankind, especially the minister of the highest form of worship, namely sacrifice, and in the case of the Mass, Eucharistic sacrifice. I told him that for myself, I had accepted that "Christ brings about a special presence in every priest, who when celebrating the Eucharist or administering the sacraments, does so *in persona Christi.*"[90] Very candidly, he then told me that he was very happy to admit to his mind that the administering priest represents Jesus himself who offers himself anew for the salvation of everybody in the whole world. This munificence, I knew full well, delighted Gunna Dan tremendously.

All this I was thinking, and indeed more, when I settled into a state of composure and of waiting. However, when I glanced sideways at my friend, I realised that he was much more composed and settled than I was. In fact, he was much more serious and more deeply concentrating than I had ever seen before.

---

90   His Holiness John Paul II, *Crossing the Threshold of Hope* (London, Jonathan Cape, 1994), 13

Chapter 20

To the High Lands on High

E very time I go to Mass, I do my best to quickly settle in and prepare myself for a spiritual journey, a journey that always involves the climbing of a spiritual mountain. Gunna Dan knew this. That was why he had said to me as we were leaving the lake, 'Let's go and climb our mountains.' And every time I go on this journey, I do so with a great sense of awe. Even from a young age, I have always admitted to myself that the great story of human life and human living is blessed and consecrated and exalted with the reality of redemption, salvation and ultimate happiness. The Mass, to and for me, has always been *the* great act of divine worship. Everything related to it oozes beauty and grandeur, magnificence and largesse. The perfection of spiritual life is found therein, and because of the closeness of the real presence in the Blessed Sacrament, one is in heaven and on Earth at the same time.

Normally this would be the way my mind would work, but on this occasion, I was ever-conscious of the presence of Gunna Dan beside me. I couldn't help but recall the alacrity with which he bounded out of the car at the church car park and how, as we walked up the slope to the side entrance, he delightfully, yet enigmatically said, 'Paddy, I'll lead the way onwards and upwards.' I had thought for a brief moment that he was imitating the cartoon kid Buzz Lightyear. The only thing I could do and did do was to continue my walk into the church, saying nothing, but greatly wondering.

But I knew this much: I knew that Gunna Dan revered the sacrifice of the Mass and the Blessed Sacrament of the Eucharist. The Mass, he had told me on more than one occasion, lifted him up and out of himself, out of this earth and into heaven itself. He was convinced that the celebration of the Mass was the conjunction of heaven, Earth and all therein. He readily admitted to me that every time the commemoration started, he could easily steady and anchor his intellect and think of nothing but the journey before him. Every time he participated in the Mass, he felt liberated and free of this world and all its limitations and frustrations. He even felt free of timely existence. He sincerely admitted to me that all impediments fast fell away from him, and as they did so, he became supremely happy. And in his happiness, he felt he was always being impelled upwards and onwards.

Normally we would sit down after a few minutes, but this time both of us remained kneeling. Normally, again, my mind would become still and quiet, but this time it was much more lively – livelier than it ever was at the start of Mass. I kept on wondering about my friend Gunna Dan. I could not help it. Then, I took a sideways glance at him. I could see that he was still composed and concentrating. He had his hands joined. His eyes were closed. And I knew, there and then, that he was on his journey. I couldn't help but take another sideways look at him a moment later. It was his growing radiance that attracted me. I knew instinctively that he was now dwelling in a great inner life. What amazed me was how total his composure was. I became increasingly certain that he was then on a mystical journey, a mystical journey far greater than the one he had had on Mullaghmore Mountain.

Because of this, it took me quite some time to compose myself. I knew that this was not going to be another ordinary Sunday morning Mass. My mind was spinning. I was thinking so much about recent events and about things done and said. What helped me first of all was the tuneful singing of the choir. It soothed me. In fact, the melodiousness of the singing transported me out of my lingering thoughts. It prepared me to become prayerful. I became more focused. I began organising the sequences of activities in the celebration of the Mass in my mind. Soon I was giving all my attention to the Confiteor, which helps me to visualise the company I am in, where I am and to where I belong. As soon as Father Hogan started it, I was able to dwell on the universality of the pleading and to imagine myself in the presence of God and in the company of all the saints and angels, the Virgin Mary, Mother of God, and all brothers and sisters everywhere. Slowly but surely, there in the parish church of Inagh, I got more and more absorbed in the journey before me.

I couldn't but notice how reflective I became at the first offering of the gifts. Normally I have to spend some time engaging myself perseveringly with the divine. I need to become quiet and still. Sometimes it comes easy, but often not. I use my own developed techniques for composing my mind and stilling my soul. But this time, I surprised myself. Very quickly I realised that I was experiencing a heightened focus. I had a splendid clarity of mind, and my awareness was very deep. I was surprised, too, and certainly delighted when I also realised that I was engaging myself totally with everything going on at the altar of God with tremendous ease and purposefulness.

When it came to the consecration, that is, to the second offering of the Mass, I felt glorious. I became more quiet and more still. I fully acknowledged that the Eucharistic sacrifice of the body and blood of the Lord is the supreme gift for the redemption and salvation of the whole world with the assurance that all sins will be forgiven, and in particular, 'the sin of the world'.[91]. For some unknown yet delightful reason, my mind began to dwell and ponder on the sublime dimension of Jesus sent to us by God the Father to be our saviour and redeemer. I recalled how I had empathised with Gunna Dan at the lakeside when, after saying the verses from Isaiah, he had said, 'This is truly powerful.' I knew what he had been implying, and in my mind I began telling myself that nobody should go through life without being greatly optimistic, without acknowledging that the experience of living is a wonderful event and that no matter what happens, all will be supremely well. Thus, with this kind of thinking and with no little pondering, I became more and more elevated and more and more purposeful.

I was fully aware of my elevated self when we stood up to say the prayer, 'Our Father'. This mysterious prayer stretches in theme and meaning back many centuries into the Old Testament and from the present into the divine world of heaven. Hidden within its few words can be found the derivation of many parables, an abundance of scriptural references and the prayers of the Old Testament prophets as they cried out to Yahweh in their entreaties to God. The prayer is a comfort to all humankind. It gives and promises sustenance, sustenance that was assured in the past with the

---

91   The Gloria; John 1:29, JB

manna in the desert and sustenance that is gifted to us presently with the Eucharist of the Mass. It is a universal prayer because all humankind can address the Godhead as 'Father'. This universality is real and sure. It is acknowledged by the fact that the prayer has been, to date, translated into 1,662 different languages and dialects.[92]

I know that a lot of people have difficulty appreciating the prayer. A good number of years ago, I even heard a well-respected commentator on the radio referring to it as 'a load of gibberish'. In fact, when I heard this comment at that time, it stimulated me to think of the Lord's Prayer more, and the more I thought of it, the more my regard for it grew. So from that time onwards, I gave more attention to the practice of creative visualisation. Every time I come to the Our Father, I visualise Jesus himself among us, among all the peoples of Earth and heaven, and, in what I can only call an application of the senses, I listen, see, hear and participate.

There, in the church in Inagh, I participated with all of my soul's senses. I listened and visualised. I visualised Jesus himself saying the prayer for us, with us and for everybody. It is his unique and special prayer. In it, he wants us to direct ourselves and our whole beings to the source of all sustenance. He wants us to recognise our existential dependence on the Father of all. This prayer gives a wonderful insight into the communion that there is between God the Son and God the Father. Jesus himself, God the Son, wants each and every one of us to be integral to this communion. What is also wonderful is that the prayer, and our praying of it, unites all Christians of whatever persuasion everywhere in solidarity. In fact, all members of humankind are united together in the divine wish that each of us is nourished, forgiven and protected.

On this Sunday morning with Gunna Dan beside me, I became more and more absorbed in my thoughts and prayers, much more so than usual. Slowly but surely, I became aware of a great spaciousness in my mind, a spaciousness that became, strangely, increasingly expansive and very silent. It contented me greatly, so much so that soon I became unaware of my surroundings, of the people in the pew in front of me and behind me. I even became unaware of my fond friend alongside me.

I was absorbed within a setting of great openness and expansiveness. I felt fully free and unfettered. As Gunna Dan had promised me, I became

---

92   'Pater Noster,' Last updated 28 April 2010. *Christus Rex et Redemptor Mundi: www. christusrex.org/www1/pater/index.html*

more and more free: free from all pain and ache; from noise and distraction; from frustration and doubt; from interference and disturbance; from time and place; from want and need; and from obligation and expectation. I was free from the need for doing. I was free from the compulsion for becoming. I rested in light and in happiness. I was free to dwell therein and stay therein.

My contentment was such that I anchored myself totally into a world that was, all at the same time, lucid and clear; silent and pure; simple and timeless; and soothing and serene. My spirit was easy, rapturously so. I was so fully conscious of the otherworldliness of it all. It saturated me. I rested in it deeply and solidly. I yielded totally and fully to it. Oh! How often in the past I willed, wished and wanted it! I couldn't but help feel so thankful. My gratitude was total.

How long I remained absorbed in this world of ease and light and contentment I do not know. For how long I was serene, composed and undisturbed I do not know. But then strangely, because strangely it was to me, a disturbance entered into the scenery of my mind. Ever so slightly, ever so weakly, I could hear faint far off voices, and they remained faint and far off for a long time. At first, I could not make them out. I tried to ignore them. Then I began to realise that they were coming, slowly but surely, nearer and nearer to me. A recollection suddenly occupied my mind, reminding me that I had experienced this sensation before. With tremendous clarity, I suddenly remembered a serious car accident I had had back in April of 1978. A lorry driver had driven his vehicle at speed from a side road onto the main road that I was on. I couldn't stop in time and continued driving under the lorry. Right in front of my face, right in front of my startled eyes, the big black circling wheels of the lorry flattened the engine of the car that I was driving. The momentum of the lorry, its weight and its speed, flung the car across the road, and it ended up in a crumpled heap by the garden wall of a dwelling house. I must have been knocked out, because what I sensed with remarkable lucidity was the crystal clear consciousness of vast white spaciousness. The serenity of it was enticingly attractive. It was so pleasingly quiet, so solid and so real. I rested in it. I even wanted to stay in it. How long I was there I do not know. What I do know is that there, too, in that spaciousness, I heard faint far off voices that came, ever so slowly, nearer and nearer to me. I remember clearly thinking, *Oh how far away from me are the voices.* It surprised me when I realised afterwards that I was not in the least bit bothered by them or interested in them. I was delightfully serene. But eventually, when the voices did reach me, the spaciousness was gone. I was now looking at the tops of some trees and the side of a dwelling house. Then I began mumbling. I ached with pain. I began to realise that people were all around me. And in my pain, I shivered with the cold. I inanely tried to assure the onlookers that I was alive and well. I struggled with myself trying to become aware of everything around me.

In the church in Inagh, in a similar way, I heard in my same serene spaciousness the far away but approaching voices. As had been true after my accident, they didn't in the slightest bit bother me. I just wanted to stay where I was. However, the spaciousness soon disappeared and I became aware that I was cold, stiff and cramped. I felt myself vibrating. I grew to realise that somebody was pushing and shoving me. Then loudly and clearly I heard someone say, 'He must be fast asleep.' What surely awakened me, however, was the stronger and the very vigorous shaking I was getting, and when I opened my eyes, I saw my godchild Clara, her hands gripping the collar of my coat. She forthrightly said, loudly and clearly, 'Paddy, we are here.'

Then I saw Cormac. He told me that as they were passing the church on their way to the house, they saw my car parked all alone in the car park and so rather than go to the house, they decided to visit the church. Like a scout on a foray, Cormac had gone in first to investigate and soon reported back that I was within. They were amazed to find me curled up and asleep on the seat. Eileen looked at me smilingly and, as always, was delighted to see me and to meet me, but she couldn't help but wonder as to why I was all alone in the church so late on that Sunday afternoon.

I looked all around me, hesitantly, yet expectantly. I kept looking, but soon I accepted that I had been all on my own. Somehow or other, I knew there and then that it would be quite some time before I would meet with Gunna Dan again.

Index

A

abstract violence 66
abundance 7, 29, 50, 93, 103, 164,
    188
acceptance of truth 57
activation energy 94
A Dhaoine Uaisle 22
Adomnán of Iona 18
aerobic respiration 29
algae 35
allegiance 28
aloneness 32, 79, 80, 95, 98, 103, 111,
    114, 130, 131, 139, 163
An Cathach 19
ancient Greek philosophers 103
angel 129
angel for everyone, an 129
angelic 79, 129
Angelus 88
angry energy 68
Annagh Dún 64
An Teach Bia, Ennistymon 25
Apple iPods 26
application of the senses 189
Aquarius, dawn of 136
aqueducts 62
Aran Islands, the 43
Ardagh Chalice 143
Ardagh in County Limerick 143
Aristotle 96
army 157, 158
Ash Wednesday 39
aspiration 72
astral matter 40
Atlantic Ocean 25
awareness 72, 83, 92, 133, 135, 139,
    182, 188

B

babies 37, 47
badness 59, 68

Ballybunnion in County Kerry 54
Ballyduffbeg Central Waste Manage-
    ment 179
Ballylin forest 165
battles and wars 97
Beannacht Ar Chách 137
bell, iron bell of Saint Patrick 38
bell, sound of 38
best, the 48, 49, 51, 80, 85, 105, 112,
    122, 129, 130, 174
be yourself 80
Biddy Early Brewery 17, 21, 73, 74
birth duties 111
Bodleian Library 23
book of Genesis 39, 79
brightness 40, 92
bumblebee 42, 43, 45, 168
Burren, the 43, 141, 142, 164, 165,
    166, 167, 171, 172
Buzz Lightyear 186

C

cardinal virtues 96
Carricknola 129
Carron 171, 181
Cassidy's Pub 171, 181
Castletown 10
cathedrals of Europe 65
Celtic high crosses 141, 143, 147
certainties 85, 87, 163
Charles Nelson 42
Chicago, Illinois, United States of
    America 155
chilblains 153
child-friendly 153
childhood 10, 16, 21, 55, 69, 70, 79,
    83, 94, 98, 106, 117, 152, 165,
    167
church bell 37
Church Hill, Ennistymon 24
Clare senior hurling team 164
Clare, the name 150

Cloonmacken Lake 6, 7, 12, 15, 40, 44, 46, 102, 120, 178, 181, 182
cognitive responses 147
coincidence 5, 172, 181
Concise Oxford Dictionary 23
Confiteor, the 158, 187
connection 87, 92, 95, 173, 177
consciousness 81, 92, 99, 105, 153, 157, 182, 190
consumption 27, 35, 72
Cormac McCarthy 21
Corrofin 32, 149, 151, 164, 165
cosmological dimension 40
cotyledons 165, 176
Council of Nicaea 19
Count Axel Oxenstierna 109
County Clare 1, 21, 29, 42, 137, 161, 164, 165, 166, 181
crap 26, 27, 28, 39
creativity 66, 79, 92, 103
criticising 127, 128
Crosaire crossword 3

D

Decalogue of Assisi for Peace 160
Declaration of Independence 102
Declaration Toward a Global Ethic 155
deduction 86
De La Salle Brothers 10
deliverance 59
democracy 67
deportment, etiquette and decorum 72
depression 2
Destructiveness 64
Destructive power 65
diminishing finite process 34
direction 2, 46, 55, 84, 112, 164
discretion 79
discrimination 79, 92
divine intelligence 79
divine kindness 119, 128, 131, 139, 176, 183
DNA structure 30
Doorty Cross 144
doubt 64, 85, 86, 93, 153

doubts and uncertainties 57
Dublin 13, 21, 26, 38, 43
Duke Senior in Shakespeare's As You Like It 96

E

Earth 28, 39, 138
Easter Sunday – dating 19
Eckhart Tolle 30
education 109, 117
eels, catching of 81
encounter 112
encounters - with Jesus 115
English language 22
enlightenment 92
Ennis 1, 4, 150, 151
Ennistymon 19, 24, 33, 47, 86, 134, 142
Eucharist 38, 158, 187, 189
euphoric 43
event - of Christianity 115
evolution 83
excellence 48, 50, 51, 63, 96

F

failure 130, 134, 135, 163
Faithlegg House 10
Fall's Hotel 24
Fall's Hotel, the 30, 134
Fanore beach 118
Father Hogan 184
feathers 43, 184
feminine, the 157
ferns 35
Food & Agriculture Organization of the UN 27
Freagh 79
free will 92
Freshford, Co. Kilkenny 21
frustration 59, 82, 127, 160
fullness 7, 49, 93, 98, 130, 131, 176
furze 41

G

Gaeilge 18, 38, 179
Gaelic 2, 18, 42
garden of Gethsemane 114
Global Ethic 159
Glounthaune 18
Golden Rule 148, 153, 155
gongs 38
goodness 43, 63, 68, 76, 97, 122, 165, 174
gorse 41
grace and blessing 105
Gratification 72

H

hazel trees 164
hedgerows 32
helium 34
helpfulness 127, 146
heron 87
high standards 48
His Holiness, Pope John Paul II 160
holocausts 135
Holy Scripture 182
Holy Trinity, the 42
human condition, the 46, 49, 104

I

illuminated books and manuscripts 143
illumination 58, 93, 173
imagination 92
importance 2, 46, 76, 96, 121, 122, 136, 153
Inagh 18, 72, 88, 160
individualisation 72
infinite goodness 131
ingenuity 92
initiation energy 94
inner life of our minds 101
insight 79, 92
inspiration 92
insulin 30
intelligence 79, 92
Internet 97, 159

intuition 86, 92, 132
Iona 19
Ireland 18, 19, 20, 22, 26, 32, 38, 42, 43, 102, 142
Isaiah, prophet 182, 183, 188

J

Jesus, the Son of God 80, 111, 114, 121, 144, 145, 146, 148, 149, 183, 185, 189
Joe's Restaurant 117
judgment 79, 92
judgment experience 183
Julian of Norwich 90, 91, 138

K

Keatings' supermarket 88
Kilfenora 141, 144, 164
Killnaboy 149
Kilnamona 21, 64, 100
kinddom 121
kindness 79, 80, 116, 119, 120, 121, 122, 123, 125, 126, 128, 130, 132, 135, 136, 138, 139, 146, 147, 148, 153, 174, 176, 183
King Henry VIII of England 22
knowledge 92

L

Lahinch 3, 32, 44, 50, 52, 54, 56, 104, 116, 124, 126, 140, 144, 170
landscape - independent 16
Latin 18, 20, 23, 96
law of conservation of mass-matter 28
leafiness power 103
Leamaneh Castle 149
lesser yellow trefoil 42
Let it be done 98
life 17, 18, 66, 82, 134, 139, 181
Linane's pub 149
Liscannor 25
Lislachtain Abbey 21
lonesomeness 9, 95, 116, 122, 140
love for our neighbour 140

Love thy neighbour as thyself 154
luminosity 58, 94, 109, 125, 135, 136, 175

M

Mallow 10
mammalian design plan 30
manifestation 104, 177
Mass, in church 37, 38, 59, 111, 158, 178, 184, 185, 186, 187
Mauricesmills 32, 35, 151, 164
mechanism for survival 49
memory 92
merry-go-flush-around 39
messianic banquet 183
Milltown-Malbay 64
mind 1, 3, 6, 11, 24, 27, 36, 45, 48, 49, 54, 55, 56, 57, 59, 60, 65, 67, 76, 77, 83, 86, 90, 91, 92, 93, 94, 96, 98, 103, 104, 105, 112, 113, 114, 119, 127, 130, 133, 134, 139, 144, 147, 149, 157, 158, 161, 167, 168, 171, 175, 181, 183, 186, 190
mindfulness 98
mosses 35
Mullaghmore 143, 164, 166, 171, 180
Mutton Island 124

N

Nathaniel Colgan 42
National Botanic Gardens, Glasnevin 42
neighbour 72, 137, 139, 146, 148, 173
nettles 56
Newgrange, County Meath 62
Nintendo Wii 26
nothingness 9, 127, 176
nothingness and nihilism 127
Nurse Kitty Mulcahy 54

O

Old Abbey 22
Onavistan 8, 41, 70

Oranmore 18
organic food 27
Our Father 188
oxygen 29, 34, 35, 36, 39, 50, 74, 76, 83, 91

P

parable of the good Samaritan 144
parents 60, 71, 97, 107, 108, 109, 149, 152, 164
Pearse College of Further Education 13
perception 92
perfect beings 49
perfection 48, 49, 50, 51, 55, 56, 57, 58, 59, 61, 65, 75, 80, 86, 89, 90, 91, 94, 98, 104, 105, 111, 113, 114, 127, 128, 131, 132, 136, 139, 175
Perfection 51, 54, 56
personal integral worthiness 138
personal largesse 121
personhood 39
philome 105, 113
philosophical imperative 57, 58, 82, 84, 104, 105, 109, 113, 136, 139, 163, 183
philosophy 175
Plato 96
Pope Martin V 22
positive determination 93
potpourri 133
pragmatic education 14
priests 65, 157, 184
Psalms 19
purposeful thinking 24
pygmy shrew 168
pyramids of Egypt 142

Q

quietness 7, 16, 111, 122
Quilty 124

R

rainbow 41

Rambler's Rest 32, 64, 70
Rayleigh scattering 75
reality 17, 32, 44, 85, 180
reason 92
recognition 92
recycling 35, 39, 45, 83, 179
red blood cells 37
René Descartes 85
retention 92
Roman script 20
Rome 62
rosary, the 38
Royal Irish Academy 21

S

sacrifice of the Eucharist 158
Saint Augustine 86, 173
Saint Columba 18
Saint Fachtna 143
Saint Lachtain 21
Saint Patrick 19, 20, 38, 42
salvation 11, 59, 145, 182, 185, 186,
      188
sanctification 174
Saragossa Sea 82
Schaffhausen, Switzerland 19
science 175
Seafield 124
search for spiritual truth 69
self-confidence 2, 25, 138, 163
self-enrichment 98
self-esteem 2, 25, 98, 126, 138
self-worth 125
senna leaves 152
seven bones in neck 29, 30, 57
Sextus the Pythagorean 154
shamrock 42
Shanagolden 10, 21, 22, 54, 70, 81,
      143, 152, 164, 165
Shankill 18
shoulders of a giant 174
silence, world of 167
silent manifestations 56
simplicity 44, 86, 173
sin of the world 59, 65, 114, 127, 188

Sir Henry Sidney 150
slaughterhouses 27
Slievecallan Mountain 21, 40, 64, 105
Socrates 96
solace 2
Solomon 96, 116, 117
sonority of bells 37
sound judgment 25
spaciousness 6, 16, 24, 58, 129, 168,
      189, 190, 191
Spanish Armada, the 129
spectrum of light 41
stillness 7, 87
Stonehenge in England 62
success 14, 15, 107, 131, 135, 163
success and failure 131
sun 28, 34, 35, 36, 39, 50, 55, 62, 75
superlative happiness 80
superlative hunger 48
supreme bliss 131
switching off 75

T

teaching 1, 2, 8, 10, 11, 13, 80, 117,
      121, 122, 138, 146, 148, 154,
      182
Temple Gate Hotel 155
Terenure 18
Thales of Miletus 153
the bad, the worse, the worst 135
The Book of Armagh 20
The Clare Champion 100
The Clare People 74
The Cloud of Unknowing 147
The Flora of County Dublin 42
the good, the bad, the indifferent 135
the good, the better, the best 135
The Power of Now, Eckhart Tolle 30
the symbol zero 9
thinking 1, 2, 8, 9, 15, 24, 31, 34, 36,
      39, 40, 45, 46, 48, 49, 57, 68,
      75, 77, 78, 84, 87, 92, 97, 102,
      104, 106, 108, 109, 116, 119,
      125, 126, 132, 138, 140, 146,
      147, 163, 164, 165, 176

thistles 56
Thomond 150
tolerance 33
transfiguration 114, 169
transience 39
Trifolium dubium 42
truth 17, 57, 146, 180
Truth 58, 101
turlough 171
Turlough Donn O'Brien 150

U

unconditional 119, 126, 139, 146,
    147, 148, 159, 174, 176, 183
understanding 1, 7, 9, 13, 15, 28, 33,
    46, 48, 56, 58, 59, 63, 76, 87,
    89, 91, 92, 106, 108, 111, 112,
    118, 129, 132, 135, 147, 163
utilitarian education 14

V

values 25, 69, 96, 97, 106
Vice Commandant Martin Devitt 102
violence 66
violet light 41
virtue 33, 63, 72, 96, 125, 128, 174

W

War of Independence 33
water 3, 12, 13, 23, 34, 35, 36, 37, 40,
    42, 51, 62, 71, 82, 89, 100, 105,
    122, 128, 149, 152, 155, 156
wee 26, 27, 28
West Clare bruschetta 1
whin 41
white blood cells 37
White Strand, Miltown-Malbay 74
whitethorn, hawthorn 34
wholeness 93
wholesome 52, 130, 131, 148, 163
wholesomeness 59, 96, 130, 131, 132,
    160, 176
William Shakespeare 23
willpower 92

winners and losers 67, 130
wisdom 23, 25, 69, 85, 97, 100, 109,
    110, 111, 112, 116, 117, 118,
    120, 121, 128, 129, 130, 132,
    135, 137, 139, 145, 148, 154,
    174
Wisdom 97, 117, 118, 174
wit 92
womanhood 157
wonky 75, 76, 91

Y

year of the Easter Rising, 1916 32